ROUTES TO RECOVERY

ROUTES TO RECOVERY

KEN GLAZIER

Capital Transport

AUTHOR'S NOTE

Title page Two aspects of coping with the acute vehicle shortages and late vehicle deliveries in the aftermath of the Second World War are captured in this picture taken at St Paul's Cathedral in September 1949. Former Green Line T 262 is substituting for a double-decker on route 6, while RT 1471, which follows it, is one of 120 with non-standard bodies built by Cravens of Sheffield to compensate for the shortfall in production of the standard type. J.H. Aston

Facing page After their sale to the British Transport Commission in 1948, the Tilling Group companies also came to the help of London Transport, albeit rather unwillingly, with the loan of brand-new standard ECW bodied Bristol Ks. Crosville K6A MB 328 (JFM81) was one of those allocated to Merton garage for operation primarily on route 118. A.B. Cross

In 1945, after six years of total war, London Transport found itself with a fleet of motor buses, trams and trolleybuses impoverished by the enforced neglect and lack of materials which were an inevitable consequence of wartime conditions. Half the motor bus fleet and nearly as large a proportion of the trams were also life-expired, many motor buses having survived a full six years beyond the point when they would have been replaced in normal times. The next five years were spent struggling to keep the elderly fleet going while catching up on the backlog of replacements and trying, by the use of various expedients, to maintain what can only be described as the least bad service until the fleet could be brought fully up to pre-war standards once more. The Board, and later the Executive, had to achieve these results while keeping as happy as it could a hard-worked, weary and impatient workforce who so often found themselves in the firing line of passengers' complaints. In this they were given the unstinting support of the Trades Unions, the most overt example of co-operation being the responsible and pragmatic approach to the post-war vehicle replacement programme which could have been a source of much disputation. Unfortunately, as so often happens, this led to many unofficial disputes when the staff lost patience with their representatives but even so, in a period of great difficulty, industrial relations were reasonably stable. It is the story of those years which is the subject of this book. Fresh research has made it possible to go into greater detail than was possible in *London Buses and the Second World War* (published 1986, and now long out of print), perhaps most notably in the case of the Hired Coaches scheme which is covered more fully than hitherto.

Many people have given me a great deal of help in writing this book. My particular thanks must go to Dave Ruddom who did the detailed research on hired coaches and supplied the original text for that part of chapter eight concerned with that subject. I would also like to acknowledge the valuable help given by Mary Upchurch and David Bathe in putting the detailed computer listings into a usable form. Dave Ruddom also helped track down suitable illustrations and kindly checked what I had written. I am also very grateful to Gavin Martin who supplied the original text for chapter five and other historical material about the motor bus fleet which I have used to enrich the narrative. As ever, Dr Andrew Gilks has been the source of much of the detailed information about vehicles and I am grateful to Laurie Akehurst for his considerable help, particularly with Green Line and Country Bus matters. Others who have helped include Brian Bunker, John Gent, Malcolm Papes and all the photographers who over the years recorded so many of these important events so that we may enjoy them fifty years later. The cover painting is by Mike Jeffries.

First published 2000

ISBN 185414 236 4

Published by Capital Transport Publishing
38 Long Elmes, Harrow Weald, Middlesex

Printed by CS Graphics, Singapore

CONTENTS

1   THE BEGINNING OF THE END

An almost deserted Uxbridge bus station illustrates the depressed state of travel in December 1944, with no potential passengers in sight. The only two buses are Country Bus vehicles, an 11T11 on route 458 and an STL, probably on the 457 or 457A, both with substitute boarding in some of their windows to save glass. LT Museum

ONE OF Winston Churchill's most famous wartime pronouncements was made following the landmark Allied victory over Rommel's Afrika Corps at El Alamein in November 1942 when he said of the Second World War that this was not the end, nor the beginning of the end but perhaps '. . . the end of the beginning . . .' Japanese advances in south-east Asia had also been halted in the summer of 1942 but their reversal was to be a long hard slog and the crucial rubber plantations in Malaya, source of the raw material for tyres, were to remain in enemy hands until the very last day of the war. In Europe, the beginning of the end came a grinding 19 months after El Alamein when the Allies launched the so-called Second Front with the invasion of the Normandy beaches on D-Day 6th June 1944. In preparation for this important event large numbers of troops had been mustered all over south-east England, including no fewer than 1.5 million American servicemen. The population of London suddenly increased and, for many months before the Normandy invasion, its streets were thronged by American soldiers with

time on their hands and money to spare. Those who could got one of the very few taxis available, but the rest had to use public transport, putting a barely tolerable strain on the heavily truncated services then running.

The volume of service provided by London Transport's road services had reached its nadir in October 1943 by when car mileage had sunk to a figure 29.4 per cent below the last year of peace in 1938/1939; but the cuts were not spread evenly. In the Country Area bus mileage was actually running at a level 16 per cent above pre-war but Green Line coach services had gone completely, pulling the combined Country Bus & Coach department's total down to a cut of 41 per cent. However, in the territory served exclusively by Country Buses the reduction in service was nothing like so great because a substantial proportion of the Green Line mileage had operated inside the Central Bus operating area. Central Bus mileage had fallen by a third, partly offset by a lower than average reduction of 15 per cent on trams and trolleybuses to give a combined figure of 27.3 per cent.

By contrast, passenger journeys were an average of only 10 per cent below pre-war but this average masked a wide variation from a drop of 14.9 per cent on Central Buses and 6.8 per cent on Trams and Trolleybuses, to an increase of no less than 82.4 per cent on Country Buses. With leisure traffic strongly discouraged and off-peak and evening services heavily curtailed or withdrawn altogether, most of the lost passengers came from those times of day. On the other hand, peak hour demand was more intensive than ever, although it had to be carried on Central Buses by 17 per cent fewer vehicles. The increase in demand for Country Bus services is all the more remarkable when account is taken of the traffic carried by Green Line before the war, because the buses alone were now carrying 55 per cent more passengers than

had the buses and coaches combined. Even allowing for the fact that much of the mileage, particularly in the Country Area, was now operated by larger buses the effect on travelling conditions of this disparity between demand and supply can be imagined.

The fortunes of war began to run in the Allies' favour at the end of 1942. By the spring of 1943 the Royal Navy had begun to turn the tables in the Battle of the Atlantic and had soon defeated the submarine threat. Imports began to flow almost uninterrupted and there was a gradual improvement in the availability of essential materials. This enabled the government to authorise some expansion of bus services and, in London, the slow climb out of the trough began in November 1943 with the addition of 43 buses to the

Central Bus peak vehicle requirement. They were used to increase frequencies on a wide range of routes, priority being given to those of greatest strategic importance, and similar improvements continued week by week until, by the end of 1943, the total of additional buses had reached 194, nearly a 5 per cent rise.

On 26th January 1944, an entirely new route was conceded, a landmark in itself, although the operation was modest enough. Route 225 needed only one Leyland Cub from Uxbridge garage to supply a half-hourly service between Northwood Hills and Eastcote Station, using the previously unserved Joel Street. This part of north-west Middlesex had been seeing a considerable increase in military activity in preparation for D-Day, including a substantial concentration of American servicemen. The 225 was a small contribution to their needs. Demand was such that the Cub was replaced by a T on an unscheduled basis from 14th May 1944, the formal date of allocation.

A month later, at the other extreme of Middlesex, another new route of modest proportions but some strategic importance, the 121, started running from Ponders End over the border into Hertfordshire to forge a link across the Lea Valley to Chingford for the first time. In recognition of the severe shortage of materials and manpower, this three-bus route (121) ran no further than was necessary, failing to reach the obvious western objective at Enfield Town and terminating in Chingford, not with all the others at Royal Forest Hotel but at the station. This careful husbanding of resources, often in defiance of normal principles of route planning, was to become the typical approach to service development during the

period of gradual recovery over the ensuing eight years.

A third 'constrained' route to start in this period was the 108A, which was introduced on 19th April. Three extra STLs were used by Athol Street to allow the extension of Poplar – Blackheath peak hour shorts on route 108 to a point euphemistically called 'Eltham' but which was actually the junction of Well Hall Road and Rochester Way. This was as far as it needed to go without duplicating other services but this sparing use of resources stopped it well short of its natural objective in Eltham town centre.

Service increases on the established network continued through the first half of 1944 and by 31st May the total of restorations had reached 239. Progress then slowed down drastically. The marauding soldiers all disappeared suddenly at the beginning of June to take part in the invasion, which in itself was probably a welcome relief. Then, on the night of 12/13th June, the first of the V1 flying bombs landed in London, starting another period of intensive aerial bombardment causing death and destruction indiscriminately. The immediate effect was to provoke another evacuation from London and those remaining in the capital drew in their horns once again and were less inclined to make non-essential journeys, further reducing demand for services.

An even more horrific bombardment started on 8th September, four years almost to the day after the first London Blitz had been launched and only one day after the government announced the capture of the V1 launch sites. On that day, the first of the V2 rocket bombs fell on Chiswick, although the government covered up the nature of the weapons until November, asking Londoners to believe that there had been an unprecedented number of gas main explosions in the capital. The combined bombardment went on until 29th March 1945, only five weeks before the end of the European war. The result was that the programme of augmentations in the second half of 1944 and early 1945 ran at only a tenth the rate of the previous eight months. A mere 32 buses were added to schedules between May and the

end of December and another 11 before May 1945, bringing the total since the trend began in October 1943, to 282 (7 per cent).

In the case of trams and trolleybuses, most of the wartime cuts in service had been concentrated in the evenings and on Sundays. The peak operation was at virtually the same level as in 1939, except in those areas most severely hit in the Blitz where some heavy cuts had been made. It took little time for the peak services to be restored to the pre-war level and by May 1944 that benchmark had been passed. Unfortunately the events of the summer of 1944 caused a temporary setback, mainly on trolleybus services, and mileage actually dropped by 3 per cent, by which time it was over 17 per cent below 1939.

As Country Bus services were already at a much higher level, it is perhaps paradoxical to talk of recovery but most of the wartime improvements had been to meet the needs of people getting to and from work. Services outside peak hours and times of factory shift changes had been severely attenuated. There were no services at all after 9pm or on Sunday mornings, other than essential factory journeys, and this remained the case until the end of the war. There were some temporary cutbacks during the preparations for D-Day as buses in the eastern and southern Country Area operated right into the restricted zone and some areas were made out of bounds altogether. The most drastic example of this was a complete recasting of routes at Grays when the A13 was designated as a store for war materials. These restrictions were gradually eased as the war progressed. Improvements were sanctioned, however, and Country Buses was able to record an increase of 9 per cent in mileage between 1943 and 1944 and a further 5.6 per cent in the following 12 months.

The recovery had begun but there was to be a long haul out of the doldrums. Expectations were high in the wake of victory and people, not least the Board's own staff, demanded a swift return at least to pre-war standards but preferably with all the social improvements demanded by a populace which was to vote for radical change in the 1945 General Election. London Transport's will to do so was strong enough but its ability was seriously limited by shortages of manpower and serviceable vehicles which were to bedevil efforts to meet the unprecedented demands for public transport over the next seven or eight years.

2 THE FLEET IN 1945

Above The oldest bus owned by London Transport in 1945 was ST1139, the Short Bros bodied prototype which had started with Autocar and East Surrey in 1929. Its latter days were spent at Windsor, where it is seen in Castle Hill working on local route 417.
Ken Glazier collection

ONTRARY TO popular belief, when the war in Europe formally ended on 8th May 1945, London Transport owned more motor buses than in September 1939 and had a substantial surplus of trams. The trams had been replaced by trolleybuses in 1939 and 1940 and held in reserve deliberately against wartime contingencies. Such was the resilience of the situation in the bus fleet that there were still 80 STs on loan to operators outside London, this total having fallen from the peak of 312 reached in 1944.

Leaving aside the vehicles then in store awaiting disposal, at the end of 1939 London Transport had 5,101 double-decker motor buses in the STL, LT, ST, STD, RT and Q classes, 1,016 large saloon single-deckers (T, Q, LT, TF, LTC) and 151 20-seaters in the C and CR classes. Between then and 1945, 166 were totally destroyed by bombing, fortuitously most of them among the older buses

in the fleet. Of the 142 double-deckers, 60 were STs, 20 LTs, 61 STLs and one a Q. There were 24 single-deckers, 11 LTs, one Q, one CR and 11 TFs, most of which had been in store at the time of their destruction.

London Transport had no policy relating to motor buses comparable to the embargo on the disposal of trams and had been surprisingly free and easy about disposing of older vehicles. Having already let go the 113 serviceable Leyland Titans in store at the beginning of 1940, the Board then disposed of 34 open-staircase STs that were either sold or converted to service vehicles. The losses in the double-deck fleet were more than made up by the intake of 445 new buses, including the remaining 140 2RT2s, 54 unfrozen buses (STLs, STDs and Bs) and 251 utility Gs and Ds, bringing the total number owned on 7th May 1945 to 5,369, an increase of 269. The situation of the single-deck fleet was more complicated and will be explained later but the total number owned on 7th May 1945 was 1,080 (927 large and 153 small saloons), a fall of 87. The whole fleet had therefore grown by 181 buses.

Needless to say, this was not the whole story. For one thing, all the survivors of that 1939 fleet were now five years older and at least half of them had become life-expired. A large proportion of them had also been subjected to abnormal wear and tear having been damaged to a greater or lesser extent by bombs or bomb blast, some on more than one occasion. There had also been 92 incidents in which bus bodies had been written off after bomb damage but the chassis had been salvaged. The Board had been allowed to build 17 replacement STL bodies following the losses in the Blitz but the other 75 salvaged chassis were matched with bodies from the overhaul spares float at Chiswick Works, thereby undermining the flexibility of the maintenance system. Finally, maintenance itself had been carried on at a much reduced level, because materials were in short supply, skilled labour was not readily available and work at night was restricted by the limitations imposed by the blackout. To add to the problems this was all done without the benefit of

the main overhaul works at Chiswick which was in use for the manufacture of war materials, most famously playing an important part in the manufacture of Halifax aircraft. As the fleet got older it needed more attention and spent more time off the road while receiving that attention, with the result that as many as 10 per cent of the fleet could be out of action for maintenance at any one time. Nevertheless, in 1945 there was no real shortage of buses as the fleet of 5,369 was more than enough to cover a peak vehicle requirement in May 1945 of 4,590, but as service levels were built up in the following years it was to become a major problem.

Although the single-deck fleet had not suffered so much direct physical harm as the double-deckers, losing only 24 vehicles in all, it had been subjected to considerable upheaval. The Board had started the war with a large number of saloons in store awaiting disposal, mainly petrol engined Green Line Ts, which had been replaced in 1938/1939. Twenty five of these had been sold or converted to lorries in 1940 but others were brought back into service at various times. At the beginning of May 1945 fifty-one Regals were sold to the War Department for use by the Control

The most common vehicle type in 1945 was the STL, which made up nearly half the double-deck fleet, their typical appearance immediately after the war being exemplified by STL 882, a 1/9STL5/2. The window of the Lyons Tea Shop in Strand has the reduced area of glass often found in shop windows at the time, either because of bomb-blast damage or as a way of economising in the use of glass.
The Omnibus Society

Commission in Germany, where they were to play a part in restoring life to normal in that ravaged country. Sadly, the disposals included the entire batch of twelve 5T4s, which had comparatively modern Weymann bodies dating from 1935 and presumably qualified only because they had petrol engines. Also despatched were the remaining nineteen 7T7s (the rear-entrance version of the Green Line T), sixteen of the 1/7T7/1s, the last remaining rear-entrance 1T1 and seven of the nine remaining miscellaneous Country Bus Regals. Although nominally owned by London Transport much of the modern Green Line fleet was not available. Forty-four 9T9s, ninety-five 10T10s, the entire stock of Green Line 6Q6s and TFs and the private hire LTCs were still in the hands of the Ministry of Health as public ambulances in May 1945. A further six 9T9s and eighty-eight 10T10s were temporarily out of stock as they had been seconded to the American Army as transports, ambulances and 'Clubmobiles'.

This left 531 large saloons to meet a peak output of 471, and 153 20-seaters for a schedule of only 44. The big reduction in single-deck requirements largely reflected the absence of the Green Line but there had also been a significant move during the war years towards using larger buses wherever possible, with 20-seaters being replaced by 30- or 34-seaters and large single-deckers by double-deckers.

The tram and trolleybus department had also suffered many losses during the war. A straight comparison with 1939 is not appropriate as there were several stages of conversion from tram to trolleybus after the outbreak of war, but in May 1945 the trolleybus fleet stood at 1,702 serviceable vehicles out of the total of 1,764 purchased between 1931 and 1943. Seventeen had been completely written off during the war either because

of war damage or because of fires. The other 45 had been victims of V1 bomb attacks in 1944, one in service in Walthamstow and the others at Bexleyheath Depot and West Ham works. Their bodies had been destroyed beyond repair but their chassis or running units had been salvaged and were now awaiting new bodies. The trolleybus fleet was younger than the average of the motor buses and therefore did not suffer the problems of ageing to the same extent but it did include the 60 so-called 'Diddlers', dating from 1931, which were by now life expired and due for early replacement.

Although the tram to trolleybus conversion had been halted in June 1940, the volume of trolleybus operation had been increased as a matter of policy in subsequent years, to maximise the use of electric traction on roads where motor buses, using imported fuel, could be withdrawn. From a figure of 1,532 in 1940, the peak vehicle requirement had risen to 1,600 by May 1945, leaving a spares margin of just over 6 per cent in the fleet of 1,702.

The tram fleet had the highest average age of the lot and had been living on borrowed time since the temporary interruption of the scheme of abandonment after June 1940. Although the same policy of optimising the use of electric traction applied to the trams, some of the areas which they served had been so devastated by bombing that traffic had declined catastrophically. Traffic to and from the City of London and in the south London docklands had been particularly badly hit and the result was that peak output of tramcars declined from 806 in 1940 to 734 in May 1945. Disposal of redundant tramcars had been halted in 1939 and in consequence there were 1,124 still in stock in June 1940. Seventy-one were lost through bombing and another seven were dismantled for various reasons, leaving a residual total of 1,046 at the end of the war. This gave a remarkable theoretical spares margin of 42 per cent. The availability of this reserve fleet had been invaluable in covering wartime casualties but a large number of them still lacked driver's windscreens and were now ripe for disposal.

Such was the situation on VE day. During the remainder of 1945 another 35 single-deck motor buses were sent off on relief work in continental Europe, five more 1/7T7/1s to the Control Commission in Germany and 30 Leyland Cubs to the Belgian Economic Commission. On the other side of the balance, sixteen 1/7T7/1s which had been in use as staff ambulances were restored to bus use. These could always be distinguished from the 1939 conversions by their front destination indicators, which extended downwards from the roof, rather than projecting above. The coaches on secondment to the United States Army began to come back in November 1945 and the last to be received was T 462 on 30th October 1946. Twelve 10T10s and one 9T9 did not return and the fate of all but two of them has never been revealed. The suspicion Sgt Bilko may have had a hand in it, or that a bureaucratic muddle may have been responsible is given some weight by the fact that two are known to have found their way to other operators, both re-registered in the process, T 460 (HB6138) to D. J. Davies of Merthyr and T 594 (BRD922) to Smith of Reading.

The remaining single-deck absentees, those working as ambulances, began to find their way back to their proper role in life just before the end of hostilities, with the return of five 10T10s in April 1945. There was then a pause until August when forty-three 10T10s and fifteen 9T9s were recovered. The last major batch of 10T10s came back in March 1946 and the rest by May. Most of the 9T9s were back as buses by March 1946 but the last four did not come home until May 1947. The return to service of the 6Q6s and TFs was a much more long drawn out affair. The first Qs were restored in October 1945, with two large batches following in December 1945 and May 1946, but the remainder were spread over the

Top right Three Green Line Ts which had been requisitioned by the Control Commission in 1945 are seen in public service at Le Touquet in France in August 1947 still with passenger doors on the right-hand-drive side. Nearest the camera is T 108, a rear-entrance 7T7 which was still equipped with its original Green Line destination indicator boxes. The others cannot be identified but were rear-entrance 1/7T7/1s with enlarged indicators for bus operation. B.J. Cross

Centre right Still at work in October 1948 with Autocars Douaisiens in France, T 263,

another of the Control Commission buses, has had a passenger doorway inserted into its T7/1 body for left-hand running. Ken Glazier collection

Right Fifty-five 10T10 Green Line coaches were still in use by the American Red Cross as 'Clubmobiles' in the summer of 1945, one of them being T 680, disguised here as 'Milwaukee'. The masked windows at the back conceal the private sleeping area for the operatives, the cooking and seating areas being in the forward part of the saloon. There was a serving hatch on the offside.
Ken Glazier collection

Above The Green Line coaches requisitioned as public ambulances were gradually returned to London Transport from August 1945 onwards but some were held back for several years and one of the last two to return, as late as October 1948, was Q 208c. It is seen here outside St Thomas's Hospital, Lambeth Palace Road some time after the end of the war by which time it had already been repainted into the post-war livery of two shades of green. D.W.K. Jones

next 29 months, the last two not reappearing until October 1948. The TFs followed a similar pattern, the first being returned in December 1945, followed by two large batches in March and May 1946, but with the last seven taking from then until July 1948 to make their way back. In the case of the LTCs all 24 were officially restored to PSV status on 19th December 1945 but then remained unlicensed until the following summer. In all cases the work of removing the special fittings with which they had been equipped as ambulances, then restoring and overhauling the coaches to operational standard, took anything up to six months. The restored coaches began to reappear in service from February 1946 with the return of Green Line Coach services.

There were also 80 of the original 312 STs, which had, been sent on loan to 'provincial' operators, still away from home in May 1945. The number continued to dwindle during 1945 and most of the standard STs were back by the end of the year but the Bristol Tramways & Carriage Company held on to 11 until February 1946 and the very last one, ST 772, stayed with Lincolnshire Road Car Company until September 1946. Many of the Tilling STLs stayed away longer, perhaps because London Transport were less anxious to have them back. Venture of Basingstoke had eight which returned between January 1946 and January 1947, there were two with Crosville (returned between October and December 1946), four with City of Oxford (returned 1946), two with Lincolnshire Road Car (returned March 1947) and, finally, two with Hants & Dorset (returned February 1948).

Meanwhile the double-deck fleet continued to grow. It is an incongruous fact that well over half the utility buses delivered to London Transport arrived after the end of the European war, when the return to normal production values seemed to be in sight. Between May 1945 and the end of deliveries in March 1946, 385 were delivered, reaching the remarkable average rate of nearly ten a week for the rest of 1945. Paradoxically, it was the prospect of the restoration of pre-war standards of manufacture that was behind this surprising turn of events. With this in mind, operators outside London became unwilling to invest in any more substandard vehicles but Lord Ashfield took a different view. He recognised that it would be at least a year before the production of post-war RTs could be started and decided that in the meantime London Transport should do all it could to rejuvenate its fleet. The Board therefore willingly agreed to taking a large part of the surplus. It proved to be a prudent move because, in the event, the delay was even longer.

The influx of Guys was all the more remarkable because, apart from the solitary example of G 137, no buses of that make had been taken for over a year and it had looked as though the Board had settled on the Daimler as its preferred model. The new run of Guy deliveries started a few weeks before the end of the war, on 17th April 1945, when Gs 176 and 178 arrived at Chiswick. They were the first of 49 to be supplied by a manufacturer completely new to London Transport, Massey Brothers of Wigan (G 174–193, G 258–268, G 312–318, G 358–368). By this time the specification for utility buses was being relaxed to allow for curved roof panels, additional opening windows, better seating, larger front indicator boxes and side indicator boxes. Massey

Left Some of the operators outside London who borrowed STs were also laggardly in sending them back, the last not returning to the Capital until September 1948. Venture Transport of Basingstoke hung on to ST 955 until October 1946 and it never again saw revenue service in London, being scrapped in May 1947. W.J. Haynes

was not yet able to make rounded panels and contrived to produce the most angular of the wartime bodies supplied to London, given even greater emphasis by their unusually deep roof panels. Their unique appearance was underlined by the use of two shades of brown paint, chestnut for the main body panels and a darker brown for the roof. They did have the full complement of windows now allowed and a well finished interior with upholstered seats. The last Massey was received on 5th September.

The next batch of Guys to arrive in London came from another Wigan manufacturer, Northern Counties Motor & Engineering Company Limited whose product could hardly have offered a greater contrast to the Massey (G 154–173, G 219–257, G 269–311). Northern Counties took the relaxed specification well beyond the interpretation applied by other bodybuilders to produce a body whose appearance was fully in line with peacetime standards of design. The company had been allowed to continue using metal framing for its bodywork throughout the war and this enabled saloon windows to be radiused, adding further refinement to the smooth handsome looks. These bodies were also painted brown, in a slightly darker shade than the Masseys, but with a light cream relief band above the lower deck on the first 41 and a cream relief in the pre-war layout around the windows on the rest. Earlier vehicles in the batch retained hinged ventilators on the front windows and also had no side indicators. The interior gave quite a different impression. The first 20 were the last of the utilities to be delivered with wooden seats and the interior finish of all of them was made gloomy by the use of brown paint on all the mouldings. Upstairs the single skin roof looked particularly incongruous. No fewer than 102 bodies were supplied by Northern Counties, the first complete vehicle (G 154) arriving on 1st May 1945. Although deliveries came at the rate of three or four a week at first, the pace later slowed down and the last, G 311, did not arrive until 28th March 1946, only two days before the very last utility Guy.

The remaining orders were allocated to Park Royal and Weymann but fate had one more surprise in store before these traditional suppliers resumed production for London. Park Royal could not meet their immediate commitments at this time and obtained authority from the Ministry of Supply to subcontract part of their allocation to Northern Coachbuilders of Newcastle who

eventually built 26 (G 139–149, G 151–153, G 194–205). There was already one of the company's own design of body in London, on G 30 whose original Park Royal body had been destroyed by bombing, but this new batch was very different. They were built to Park Royal's own design using materials supplied by the Middlesex company and were indistinguishable from the real thing except in three respects. Most strikingly from outside, they were painted in a scheme of dark brown with a bright yellow ochre relief, applied pre-war style around the saloon windows. Inside their appearance was made more attractive by the pleasantly warm orange and brown material used to cover the seats, which came from

NCB's own stock and was a deal more cheerful than Park Royal's leathercloth. All carried NCB transfers on the side of the staircase. They were delivered between 4th May and 31st August 1945.

The Guys from NCB gave a preview of the revisions adopted by Park Royal for the relaxed austerity design, which proved to be minimal. The basic shape of the body shell did not change, the improvements being confined to extra opening windows, a curved rear dome and better seats. The 57 bodies were split between two orders, thirteen to complete the work started by NCB (G 206–218) and a final forty-four on which the specification was further enhanced by the use of tubular steel seat frames, and winding windows (G 319–357, G 431–435). All were painted red and white. They were delivered between 1st October 1945 and 30th March 1946, when G 435 was the last utility of all to join London Transport.

Later events will show how reluctant Park Royal seemed to be about moving away from its basic wartime body shell but one vehicle produced as part of its 1945 orders was an experimental metal framed unit, in anticipation of post-war production, G 150. Although its overall shape was similar to its contemporaries, G 150 could be recognised by its radiused windows and sliding vents. Internally it looked very modern with rounded window cappings covered in brown leathercloth which were very similar to the RT design.

The balance of sixty-two Guys (G 369–430) was supplied by Weymann, who resumed deliveries to London after a break of over two years, apart from the experimental Gs 136 and 137. Their relaxed austerity design was also very similar to the earlier utilities but the rear dome was rounded from the waist upwards. Inside, the seats were tubular framed and the opening windows were of the winding type. They were delivered

between 31st August and 5th December 1945. Most of the Guys had the same basic mechanical specification with sliding mesh crash gearboxes but thirty-four were equipped with a new constant mesh box (G 301–311, G 340–357, G 431–435).

Deliveries of Daimlers also continued throughout this period. There were already 92 Duple and Brush bodied Ds in stock on VE day out of an eventual total of 181 and delivery of a second batch of 35 with Brush bodies began on 12th May (D 93–127). Broadly similar to the first batch, they had rounded domes fore and aft and the other improvements of the relaxed specification. All but one was received by 5th July and all went to Merton garage to join the earlier 92. The latecomer was D 127 which arrived on 20th August and the reason for the delay was that it had a different mechanical specification, incorporating the new Daimler CD6 8.6 litre engine and a new Daimler rear axle. It was the first of a total of 13 CWD6s, the only one with Brush bodywork. Visually these buses could be distinguished by their slatted radiators and the flatter profile of their rear hubs but their greatest difference was in the sound they made, which had a distinctive heavy beat.

The final run of fifty-four utility Daimler deliveries was supplied exclusively by Duple, four with lowbridge bodywork (D 128–131) and fifty highbridge (D 132–181). The lowbridge buses were needed to complete the allocation of route 127 and were delivered between 1st and 10th November 1945. Delivery of the remainder was spread over the next four months, the last two being received on 11th March 1946, nineteen days before the last Guy. The 12 CWD6s and one CWA6 (D 132) were painted red and allocated to Merton but the remaining 37 CWA6s were delivered in Lincoln green and white with brown roofs and carried Green Line fleetnames and no fewer than five 'Green Line' bullseyes on the upper deck panels. They were to be allocated to Romford (London Road) garage for the resumption of coach services in March and April 1946.

While the first of the final batch of Daimlers was going through the shops at Duple, they were joined by some of the third make of chassis to be allocated to London Transport in 1945, Bristol. The Brislington company had been authorised to resume chassis building, using the AEC 7.7 litre engine as the power unit, at the beginning of 1944 and London Transport had been allocated a batch of 20 from the third sanction. Apart from minor differences to accommodate the lower position of the new PV2 radiator introduced with this sanction, the bodies were identical to those supplied on the Ds, including the use of moquette covered tubular framed seats. The low bonnet and radiator gave these buses a very modern appearance which was not let down by the handsome bodywork. B 10–29 were received from Duple between 30th November and 31st December 1945. All were allocated to Hanwell (later renamed Southall).

That is not quite the end of the story. The Ministry of Supply's final allocation to London Transport for 1945 covered not only the last 37 Guys, four lowbridge Daimlers and the 20 Bristols already mentioned, but also another batch of 20 vehicles which proved to be in marked contrast to the others. The Board's traditional supplier, AEC, had been authorised in March 1945 to resume chassis production and London Transport was allowed a share of the first production batch of Regent IIs which came on stream in November. Weymann built the bodies and although they were going through the shops at Addlestone at the same time as the Guys, their appearance could hardly have been more different. Weymann had decided to waste no time in moving to produc-

tion of its post-war metal framed body as quickly as possible and it was that classic design, a development of their pre-war model, which graced the new buses. In sharp contrast to their contemporaries, these bodies had elegantly curved front and rear profiles and, their most distinctive feature, flared skirt panels – breathtakingly good looking to eyes that had grown accustomed to the crude products of the war years.

The chassis were similar in most respects to the unfrozen Regents and equally lacking in refinement, having 7.7 litre engines with iron crankcases, and crash gearboxes. They were numbered STL 2682–2701 and came to be known almost universally by their Chiswick code 18STL20. Their mechanical specification included 7-inch dynamos which did not have

Above Thirty-seven of the final Duple-bodied batch of Ds were painted in Green Line colours for use on routes 721 and 722 from Romford when the coach services were restored in March and April 1946. The peace and quiet of a typical country town of the late 1940s, Brentwood, provides the setting for D 137 during the first two months of operation, when the blinds had white lettering on a black background. The GREEN LINE name can be seen six times from this angle and appeared three times more, twice on the offside and once on the rear, the repetition perhaps being thought necessary to reassure a disbelieving public that they really were Green Lines.
The Omnibus Society

Left Duple bodies were also mounted on the batch of 20 Bristol K6As delivered at the end of 1945, and their simple but stylish lines nicely complemented the elegance of the newly introduced low-slung PV2 radiator and bonnet. Accompanying B 23 and 28 at Empire Pool Wembley is an unidentified Alperton Guy from Weymann's last batch, which were new at about the same time. D.W.K. Jones

being absorbed into the fleet while service levels
were being improved was to cause quite a lot of
disturbance to vehicle allocations. The overriding
factor which influenced the spread of allocations
of most of the utilities was that their overall
height was about six inches greater than the standard Chiswick built fleet and there were many
garages which could not accommodate them. In
the case of the Central Bus Daimlers what effectually determined their allocation was the
decision of the Ministry of War Transport to
include six lowbridge examples in the first allocation to London Transport. These were needed for
route 127 operated by Merton, one of the largest
garages in the fleet and therefore well placed to
become the home of all 144. They dislodged a like
number of STLs, which were put to good use at
other garages as a contribution to the augmentation programme.

The larger number of Guys was spread more
widely. Before the 1945 influx, the class was operating from four garages, Tottenham, Hanwell,
Alperton and Barking, being in a minority at all
except Alperton where they covered nearly three-
quarters of the scheduled output. The first
garages to receive the new intake in May 1945
were Alperton, replacing STLs on route 79 and
Barking, where they took over from LTs on routes
23B, 23C, 62, 145 and 175. Curiously the 23,
which already had a mixed allocation of Guys and
LTs, did not have its allocation completed until
October/November after which route 87 was the
only one operated by LTs, except for the Sunday
only allocation on route 9. The original decision to
put the underpowered Guys onto the 23, a busy
trunk route passing through the heart of the West
End, has always seemed a strange choice. The
decision to delay its completion begs the question
whether thought was being given to transferring
them to the less unsuitable suburban route 87.
Perhaps intervening events at Victoria garage had
some influence on the decision.

Victoria, a modern garage only five years old
and with the necessary headroom for utilities,
had already been the home of the unfrozen STDs
for three years when it was chosen for a substantial allocation of Guys in July 1945. Forty-five

enough output for operation in the Central Area,
and although the first three were painted red and
white they were all allocated to Country Buses.
The remainder were finished in the standard
Country livery of the time, green and white with
brown roof. The first to arrive was STL 2683 on
26th November 1945 and all twenty were in stock
by 7th February 1946. The entire batch was allocated to Watford High Street garage for operation
on route 321.

In the ten months between the end of the
European war and the arrival of the last utility
Guy, the London Transport double-deck fleet had
grown by 405 vehicles. The return of STs from
other operators added another 79 to the available
fleet, which now stood at 5,774, a useful 673
above the 1939 level. At first the extra buses were
used to replace, directly or indirectly, older buses
in the Central Bus fleet, continuing a trend which
had been in evidence since mid-1944. The class
most heavily hit was the ST whose peak vehicle
requirement sank from 511 in the summer of
1944 to only 345 in September 1945, but the
substantial improvements in service levels over
the ensuing six months saw a revival in their
fortunes, over 200 being returned to service.

The coincidence of so many buses of new types

were sent there for routes 52 and 77A, replacing RTs and STLs on these important central London routes and allowing the pre-war STDs then allocated to route 22 to return home to Hendon, where they replaced STs. The loss of RTs and STDs with their high standard of performance, in favour of the lumbering Guys soon fermented discontent among the drivers at Victoria and it was not long before an exchange was organised with STLs from Enfield garage. This took place in October by which time Enfield had started to receive an allocation of new vehicles, which together with the transfers replaced the STs on route 121 and STLs on all but route 128. Guys could not run on route 128 because the railway bridge in Church Street, Edmonton, was too low. In the meantime, Hornchurch had been added to the Guy portfolio, releasing a mixture of STs, LTs and STLs and subsequently Upton Park became the last garage to receive new deliveries, again losing STs and LTs. While Upton Park's large assignment of Guys was going into service, the 20 Duple bodied Bristols arrived and were sent to Hanwell to join the original nine. There they replaced a similar number of Guys operating on routes 92/A.

For the most part, the settled pattern of vehicle types in garages was not disturbed by the wide-ranging redeployment of buses replaced by the utilities, as most of the LTs and STLs could be transferred to garages already operating the types for the augmentation of services. The one major exception was at Palmers Green, where the seeds of discontent (which may have had long-lasting consequences) were sown when, between October 1945 and January 1946, the entire allocation of STLs was replaced by LTs made surplus at Barking and Upton Park. A smaller exception, which worked the other way, was the unexplained decision to allocate STLs to Muswell Hill for route 125 in place of LTs. Another of the consequences of these redeployments was the removal of the last remaining petrol engined STLs from Catford. The STs were not so readily accommodated and settled instead into a somewhat 'Cinderella' role in which they were used to top up allocations where the correct type was not available in sufficient numbers. They therefore began to appear in small pockets all around the fleet.

London Transport now confidently expected to be able to enjoy the fruits of its wartime research and planning with the delivery of the first of its fleet of post-war RTs. AEC had already started building the chassis and the first was received by the Board in March 1946, after which production soon built up to a regular flow. Unfortunately, the new principles which had been adopted for the bodywork, involving jig building to fine tolerances, were obviously causing difficulties at the bodybuilders, Park Royal and Weymann. Despite repeated assurances of an early delivery date, it was to be over a year before the first completed bus was received. If London Transport had any ideas about making do with standard manufac-

turers' bodies on the RT chassis they quickly resisted the temptation but they did continue to take non-standard buses into the fleet as short-term stop-gaps. The Ministry of Supply was still at this time responsible for allocating chassis and they authorised another 100 Daimlers, 96 Leylands and 50 AECs for delivery during 1946. The AECs and 31 of the Leylands were to be single-deckers, the first new to London since 1939.

The first of this 246 to be received were the AECs but developments in the single-deck fleet will be covered later in the chapter, so that the double-deck story can be concluded without interruption. The first of the double-deckers to arrive were the Daimlers. The Coventry company had by that time launched its post-war CV model but London Transport chose to take CWA6s, presumably in the interests of standardisation, and these were the last of that model to be produced at Coventry. The only differences from the earlier batches were a different make of exhauster for the servo brake and the use of the CWD6 type of slatted radiator shell.

The government no longer controlled the allocation of bodywork contracts and the Board was free to place the work with one of its traditional 'outside' suppliers. Weymann was approached but did not have the capacity to take on the work, otherwise London might have been graced with another hundred buses bearing the same distinctively handsome design as the 18STL20s. The contract was therefore placed with Park Royal who were able to do the work but were not yet in a position to switch fully to peacetime standards of construction. The basic design of the resulting bodies was therefore the same as the wartime models, apart from a more rounded rear dome, and they had wooden framed body structures. Because suitable quality materials were still in short supply, the company was

The Park Royal bodies on the 'Sutton' Daimlers had the same profile as the austerity version but had all the trimmings of a peace-time product, including a full set of route and destination blinds although these were fated never to be used. As can be seen on the one in the background, the box at the rear projected untidily breaking up the smooth lines of the bodywork. These were the only post-war buses to be given a number box in the rear display, surprisingly as the decision had already been taken to eliminate the separate rear number. Apart from D 209 and its unidentified sibling, there are two of Merton's utility Daimlers, marking Morden out as the heart of London's Daimlerland. LT Museum

obliged to use unseasoned timber, thereby storing up trouble for the future. Nevertheless, the return of half-drop opening windows to the front upper deck and the inclusion of a full set of 3-piece indicators front and back transformed their appearance to give them an authentic peacetime look. The rear profile was somewhat marred by the need for the indicators to bulge outwards. The break with wartime practice was given further prominence by the application to the whole batch of a new livery which had first appeared on overhauled STLs in November 1945. It resembled one of the styles tried out on RT 1 in 1939, the whole of the body being painted red apart from black wings and two thin cream relief bands, one above the upper deck windows and the other between the decks. The Daimlers were the only new buses to receive this scheme, which was otherwise applied only to STLs and three 2RT2s and had already been superseded before the last D was delivered.

The interior was finished in a style similar to that of pre-war years, brown below the middle of the windows and cream above, with a light green band above the windows. The seats were of the same tubular steel pattern that had been used on more recent utilities but were covered in the standard post-war moquette, the first time it was used on a double-decker. Another novel feature was the appearance for the first time on a motor bus of the lower deck bell cord, which was to remain a feature of London Transport buses for nearly forty years.

It might have been expected that the opportunity would be taken to use some of the new buses to clear out the remaining STLs from Merton but this was not practicable because the Park Royal bodies were too high to go through the main door-

ways of that garage. By chance, Merton was the engineering parent of Sutton garage, which needed 100 buses to cover its peak vehicle requirement of 92, and this settled their fate. They were destined rarely to stray from their home base, fully justifying the nickname 'Sutton Daimlers', with which they were labelled almost from the start.

The last of the non-standard double-deckers was a batch of 65 of Leyland's new PD1 model Titan with the company's own metal-framed bodywork. In overall appearance they bore a marked similarity to the pre-war STDs, even down to having a roof route number box at the front. Unlike the Daimlers, however, they had no provision for indicators at the back, other than the usual single aperture display above the platform. Apart from this, they could be distinguished readily enough because they had a new type of chromium plated, slatted radiator shell, with a distinctively offset filler cap, and a heavily curved rear end, somewhat similar to the new Weymann bodies. They were also painted in a new colour scheme which included a band of cream relief around the upper deck windows as well as the one between decks. Like most recent double deckers, the Titans were above standard height, which restricted the possibilities for their allocation.

The chassis specification included the new 7.4 litre engine, which had been developed from a unit supplied for use in tanks during the war and was capable of developing the same power output as the pre-war 8.6 litre engine, a synchromesh gearbox and vacuum servo brakes. The sound of this combination was completely different from the deep throated roar of the pre-war model, more strangulated tenor than fruity bass and, to many ears, less refined and a great deal noisier. They were numbered STD 112–176 and classified 4STD3.

STD 112 was the first into stock on 28th August but it was a month before any more arrived. After that they came quickly, at the rate of five or six a week and the last, STD 165 out of sequence, arrived on 16th December. If earlier practice had been followed the Titans would probably all have gone to one garage but this comparatively small batch was at first spread between five garages and ultimately four. The first four of 22 went into service on 1st October at Victoria garage where they were spread around all its routes in small numbers. This was a slightly surprising choice as, apart from the unfrozen STDs, this garage had a fleet of relatively modern STLs but at least this time the drivers apparently accepted them and they were to remain there for seven years. Victoria now achieved the distinction of having operated all three types of STDs at different times, the only garage to do so.

Next came Potters Bar, seemingly a more deserving recipient because at that time it had an allocation of open-staircase LTs, STs and petrol-engined STLs. Eight STDs were allocated between 11th and 23rd October for the important

Hanwell garage built up a surprisingly varied fleet in the mid-1940s, when the incumbent LTs and STLs were joined successively by Bristols and Guys and finally by some of the post-war STDs, including STD 159 seen laying over at Greenford on route 55. These were the first new buses to have the 1946 livery with cream around the upper deck windows which then became standard until 1950. This type also ran on routes 92/A for a time. D.W.K. Jones

trunk route 134 on which the LTs normally ran. Whether or not it had been intended to complete the allocation to route 134, which needed 29 buses, is not known but no more were sent to Potters Bar and on 20th November these eight were abruptly removed and transferred to Loughton, for route 38A, in exchange for LTs. No reason for this decision has yet been discovered but the most likely explanation would seem to be that the drivers at Potters Bar preferred to wait for the new RTs than to accept new buses with manually operated gearboxes on this busy and arduous route. Unfortunately, this episode seems also to have gone unrecorded by photographers and remains ephemeral.

The third allotment in October was to Loughton, which operated a fleet of open-staircase LTs on routes 10A and 38A. Together with those transferred from Potters Bar, Loughton took 25, the largest single allocation at the time and only five short of covering the total schedule at the garage. Another surprising allocation, of nine, was to Hanwell, which already had a very mixed fleet of LT, STL, B and G. Although the STDs went onto STL-operated route 55, the displaced STLs were used to replace LTs on route 105. A more understandable allocation was to Croydon, as this garage operated almost entirely petrol engined STLs and STs which were ripe for replacement but the nine which went there in December hardly made a dent in the problems of that garage. Croydon was chosen because the route to which six of them were allocated, the 115, was also operated by Sutton who supplied brand new Daimlers. It was the only route other than the 10A to have a full complement of the type, the balance of three being put to work on route 133.

The arrival of the STDs, which completed the delivery of non-standard double-deckers, triggered the withdrawal of four open-staircase LTs and a standard ST but none was scrapped immediately. A more interesting and surprising consequence of the allocation to Croydon was that eight Tilling STLs were transferred in December 1946 to Country Buses, the first time that the type had strayed away from the former Tilling garages in south-east London. They were used at first on the many works services operated by Two

Below Although officially intended for use on works services the Tilling STLs sent to Country Buses were often used on regular services, as is the case with green STL 117 working a through journey to Hemel Hempstead on route 302 at Bushey Arches. Gavin Martin collection

Waters garage but four of them were reallocated in February 1947, two each to the two Watford garages, High Street and Leavesden Road, for use on similar services. These were joined later by one more at Leavesden Road. Even more surprisingly, six of them were repainted in the Country Bus green and white livery in which they looked fine but alien.

Despite its preoccupation with post-war recovery, the Board did not lose its taste for innovation and, with an eye to possible future trends, undertook a remarkable experiment with payment of fares to a seated conductor. The purpose was to test the theory that the efficiency of fare collection could be improved, in other words that it would ensure that everyone paid a fare, and that the work of the conductor could be made more comfortable. For this to work, the layout of the entrance had to be altered radically to make room both for a cash desk and for an area where passengers could stand while waiting to pay. Power operated doors would also be needed.

Five vehicles were adapted for the trials, two trolleybuses and three buses all but one of which had suffered war damage. The exception was trolleybus 61 which was chosen because it already had a centre entrance with platform doors and could most easily be altered to accommodate the conductor at a desk partially under the stairs. This was fitted with a large till with a lockable sliding lid. Buttons to operate the power doors were provided on the desk on this and all of the conversions but on the two trolleybuses they were also installed in the driver's cab as he might have to operate the doors while the conductor was changing a frog or attending to the trolley poles. Three nearside seats were removed to provide circulating space and the single step stairwell was filled in to give a flat floor throughout. The longitudinal seat alongside the driver was removed and a full width bulkhead installed so that a rearward facing seat for five could be provided and more circulating space given for waiting passengers. The capacity was reduced from 74 to 69 as a result.

The second trolleybus was C3 class number 378. This kept its rear entrance and was fitted with power operated platform doors and an emergency exit in the rear wall. The platform was enlarged by moving the staircase forward and a flat floor was created by extending the lower saloon level right up to the entrance steps. The conductor was seated under the new spiral staircase at a desk with a till similar to number 61 but smaller because on this bus an ordinary TIM machine was used. The changes reduced the seating capacity from 70 to 64. A similar conversion was made to RT 97 which also retained its rear entrance, except that the staircase was moved even further forward and the conductor sat on the

nearside just ahead of the entrance. This created a large full-width platform capable of holding 19 passengers, rather reminiscent of the arrangement on the LTs and STs. Upstairs there was another echo of older times as there was a full width seat across the back of the bus. The finished vehicle seated only 50 passengers.

Two different ideas for a centre entrance layout were tried on the two STLs. STL 1793 had a doorway ahead of the rear wheels immediately opposite a staircase which ascended rearwards over the wheel arch. The conductor's desk was alongside the stairs in the front section of the bus and the circulating space for eight passengers was in the area between the stairs and the nearside longitudinal seat over the rear wheel. This conversion was interesting in that the emergency exit for the lower deck was the same type of Y-shaped window as used on the upper deck, so that a full width bench seat could be provided. The seating capacity remained at 56. The modifications to STL 2284 were more radical as it was

the only one of the five to have separate entrance and exit doors, each two feet wide. The entrance was at the extreme front and the exit in the third bay, with the conductor's desk fitted snugly in between. The rearward ascending staircase was situated opposite the exit door and the whole area around the desk and ahead of the stairs was the circulating space. To avoid the loss of too much seating capacity at busy times the rather illogical step was taken of having four tip-up seats, whose use was intended for those times when the circulating space would be most needed. There were only two rows of forward facing seats on the lower deck, at the extreme rear, the rest being longitudinal over and ahead of the wheel arches and the total capacity was reduced to 54. Both STLs had a bench seat for four across the rear of the upper deck.

The 'Pay As You Board' experiments were carried out at first on bus route 65 and trolleybus route 604, starting with STL 1793 which entered service on 25th October 1944. Trolleybus 61

Above left STL 1793 had an STL 14/1 body dating from October 1937 which had been damaged by bombing and rebuilt for the experiment. The platform was moved forward to the second bay and enclosed by a power-operated sliding door immediately opposite the repositioned staircase. The box for the intermediate point display above the doorway was smaller than usual on an STL and was fitted with a blind from an ST. It is seen in the winter of 1944–45, still fully dressed in wartime trim, sharing the stand at Argyle Road, Ealing with an ST. *The Omnibus Society*

Above right The rear of STL 1793 was interesting in having a full width window on the lower deck with an emergency exit of the same type as normally fitted on the upper, rather than a hinged door in the centre as was fitted to STL 2284.

Left The lower deck interior of STL 2284, showing the leathercloth covered longitudinal seats in the rear half and, on the front bulkhead, one of the four tip-up seats, while, ahead of the exit doorway, the conductor's desk with change-giving and ticket machines can be seen. The compactness of the spiral staircase is also well illustrated. *Ken Glazier collection*

Far left One of the tickets issued from the cash register-type machines, in this case for a 2d fare.

followed on 14th March 1945, STL 2284 on 13th November, trolleybus 378 on 1st December 1945 and RT 97 on 2nd January 1946. RT 97 later moved onto Green Line route 721 between 18th April and 2nd July 1946, after which it was withdrawn for its experimental modification as RTC 1. STL 2284 also saw service elsewhere in PAYB form, on route 445 at Windsor between 22nd May and 25th June 1946, after which it was withdrawn. STL 1793 had already been withdrawn on 6th March 1945, returning to normal operation on route 11 from Dalston garage. Trolleybus 61 went back to normal in October 1945 and 378 on 22nd March 1946.

Not surprisingly, the buses were found to be too slow in operation, causing disruption to the service and there were many complaints from passengers who did not warm to the idea of waiting in the open air while others ahead of them paid their fares. The one thing that probably was successful was the increased comfort and ease for the conductor but the mechanical ticket issuing machines did not increase the speed of ticket issue as much had been hoped. Although every passenger had to pay a fare, the checks on over-riding were not so secure and there was an increase, much as was to be experienced many years later with driver only operation. The experiments were declared a failure and the post-war replacement programme was based on conventional open platform buses with roving conductors.

In the meantime, the single-deck fleet had also been refreshed. The new buses were the first single-deckers acquired by the Board for over six years and the first large saloons for Central Buses since the 5Q5s ten years earlier. The 50 AECs were Regal I 0662s and, like the 18STL20s, were a standard Southall product with crash gearbox and the A173 7.7 litre direct injection engine which was already used in large numbers of STLs. The Board again chose Weymann to supply the 35-seat bodywork which in this case was of composite construction. The vehicles that emerged from the Addlestone factory carried another elegant design based on the company's most recent pre-war models, and the bodies were clearly direct descendants of those fitted to the 11T11s. They became T 719–768 and were classified 14T12. A new single-deck livery was unveiled on these buses, mainly red with a thin cream band around the saloon windows, echoing the 1945 double-deck scheme which had been so quickly discarded. This basic arrangement was to survive for 25 years. With the single exception of G 150 these were the first motor buses delivered new to London Transport with sliding vents on their saloon windows and were also the first to have the new standard moquette which was to feature on the whole of the post-war RT family.

T 726 was the first to be taken into stock, on 7th March, nearly seven weeks before the first of the 'Sutton' Daimlers, and deliveries were completed on 30th October. The first garage to receive an allocation was Uxbridge, who used them on route 223. By happy coincidence this put them at close quarters with their larger STL siblings in service on route 321 at Uxbridge station. Later deliveries went to Kingston for routes 206, 215, 218, 219 and finally to Muswell Hill for route 212.

In most cases the 14T12s replaced single-deck LTs but on route 206 they took over from Cubs when it was extended to Hampton Court. On route 218 they replaced older Regals but the 14T12s were too heavy to cross Walton Bridge and were therefore confined to the Kingston – Walton-on-Thames short workings. The Cubs joined the stockpile of spare 20-seaters but the Ts and LTs were redistributed around the fleet to provide the resources for the augmentation of services which added 59 to the Central Bus peak vehicle requirement during 1946.

The last of the 'stop gaps' were the Leyland single-deckers which began to arrive on 3rd December 1946, a fortnight before the last of the STDs. They were Tiger PS1s, effectually a single-deck version of the PD1 with the same engine and transmission, and were given fleet numbers

The body of RT 1 was transferred to RT 19 in November 1945 in connection with its role as the prototype 3RT and the chassis was scrapped in September 1946. There were various small variations on RT 1's body compared with the RT2, perhaps the most prominent being the curved top to the driver's cab door, which can be seen in this photograph of RT 19 taken at Aldgate.
A.B. Cross

Leyland trolleybus 407 was one of 26 whose bodies were damaged beyond repair when Bexleyheath depot was hit by a V1 flying bomb on 29th June 1944. These and 19 others similarly damaged were given new bodies between 1945 and 1948. No. 407, which had originally carried a Metro-Cammell body, was one of 25 for which East Lancashire supplied these handsome bodies, similar in many respects to the L and M classes delivered at the beginning of the war. The suffix 'B' was added to the fleet number and to the classification, making it a D2B. It is seen at the head of a line of others on the stand at Woolwich Ferry. *Vanguard*

TD 1–31. They had the same handsome Weymann bodywork as the 14T12s but with a straight bottom edge to the cab window which gave them a crisper and more modern look and seating only 33, undoubtedly because the bonnet was longer. Deliveries were slower than the double-deckers and there were none at all from late February and for much of March, probably as a consequence of the severe winter weather which had exacerbated fuel and power shortages, so that the last did not arrive until 19th June 1947. Unlike the STDs, these 31 buses were concentrated at one garage, Muswell Hill, where they provided the entire stock for route 212, with the few left over running on route 210 although, in practice, LTs still appeared frequently.

This displaced the 14T12s so recently allocated to route 212 and which for a time ran alongside the new TDs, providing an interesting comparison of the competing models from two major manufacturers. Five went to Uxbridge for operation on route 222 and the remaining 15 to Sidcup where they formed a mixed allocation with 5Q5s on route 241.

While all these developments were taking place in the motor bus fleet, the Tram & Trolleybus department was taking steps to recover some of the trolleybuses damaged in the V1 Blitz. The contract for supplying new bodies for the 45 salvaged chassis was split between East Lancashire Coachbuilders, who had never before built anything for London Transport, and Northern Coachbuilders, who had supplied some bodies on

Guy motor bus chassis. There were 16 AECs and 29 Leylands and both manufacturers rebodied both, although it might have simplified construction had they been divided by make of chassis. East Lancashire dealt with 19 Leylands and six AECs, NCB with ten of each. In all but two cases the vehicles kept their former type classification and fleet number with the addition of the suffix 'B' for East Lancashire and 'C' for NCB. The exceptions were 97C and 98C which had been short-wheelbase B2s but had had their chassis lengthened when they were rebodied; they were reclassified D2C. The first East Lancs example was delivered to the Board in October 1945 but they did not complete their contract until April 1948, at the rate of one or two a month and with a complete break in production between April and December 1947. This was partly due to shortages of both material and labour but there was also a dispute about the price of the contract. Northern Counties were much quicker, delivering their 20 between December 1945 and September 1946. The Leylands were all allocated to Bexleyheath depot, the B-suffix AECs to Highgate (except for 1385B which went to West Ham) and the C-suffix AECs to West Ham. The extra resources were used mainly to provide badly needed spares back-up to the rest of the fleet but did also allow some augmentation of services.

The East Lancashire bodies were metal-framed and very similar in appearance to the standard bodies of the later pre-war designs, differing only in a few details which were nevertheless an aid to identifying them in a crowd. The design of the front upper deck corner pillars was particularly notable and appears to have set the standard for the company's post-war styling. East Lancs were responsible for ten D2, nine H1, three J2, two M1 and a single N1. One of the J2s, 1001A, was unique in having been rebodied already as part of the programme carried out by Weymann in 1941/1942. The NCB bodywork, of composite construction, had a softer more rounded profile than that from East Lancs and could be recognised by the distinctive curve of the rain-shields on the front dome. This shape was to feature on their subsequent standard bodies. NCB bodied eight D2, three E1, two E2 and five E3.

With the lifting of the government wartime embargo on the disposal of roadworthy vehicles, London Transport took the opportunity during 1946 to rid itself of a number of non-standard or experimental buses. In truth their retention in the fleet was a mere nod towards the law as most of them had not seen service for a good many years. In the experimental category were Q 1, TF 1 and C 1, all of which were sold in January 1946, the four remaining double-deck Qs, 2, 4, 5 and 188 sold in March and LT 1137 which was scrapped in July. The non-standard buses were STL 558 and ST 1029, both formerly owned by Independents, and Ts 274 and 305 which had been fitted experimentally with 8.8 litre oil engines. Eight Tilling STs, four of which had seen no London service since 1941, were also scrapped but perhaps the saddest casualty was the chassis of RT 1 which was broken up in September.

After this clearout and the return of the single-deckers still on one or other form of war service, the fleet of large single-deckers stood at a total of 942, of which 25 more were private hire coaches. The 917 service buses and coaches provided an 18 per cent margin over the fleet-wide peak vehicle requirement of 776 in the summer of 1946. The 20-seater fleet was even more generously endowed, with 122 vehicles to cover a schedule of forty-one. However, nearly one third of the large saloons, comprising 83 Ts and 190 LTs nearly all in the Central Bus fleet, qualified for inclusion in the 'obsolete fleet' category and were overdue for replacement. The double-deck fleet now comprised 5,923 vehicles, a total that was 554 more than in May 1945.

In this microcosm of the early post-war dilemma, an anxious queue waits for a 49 in Kensington High Street while three well-laden buses make their way towards Hammersmith on routes 9 and 73. The leading bus is open staircase LT 106, an LT2/1 with rounded cab, being used to cover shortages in the oil-engined fleet represented here by LT 555, a 1/12LT3/3, and LT 193, one of the original oilers (4LT5/4). Gavin Martin

3   THE AUSTERE PEACE

The 321 was one of the first routes to have its Sunday morning service restored in October 1945, perhaps reflecting its importance as a major contributor to Watford's town service network as well as providing important trunk links. During the following July 'Bluebird' ST 1070, a 48-seater dating from 1932, waits outside the Post Office in Market Street Watford for a fresh crew to travel up from High Street garage. *A.B. Cross*

Right Route 52 had its late evening service restored closer to its pre-war level from 13th March 1946 lifting the impoverished wartime frequency to 18 an hour. One of the more interesting buses to be found on the 52 at that time was STL 268, a 1/16STL18, which still had a glazed staircase window. *G.F. Ashwell*

ERMANY capitulated on 7th May 1945 but no official announcement was made immediately and it proved to be a strange day in twilight between war and peace. The news leaked out as soon as German radio started broadcasting instructions to German troops to surrender, provoking an announcement on the six o'clock news that the following day would be VE Day. Even so, it was not until the afternoon of 8th May that Churchill formally announced the end of the war. The delay was in deference to Joseph Stalin who did not accept the submission as valid until the German command on the eastern front had surrendered to a Soviet general. This did not stop people wanting to do something to celebrate; during the beautiful spring evening of the 7th people began to drift into the West End in increasing numbers and London exploded joyously into a spontaneous celebration on the streets. The West End became one mass of people dancing, singing or just walking around happily (or as some said 'vacuously'), completely blocking roads and forcing the diversion of buses far and wide. Elsewhere, all over London, people were hanging out flags and bunting which had been stored 'for the duration'. On VE Day

itself, commercial advertisements were illuminated and public buildings floodlit for the first time since the summer of 1939, adding an ephemeral touch of fairyland to the even more wild celebrations which took place, again effectively closing the West End to traffic. All over London spontaneous street parties took place, usually around the inevitable bonfire.

The extra demand on services to and from the West End put an almost intolerable burden on a system already under considerable stress. The Board later admitted that it had been embarrassed by the demand but in the atmosphere of that joyous day, nobody was complaining about travelling problems. That would come soon enough as the realities of the post-war situation bore down on an exhausted public. Some families were less inclined to celebrate just yet because, while these wild celebrations were taking place, there was still a serious and nasty conflict with Japan raging in the Pacific. Although the Allies were making ground doggedly it was against a fanatically suicidal enemy and, at the time, it seemed that that war was likely to go on until for at least another 18 months or, according to some sources, even as late as 1950. This had important implications for London Transport, notably that supplies of rubber would continue to be limited and that the personnel to drive, conduct and maintain the extra buses trams and trolleybuses needed for the gradual restoration of services were not yet being released from the armed services. For the whole of London Transport, including the Underground and general administration, the number of staff on national service was 22,794, and there was little prospect in May 1945 that many of them would be returning in the near future.

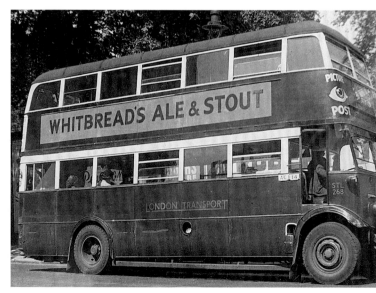

Nevertheless, improvements were sanctioned. The basic petrol ration was reintroduced on 6th June and at the beginning of July the Ministry of War Transport announced that the operation of private hires could be resumed, subject to the sanction of Regional Traffic Commissioners. The maximum return mileage was still restricted to 70 miles, with a further restriction in London to 50 miles for holiday and recreational trips. In August and September recreational and holiday coach trips which returned on the same day were allowed on Sundays to resorts on the coast between Clacton and Southsea but long distance services, including Green Line, were embargoed.

Wartime controls were removed with agreeable rapidity during the summer of 1945, most of those affecting public transport being discontinued in June and July. The wartime powers which enabled Regional Traffic Commissioners to restrict what they deemed unnecessary services, continued for the time being but some easements were allowed. On services operating outside the Metropolitan Traffic Area, there were curfews, which had been in force since May 1943, forbidding the operation of any but essential works services after 9pm on all days of the week and before 1pm on Sundays. The whole of the Country Area and 18 Central Bus routes were caught in this net. However, the evening curfew applied to only three of the Central Bus routes and then only on Sundays. The Central Bus routes were restored at these times from 11th July but Country Buses, having made a start with restoring late evening services to 117 routes on 4th July, were unable to move as quickly because they did not have enough staff.

The first group of routes to have their Sunday morning services restored, on 17th October, was mainly in the west and north-west, covering services operated by Addlestone, Amersham, Luton, Staines, Tring, part of Two Waters, Watford (High Street and Leavesden Road), Windsor and also in the east at Epping and Grays. Further programmes followed on 21st November, in the south at Chelsham, Crawley, Dorking, Godstone, Guildford, Leatherhead and Reigate; and 5th December in the north and north-east at Hatfield, Hertford, Hitchin, St Albans and the rest of Two Waters. The Country Bus programme of restorations was not finished until 6th February 1946, when the routes in the South East District from Dartford, Dunton Green, Swanley and Northfleet were rescheduled. Interestingly, these had been among the first to have their late evening services restored in July 1945 but in all other cases where the evening restoration had not been made at that time, it was effected at the same time as the Sunday changes.

Central Buses continued to make small improvements through the summer of 1945, adding 46 double-deck and five single-deck buses to its peak schedules. Increased capacity was also given to route 243 on 12th September when its single-deck LTs were replaced by STs, and to the Uxbridge to Stanwell service on route 224 from 3rd October, when Ts replaced Cubs. Country Buses made a few small improvements to frequencies and route 497 (Gravesend – Dover Road Schools) was changed from single-deck to double-deck operation on 31st March 1945. Otherwise, apart from the removal of the curfew on Country Buses, little changed.

Following an approach from London Transport, who had had representations from the Trade Union, one of the other emergency measures which was altered but not entirely removed, by the Regional Traffic Commissioner was the wartime relaxation of the rules concerning standing passengers. From 10th November 1945, the number of standing passengers allowed in off-peak hours on vehicles seating 24 or more, was reduced from 12 to eight. This was not good enough for the staff and a different approach was negotiated, culminating on 15th May 1946 in a return to the pre-war practice of allowing five standing only during peaks and after 10.30 pm.

Below Route 2 lost its interesting peak hour extension from Golders Green to Arnos Grove in February 1946 but the 'round-the-corner' link from south to east at Whetstone was continued by new route 251A between Arnos Grove and North Finchley operated by Muswell Hill garage with LTs. LT 920 is seen opposite Arnos Grove station. *Peter Mitchell*

Bottom Park Royal bodied G 114 and Weymann G 372 are at Kew Green on the 83A summer Sunday variant of route 83, restored in May 1946 after a lapse of four years. *J.H. Aston*

Hampton Court again became a summer Sunday destination in 1946 and Vrow Walk once more thronged with buses, especially on Bank Holidays when the area behind RT 77 on route 14A would often be filled with a snaking queue of enormous length. J.H. Aston

Although the Press, uncharacteristically, played down the implications of this drastic reduction, the loss of anything between ten and 15 per cent of capacity was to have a serious effect on the adequacy of services. A fuller account of this dispute can be found in Chapter 6.

Meanwhile, the war in the Far East came to an abrupt and brutal end on 15th August following the dropping of the two atomic bombs on Hiroshima and Nagasaki. There was a delay between the 10th August, when the Japanese government decided to surrender, and the 15th August when the formal capitulation was announced but many Londoners were impatient to celebrate. Crowds began to accumulate on the 10th August and traffic in Piccadilly was brought to a standstill frequently while London had the strange experience of a kind of New York ticker-tape celebration as people tore paper into shreds and dropped it from windows. On VJ Day itself, 15th August, London again went wild with relief and joy and there was a repeat of the bright lights, bonfires and general traffic disruption which had characterised VE day three months earlier.

Everybody thought and expected that now it would be possible to concentrate on restoring peacetime standards and London Transport looked forward to the demobilisation of the armed forces and the return of its many staff to provide the manpower for the desired improvements. As things turned out, not everyone who was released came back to work for the Board. By the time nearly all had been released from the armed services at the end of 1947, the shortfall for the whole of London Transport was nearly 19 per cent of those who had been called up. Being a bus-man was no longer such a prize as it had been before the war. Up to this time the employment of women in 'men's jobs' was regarded as a temporary expedient and the intention had always been to return to an all-male workforce as soon as the men were available. The changed circumstances of the post-war labour market led London Trans-

port to reverse this policy from 1st February 1947. This subject is another that is covered more fully in Chapter 6.

The winter schedules on 10th October (Central Buses), 17th October (Country Buses) and 21st November (Trams & Trolleybuses) did contain some important changes. Most significantly, the usual reduction in Sunday services from summer to winter did not take place. Instead there was an increase which took the number of vehicles in service on Sunday above the level of the winter of 1944 by 9 per cent on Central Buses, 14 per cent on trams, 12 per cent on trolleybuses and 5 per cent on Country Buses. Most Central Bus Sunday schedules did not change but some were increased and in total were 1 per cent higher than for the summer, the total number of allocated buses rising above 2,800 for the first time since the summer of 1939. The practices of bringing the evening peak an hour earlier during the winter and shortening the traffic day, also came to an end. The reduced and curtailed services which had operated in blackout hours continued to apply for the time being but were no longer related to the main hours of winter darkness, the later summer starting time being kept in operation into the winter. Lack of staff restricted the extent to which evening frequencies and later finishing times on Central Buses could be restored.

At the beginning of 1946, the Board announced what it called its immediate tasks. All services had to be restored to a high standard of adequacy, comfort and convenience as quickly as possible and the development of services in 'outlying areas' should be resumed. It would also be necessary to replace the south London trams by 'a more modern and attractive form of transport', although at this stage the door remained open to either motor buses or trolleybuses. Arrears of maintenance of rolling stock had to be overtaken and life-expired vehicles replaced. The 1935–1940 New Works Programme was also to be brought to a conclusion. During the year considerable progress was made towards restoring services.

The Country Bus department was to be very busy during 1946, notably with the restoration of Green Line services (see Chapter 5) but also with significant improvements to bus services. On 16th January, double-deck buses were substituted for single-deckers on route 418 and in order to make this possible, two major alterations were made to the route. The wartime extension to Guildford over the former Cub-operated 432 was withdrawn and the 432 re-introduced as a two-man route using 4Q4s, but meeting the 418 end on at Great Bookham instead of Effingham as in former times. The 418 was also withdrawn from the deviation via Horton and sent by a more direct route via Hook Road. The Horton loop was served by a new single-deck 419 between West Ewell (Bungalow Stores) and Epsom Station.

The reinstatement of the last group of Sunday morning services in the south-eastern area of Country Buses prompted a programme of changes on 6th February which involved no less than the complete restructuring of the Thames-side services in north Kent. Route numbers 401A (Dartford – Horton Kirby), 407 (Sidcup – Horns Cross/ Gravesend) and 492 (Belvedere – Horns Cross/Gravesend) disappeared and were replaced by changes to routes 477, 480 and 496 and the introduction of three new routes. The 477 was extended from its Monday–Friday terminus at Horns Cross and on Saturday and Sunday from Gravesend, to Denton, and route 480 was given a more frequent service between Dartford and Erith. The 496 was extended from Northfleet to Dartford in evening peak hours. The new routes were the 467 (Sidcup Station – Bexley – Dartford Horton Kirby), 475 (Works service Lower Belvedere Crayford Ness) and 491 (Lower Belvedere – Northumberland Heath – Barnehurst – Crayford – Dartford – Horton Kirby). Route 491 ran via Chastilian Road, Dartford, a road previously unserved, and in so doing began the fulfilment of one of the Board's declared tasks, to introduce new services to outlying areas. In this respect during the early post-war period, the Country Bus department was to be ahead of Central Buses which concentrated instead on restoring services to at least their pre-war level and to tackle inadequacies on the existing network. There was also some improvement in service levels over various sections of route, in pursuit of improved standards of comfort and adequacy.

The single-deck routes radiating south from Gravesend were also restructured and augmented in this programme, principally by an increase in basic services to hourly on routes 451, 490 and 490A, which called for four extra Cubs. The capacity of the services to Northumberland Bottom and Singlewell was also increased by the expedient of exchanging these sections of 20-seater Cub-operated routes 451 and 490 with an extension of route 489 (as, respectively, 489A and 489), which was operated by 35-seat 4Q4s.

The Central operating departments began to tackle the matter of late evening services with a programme on 13th February 1946 covering 45 bus, five trolleybus and two tram routes. This not only involved the restoration of frequencies and the introduction of later last journeys but also the reinstatement of those sections of routes that had been withdrawn during blackout hours. In this programme, for example, the evening service on route 7 was extended from Acton Vale to the daytime terminus at Kew Green, the 8 from Willesden to Blackbird Cross, the 38A from Leyton to Victoria, the 88 from Clapham Common to Mitcham ('The Cricketers') and the 239, which had been withdrawn altogether in blackout hours, was reinstated. The process continued in three further stages at roughly monthly intervals until it was completed with the summer programme on 22nd May.

This did not mean that there was a total return to the standards which had applied before Sep-

tember 1939. Until then Central Bus, tram and trolleybus services had generally operated until about midnight and many trunk routes had continued until 1am or later. For example, the last bus of the day service on route 9 to Mortlake left Piccadilly Circus at 1.04am in August 1939 but after the war the main service closed at 11.42pm, with just a single journey retained at 1.07am The last 13 left Aldwych at 12.25am in 1939, 11pm after the war. Even in the suburbs, important routes had run very late. The last 33 to Hounslow left Hammersmith at 1.03am (passing Richmond at 1.28 and arriving at 1.50am) compared with a post-war time of 11.09pm and the last 86A left Bow for Hornchurch at 12.46am compared with 11.12pm Not all routes had such startling differences but in broad terms last buses, trams and trolleybuses were at least an hour, sometimes more, earlier than they had been. Although this did not matter too much in the London of 1946 when night life was at a minimum, it did tend to put a greater strain on the last few journeys on many routes and London Transport started a poster campaign urging people not to wait until the last bus.

The February changes had included a few other fairly minor alterations. One was a good illustration of how resources had to be husbanded and how the need had diminished for routes linking distant residential areas with factories which had been important in the war effort. The peak hour extension of route 2 to Arnos Grove had continued throughout the war, even though the section of the main service which duplicated trolleybuses had been cut back from North Finchley to Golders Green as a fuel saving measure at the beginning of the war. It had been retained as an important strategic link to the New Southgate factories but was now cut back and replaced by a shorter peak hour only route 251A from Arnos Grove to North Finchley. The resources saved were used to give the rest of route 2 a much needed boost in service. The Greenwich terminus of the truncated 53 at Blackwall Lane had been

When wartime route 231, which had served munitions factories in Waltham Abbey and Quinton Hill, was withdrawn as redundant in May 1946, the section of road between Waltham Isolation Hospital and The Wake Arms, Epping Forest, was covered by a daily extension of route 242. Former Tilling T 309 is at Waltham Cross working from Enfield garage on the extended route.
D.A. Thompson/LTPS

unsatisfactory from the start and the route was now extended to Blackheath Hill, not quite reaching Deptford and still a strange place to turn, but at least enabling interchange with route 53A. The other change involved the equally frugally designed route 108A, which was given an off-peak and evening service between Bromley-by-Bow and 'Eltham' (Rochester Way).

Another interesting reversal of a wartime change also took place on 13th February when the arrangement by which routes 14, 63, 68, 77 and 77A had used the coach station in Crestfield Street, King's Cross, as a fuel saving measure, came to an end. Coach services were now returning and the buses reverted to York Way to release the coach station for its proper use.

There were a few other interesting changes in the Central Area. On 13th March two apparent restorations of evening services took place but in both cases there was an improvement compared with 1939 as no such services had existed then. The 135 became an all day service to Brimsdown, which had been served only by works journeys on route 69 in pre-war days, and the 151 got an off-peak and evening service. The 151 had been one of those rare creatures, a route newly introduced during the war to serve new areas, in this case between Morden and Hackbridge and linking them to North Cheam. On 17th April, another of those frugal wartime innovations, the 225 which had started with one Cub but had by now graduated to a T, was extended at both ends to run between Eastcote Lane (Eastcote Arms), still a bit in the middle of nowhere, to Northwood Station. It was also upgraded from single to double-deck using STs. Another minor double-deck operation on a single-deck route started the same day with

one LT running between Sidcup Station and Chislehurst on route 228.

As already noted, unlike motor buses, tram services had not been cut during the war except those that had lost so much traffic because of bombing that their services had been reduced for purely traffic reasons. Their late evening services had been curtailed, however, and these were restored for most routes on 17th April 1946, the 68 and 70 having preceeded the others on 13th February. Other examples of at least partial restoration of pre-war operations on 17th April were the extension of the 26 on Sundays from Savoy Street to Blackfriars and the 48 on Saturday afternoons and Sundays from Elephant & Castle to Borough Station (known as St George's Church, in accordance with LCC policy, until the very end of tramway operation). The 26 extension could hardly have been a money-spinner, given that the eastern end of the Embankment was, like the rest of the City, dead on Sundays, so it was not surprising that it lasted only until 9th November 1947. Another event in 1946 was the allocation of route numbers to night trams (and trolleybuses) for the first time. The four routes which had no recognisable daytime equivalent used the now vacant north London numbers 1, 3, 5 and 7, possibly using route number stencils redundant since 1938, while the night services over parts of the 26 and 35 took their numbers. One short extension took place on 16th August when route 42 was extended from 'The Greyhound', Croydon, to Coombe Road, although the trams had been doing this 'dead' since at least 25th October 1944.

For the remaining months up to its summer programme, Country Buses concentrated its efforts on the restoration of Green Line services.

The summer seasonal services to Whipsnade Zoo were re-instated in May 1946 but staff shortages prevented their return in 1947. Red ST 588 was photographed opposite St Albans garage at Easter 1948 when the final restoration took place. ST 588 was one of those which had been converted to operate with producer gas between 1943 and 1944.
A.B. Cross

However, a small augmentation on route 441, which included the withdrawal of route 417 between Windsor (Bus Station) and Old Windsor (except for hospital journeys), took place on 6th March and another 'outlying area' got a bus service on 1st May. Route 401 was extended from Bexleyheath to Upper Belvedere with a peak extension to Lower Belvedere, bringing buses to Long Lane and Picardy Road. This was a curiosity as the area was well within the Metropolitan Police District and would normally have been regarded as Central Bus territory although it may have been difficult for them to cover it efficiently.

The Central Bus summer programme on 22nd May was another important milestone on the road to recovery, marking as it did the introduction of summer weekend extensions for the first time for four years, five years if the perfunctory two-week operation in 1942 is discounted. Sixteen routes were involved and the opportunity had been taken to modify the network compared with 1939. Three operations which had not operated between 1940 and 1942 did not reappear now, included the 40 extension from Wanstead to High Beach, which meant that the section of Epping New Road from Woodford to Rangers Road finally lost its summer service which had first operated over 30 years earlier. Others were the 69 to Rye House, but that route had disappeared anyway, and the seasonal 96A (Putney Common – Loughton) and a Sunday service on 96. Others which failed to return were the 73 extension from Richmond to Hampton Court via Kingston and the 74 extension from Putney Heath to Wimbledon. The 35A was another which had not run between 1940 and 1942 but this one did reappear, although re-routed via Wood Street and Highams Park, rather than Whipps Cross and Woodford. One which took a different form was the pre-war 109 extension from Collier Row to Chigwell Row which was attached instead to the 247. The 109 had been withdrawn in November 1940 but the 247 had not been extended in 1941 or 1942. There was one entirely new operation numbered 139A, (Dagenham – Chigwell Row), a summer Sunday variation of the 139, which had been another of those rare wartime innovations.

There was also the usual general seasonal increase in Sunday services fleetwide and during the summer further increases were made until the number of buses scheduled for Central Area service reached 3,503, only 128 short of the summer of 1939 and 26 per cent higher than in 1945.

In this programme Loughton garage lost its small allocation of single-deckers with the withdrawal of both route 231 and the infrequent extension of route 205 from Chingford to Loughton. The 231 was an interesting route as it had started in 1942 as Country Bus 340 between Epping Town and Waltham Abbey 'Royal Gunpowder Factory', with some journeys double-running to the similarly named factory at Quinton Hill. Within two months it had been taken over by Central Buses as 231 but by 1946 it

had served its strategic wartime purpose and could be withdrawn. The stretch of road between Waltham Isolation Hospital and The Wake Arms was covered by a daily extension of route 242.

The Country Bus summer programme on 29th May also included the reinstatement of seasonal services, (368 and 376 to Whipsnade Zoo) and a substantial uplift in the level of service generally. The policy of expanding the network was continued with the introduction of services for the first time to Chorleywood Gate (Route 361 extended via Common Road and Chenies Road), Langley Vale (route 419 extended) and between Ewell and Chessington North (new route 468). The latter had been planned as a Central Bus service in 1939 but the war had intervened to prevent its introduction. Significant increases were made to local services in Watford, which were reorganised and simplified at the same time, routes 315, 315A and 324 being replaced by a diverted 321 and new 334

Top An interesting new route introduced on 29th May 1946 was the 468 from Great Bookham to Chessington Zoo covering a new section between Epsom and Chessington planned as a Central Bus route before the war. ST 1124, seen in Epsom, was one of 42 with Ransomes Sims and Jefferies bodies supplied to East Surrey in 1930, hence the Surrey registration. D.W.K. Jones

Above New to Watford from 29th May 1946 were routes 334/A which replaced parts of routes 315/A and 324. Bluebird ST 1072 carries the destination NORTH WATFORD THE DOME, an important terminal for short workings on town services Gavin Martin collection

and 334A. In Redhill and Reigate improvements were achieved by absorbing route 449 into an extended 447 and new route 440A. Another bit of restructuring in the Addlestone area enabled considerable improvements to be made with the injection of just one additional bus. New route 463 (Walton – Woking via New Haw) helped establish the neatly interlocking group of services which provided a frequent network between Staines, Walton and Woking via Addlestone on routes 436, 461, 461A, 462 and 463. A relic of the double-decking in 1943 was the isolated single-deck section of route 461 between Hersham and Walton which was now withdrawn as was the 437A Old Woking circular. The frequency of the 219 had been increased in the previous week's Central Bus programme.

Also included in this programme was another example of Country Buses withdrawing from territory covered by the Central departments. Route 310A was withdrawn from its traditional route through Ponders End and Hertford Road to run instead via Great Cambridge Road. This was an odd decision because the same had been done to route 310 in 1942 to provide a replacement for the Green Line over that section. Logically, with the reinstatement of the coaches the 310 should have rejoined the 310A on its pre-1942 route, rather than the other way around. It had the remarkable effect of increasing the total service via Great Cambridge Road from four an hour in 1945 to 11 an hour. This area had been a bone of contention

ance of special services to sporting events, starting with Derby week operations to Epsom Race Course between 4th and 7th June. Central Buses ran their time-honoured service from Morden Station to Buckles Gap, Epsom Downs for which buses were scraped together from garages all over the fleet by making discreet reductions in normal services. Although this may sound a brutal method, in those days before mass television ownership the Derby was still such a major draw that demand for bus services elsewhere was reduced quite significantly. Country Buses operated their two services from Epsom Town (406E) and Station (406F) using buses from nine garages in the southern country area. The two special services for Wimbledon Tennis from Southfields and Wimbledon made their post-war debut on 14th/15th June for the Wightman Cup and then again between 24th June and 6th July for the main championship fortnight. Special services on route 83 for Speedway at Wembley and Greyhound Racing at Hendon stadium were also resumed on 15th August. In the absence, for most people, of private transport the Board's services were also the main means of visiting race meetings, football matches and other sporting or cultural events and extras were operated for many of these during the year.

In the meantime, on Saturday 8th June the centre of London was closed down for a major celebration of the ending of the Second World War. The Victory Parade was in two parts. A marching

The four buses which took part in the Victory Parade on 8th June 1946 are lined up at Chiswick before the event. Representing London Transport, RT39 was finished in a version of the 1945 mainly red livery which was used on only two other 2RT2s, and RT4 displayed the new livery about to be introduced which became the standard until 1950. The 'provinces' were represented by Halifax Corporation Park Royal-bodied AEC Regent number 10 which claimed to be the first to come to London in 1940, and a Manchester Metro-Cammell lowbridge Leyland Titan. All have been done up in blackout trim and treated to window netting. The netting was fixed to the outside of the windows rather than the correct position inside, presumably to make it easier to fix and remove. LT Museum

between the two departments for many years and it can only be assumed that this was a final redrawing of boundaries. Twenty-four years later, when Country Buses became LCBS, these old rivalries were to be revived.

The summer of 1946 also saw the reappear-

column followed a route from Marble Arch via Oxford Street, Charing Cross Road, Victoria Embankment, Parliament Square, Whitehall and the Mall. A mechanised column went on a much longer route through some of the areas of greatest devastation, to join the marchers for the salute to the King and Queen in The Mall. The importance of public transport to the war effort was recognised in both processions. Inspector Waller led a contingent of 72 London bus drivers, conductors (including women conductors Lily Brokes and Dorothy Hunt), cleaners and inspectors, as well as representatives of the Underground, and the Board's Civil Defence and Home Guard units. The vehicles were represented by two 2RT2s and vehicles from Halifax and Manchester, in honour of the part played by the 'provincial' operators in supplying buses to London during the Blitz. The 2RT2s each had a different new livery. RT 39 had the style which had been applied to some STLs and the Sutton Daimlers, while RT 4 revealed the livery which was about to become the standard for the next four years, red with a cream relief around the upper deck windows and between decks. Both were also fitted with wheel trim discs at the front, of the type used on buses and coaches delivered in 1938/1939, but this did not augur their adoption as standard.

Within the area surrounded by the mechanised column, roads were closed and a Coronation-style boundary was imposed on bus, coach, tram and trolleybus services. From 5am they terminated at Camberwell New Road (Vassall Road), Kennington, County Hall, Lambeth North, Elephant & Castle, Aldwych, Great Dover Street, Tooley Street, Eversholt Street, Hampstead Road, Albany Street, Park Road, Edgware Road (Church Street), Praed Street, Bayswater Road,

Knightsbridge, and Victoria. From 8am onwards they were cut back further to Angel, Kingsland Road, Mare Street Hackney, Mile End, Commercial Road, Brixton Road (Cranmer Road) and Vauxhall. Trams and trolleybuses used the nearest crossovers or turning loops to these points. The area was progressively re-opened as the processions passed and full operation had been resumed by the end of the day.

Green Line coach routes were split to turn from each end in London, most of them at Eccleston Bridge whether or not they normally went there, and diverted to avoid the processional routes but the 715 and 724 were allowed to run to Oxford Circus. Otherwise coaches were cut back only for short periods when the mechanised column passed Elephant & Castle, Vauxhall, Lancaster Gate, Marylebone, Great Portland Street, Stepney Green and Commercial Road.

There was a firework display on the Thames at 10pm that evening and many public buildings were floodlit, bringing a rare sparkle to the drab post-war scene. During the week of celebrations special late services were run on most tram and trolleybus routes until 2am and on 46 bus routes until 1am, with Green Line coaches finishing between midnight and 12.30am. All had to be supplied within existing resources and the whole operation depended on the willing co-operation of staff and Trade Unions in working overtime and Rest Days.

VICTORY CELEBRATIONS

TRANSPORT ARRANGEMENTS

LONDON TRANSPORT AT LONDON'S SERVICE

The leaflet produced for the Victory Celebrations in June 1946, the first major event with which London Transport had to cope after the war.
Ken Glazier collection

A closer view of RT 4 shows the new red and cream livery and the experimental vertical route number plate on the nearside pillar which had just made its appearance. Both RTs had disc trims attached to their front wheels for the occasion, of the type which had been used on the later deliveries of buses and coaches before the war, but this did not herald their introduction on post-war buses. LT Museum

London Transport considered this to have been the biggest traffic problem with which it had ever dealt. Apart from carrying the crowds in and out of London, they also had to provide transport into central London for police and to and from transit camps for troops and industrial workers taking part in the parade. Transport was also supplied during 'Victory Week' for 120,000 school-children who went on outings arranged by the London County Council. All was exacerbated on the day of the parade, as ever, by the weather which turned to rain towards the end of the morning, encouraging people to go home and return later for the evening celebrations. During Victory Week as a whole, the Board carried 90,000,000 passengers on all its services, an average of 13,000,000 a day, two million more than a normal average day. Although no separate figures were issued for road

services it is reasonable to assume that this 15 per cent uplift applied equally to them as to the Underground.

While these celebrations were in full flight, London Transport's conducted coach tours were resumed on 11th June. It was a puny programme compared with 1939, when there had been nine tours covering a range of destinations in London and the Home Counties. There were just three tours, a morning Westminster and City, an afternoon West End and Northern Heights and an afternoon trip to Hampton Court and Windsor, all of which could be covered by two coaches. The fleet of coaches available for such operations had been reduced drastically in 1940 when bombing had destroyed 11 of the 12 Private Hire TFs. It was the sole survivor of these, TF 9, which became the backbone of the tours, with the help of LTCs.

The summer schedules for motor buses in 1946 called for 5,106 double-deckers from the total of 5,762 owned at that time, giving a margin of 13 per cent, dangerously tight given the condition of most of the fleet. In the second half of the year, therefore, the pace of scheduled service improvements which required extra buses slowed down and by the autumn was at snail's pace. The arrival of fresh supplies of Ds and STDs did allow some expansion by Central Buses. The largest programme was on 28th August when 27 double-deckers were added to the peak vehicle requirement but between May and December the total reached only 74 double-deck and 28 single-deck, only a quarter of the rate achieved between January and May. Apart from a number of cases where off-peak improvements were made or services restored on Sundays or during evenings, most of the service changes were straightforward increases in frequency. In one case on 28th August this was done by extending the Acton Vale to Holborn shorts on route 7 to London Bridge station thereby creating new route 7A. There was one rare case of new roads being served when route 206 was extended from Imber Court to Hampton Court on 11th September. The availability of the new 14T12s was obviously a factor in this as these were used to replace the one-man Cubs at the same time. One of the Sunday improvements was interesting in that it removed the long-standing anomaly of having two routes serving Chipstead Valley on Sunday and none to Old Coulsdon. Route 159 was switched from one to the other on 9th October.

Country Buses were even more circumspect and made only the most minor of changes, but it had had an exceptional first half with the restoration of Green Line services. Trams and Trolleybuses changed hardly at all in those six months. Nevertheless, it had been a record year. Car miles operated by road services had increased by 28 per cent compared with 1945, the largest annual gross increase ever recorded, and by the end of the year the running rate had crossed the magic boundary and had reached 2.6 per cent above pre-war. The lion's share of this increase

Fresh supplies of new Daimlers and STDs provided the resources for limited improvements to services in 1946. There were heavy storms in August that year and it was perhaps during one of those that this scene between Belmont and Banstead was photographed with brand new Sutton Daimler D 236 heading north, squeezing past a Merton bus on loan, Duple-bodied D 87 making for Tattenham Corner.
The Omnibus Society

was on Country Buses & Coaches which went up by 57 per cent compared with 1945 and 55 per cent compared with pre-war but since 1945 Central's had also increased by nearly 30 per cent and trams and trolleybuses by 13 per cent. Passengers carried had increased in the same period by 18 per cent, another record gross increase, and now exceeded the pre-war level by over 11 per cent. The largest increase since 1945 was on Central Buses, 21 per cent, but compared with pre-war Country Buses and Coaches showed the remarkable increase of 82 per cent.

Even a cursory glance at these figures shows that increased demand was not being matched by extra capacity. This situation was set to get worse and very few improvements of any kind took place during most of 1947. The main source of the problem was the complete failure of the body builders to deliver a single one of the 500 new RTs which had been ordered for 1946, despite AEC being fully up to speed on delivery of chassis. Throughout this period there was a small surplus of single-deckers and the Board took the decision in the spring of 1946 that these should be used as emergency support for the double-deck fleet. When London Transport announced its intention to press 60 single-deckers into service as 'Rush Hour Reliefs', the Press characteristically glamourised the event with headlines like 'Cruising Coach Fleet To Tour Bus Queues' as though they were some sort of concert party.

The reality was that the largest single group of vehicles were from the CR class, diminutive rear-engined 20-seaters as far from being a coach as anyone could imagine in either comfort or standard of ride and they were also notoriously prone to break down. These went into service on 17th June initially on routes 12, 16, 23B, 56, 68, 73, 88, 96 and 133 and, although designed for one-man operation, were obliged to carry a conductor. There were also a few C class Cubs on the 23B and there is photographic evidence that they also ran on routes 73, 96, 175 and possibly 103, but passengers on routes 3, 54 and 137 (and others later) had the pleasure of the comfort offered by 9T9s. Gradually more were brought into operation during the rest of the year, including spare former Green Line 1/7T7/1s which were to be found on routes 3 and 6. It now became common to see almost any type of single-decker which happened to be available plying the streets of central London, most commonly 1T1s, 11T11s and single-deck LTs but increasingly as time wore on, LTCs too.

Country Buses also used spare single deckers to cover shortages but in both more and less for-

Travelling conditions were so bad in 1946 that the LPTB thought it worthwhile to run 20-seat CRs at disproportionate expense on busy routes to help in their 'Battle of the Queue'. Apart from the routes officially specified, they sometimes found their way onto others, as is the case here with CR4 waiting to do a spell of work on route 118 from Streatham garage
Capital Transport collection

Route 7A started in August 1946 as an extension of short-working 7s from Holborn to London Bridge. A few years later at London Bridge station, Tilling ST 850 acts out its role as general factotum for Middle Row garage. Although surrounded by severe bomb damage, the view in this direction had hardly changed for several decades, even the bus stops being those supplied originally by the LGOC.
Vanguard

A bus with a complicated history, T 120 picks up in Regent Street while working from Norwood garage as a peak hour relief. It was the last survivor of the original 150 7T7 rear-entrance Green Line Regals but had received a front-entrance T7/1 body in 1945 after serving as a staff ambulance during the war. Gavin Martin collection

mal ways than Central Buses. Many double-deck routes were given formal allocations of single-deckers, while at the other extreme makeshift substitutions were made from day to day. Country Buses lent a lot of single-deckers to Central Buses but there was one interesting reverse loan when 12 LTCs were sent to the Country Area on 1st July 1947. They were originally intended primarily for use on Green Line route 703 but it was decided that the type was not suitable and they were generally used on bus routes at Epping, Hertford, Luton and Northfleet, all garages with supplies of petrol. They were occasionally used as reliefs on the Green Line. Continuing problems

during 1947 led the Board to desperate measures and they turned eventually to the private coach sector for help. An agreement was made with the Passenger Vehicle Operators' Association for the hire of coaches. The history of this episode can be found in Chapter 8.

The struggle to deliver adequate services suffered a devastating setback in the winter of 1946/1947 which was one of the worst on record. A long cold spell set in at the end of December 1946 and severe wintry conditions began to spread across the country in the middle of January. London was not affected until the afternoon of 28th January when a fierce blizzard unexpectedly hit the capital with great force taking the road authorities by surprise. Council workmen were unable to keep pace with the frequent bouts of snow and the tendency for road surfaces to freeze even in the middle of the day, making many hills impassable for several days. Some sections of road lost their services sporadically, those most often affected being Aylesbury to Tring, Westerham to Brasted and to Keston, Sevenoaks to Weald, Coulsdon to Old Coulsdon via Marlpit Lane, Potters Bar to Cockfosters, Shirley to Hayes, and Muswell Hill. Trams were not affected by hazardous road surfaces but they had their own special problem in the conduit system. Snow sometimes froze solid in the slot creating a blockage that was no friend to ploughs which could snap under the pressure, leaving the tram disabled and bringing the whole service to a standstill. On at least one occasion when this happened at a junction, the tram was derailed in the resulting mayhem. The stoppages could last as long as an hour and there was one report of 30 trams being caught in one hold-up at Kennington Gate.

Melancholy weather records were set, 29th January being the coldest January day since 1929 and the coldest night since 1894 and these daunt-

Some frustrated passengers were able to relax to the balm of travelling in luxury on LTC Private Hire coaches which, with limited work of their own type available, were put to good use working peak hour reliefs. On the occasion of this photograph the type graced two consecutive departures from Victoria on route 52, LTC 10 leading and an unidentified one bringing up the rear. Capital Transport collection

ing conditions continued throughout February. As time wore on, the effect of all this on the vehicles themselves began to be felt as many were put out of action, leaving services seriously depleted. Apart from the surfeit of broken plough carriers, electric traction motors on trams and trolleybuses were vulnerable to penetrating snow and bus radiators often froze while buses were on the road. All of which was made worse by the effect this and a serious fuel shortage was having on industry. Output of essential spare parts was curtailed and this too created vehicle shortages. Tram and trolleybus services were cut by 12 per cent to save power and lesser cuts were made on buses, but these had less effect than might be thought because reductions in factory output meant that many people were unable to work. People also cut out non-essential travel because it was no pleasure to go out and this led to temporary cuts of about 10 per cent in Sunday services.

Very few improvements in scheduled services were possible during the whole of 1947 and 1948, mainly because the vehicles were not available. The total number of buses, coaches, trams and trolleybuses scheduled for peak service increased by only 53 in the 24 months, compared with the 710 added during 1946. Most of the increase happened during the first half of 1947, no fewer than 21 being added by Central Buses on 1st January 1947 using the small surplus created by the delivery of the 4STD3s. Nearly all were used for straight frequency enhancements but route 62 was also extended from Chadwell Heath to Chigwell Row over roads previously served only on Sundays and by some works journeys during the war. Strict observance of the policy of concentrating on improving existing services was again relaxed on 26th February when a new single-deck route 150 was introduced between Manford Way, Hainault and 'The Old Maypole'. This provided an urgently needed service for the village of pre-

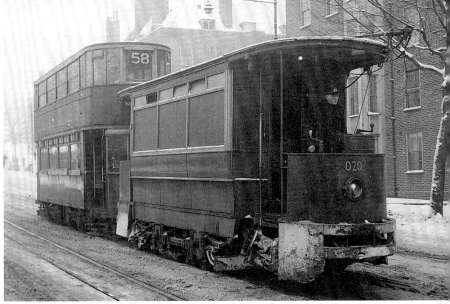

Top The relentless cold snowy weather of January 1947 left many roads impassable because of compacted snow and ice. Some idea of the conditions which were encountered day after day can be drawn from this photograph of Tilling STL90 and an unidentified STL5 on the stand in Crystal Palace Parade surrounded by solid snow. D.W.K. Jones

Centre At home these waiting hopefuls were plagued by power cuts and had little coal for heating during the winter of 1947, when travelling conditions were also foul, as this scene at London Bridge station illustrates so powerfully. London Bridge station was badly hit in the Blitz leaving

little to be seen behind the buses, which are facing north. Capital Transport collection

Bottom Trams were particularly hard hit by the wintry conditions, especially when ice solidified in the conduit slot laying a trap for an unwary plough which then snapped on impact. Snowbroom 020, rebuilt from a former LCC B type car, has come to the rescue of an HR/2 on Dog Kennel Hill where the points at the bottom were jammed with snow. The conditions must have been foul for 020's driver who, without the protection of a windscreen, was exposed to anything nature cared to throw. D.A. Ruddom collection

A rare example of a new route serving virgin territory emerged on 26th February 1946 when route 150 started between Hainault and 'The Old Maypole' Barkingside at first as a single-decker but then double-deck from 10th December. The route was then also extended to Chigwell Row, where this photograph of LT1 was taken, still carrying its original body but now with a rounded cab.
Gavin Martin collection

STL1971 in Market Street, Dartford on route 486, which was introduced to serve the Fleet Estate on 26th March 1947.

fabricated houses which had grown up around Manford Way, some distance from both bus and rail services. The area served by the 150 grew in the next few years into one of the LCC's large 'out-county' housing estates, which were built to relieve overcrowding in inner London. The service also broke the rules about route numbering but only until the road under the railway bridge could be made suitable for the intended double-deckers which were substituted on 10th December, when the route was simultaneously extended to Chigwell Row.

Country Buses made a few improvements on 26th March 1947, the most significant being a new route 486 primarily to serve the Fleet Estate at Dartford but bringing buses newly to Burnham Road, Thames Road and Crayford Way on its way from there to Upper Belvedere. Other new places served at tiny cost were Chalfont Common (305A)

and St Leonards (348), both by modest extensions of shortworkings. Otherwise, improvements were confined to times when extra buses would not be needed, such as the introduction of route 7A on Saturdays from 1st February and the introduction or restoration of Sunday services on a number of routes. Things were so tight that Country Buses could not even afford to operate its two seasonal bus services to Whipsnade Zoo in 1947, let alone go ahead with a planned extension of route 343 from St Albans to give Marshalswick Lane, The Ridgeway and Kings Hill Avenue a service. Their failure to do so raised the hackles of Marshalswick residents whose resolute protests eventually forced London Transport to yield a 'shuttle service', the common man's solution to all transport problems, from 27th August.

The delayed winter programme on 12th November brought with it an array of service alterations, many if not most of which were a direct result of the new scheduling agreement. Famous changes in this programme included the exchange of northern terminals between route 53A (West Hampstead) and routes 59, 59A and 159, which had traditionally gone to Camden Town; and the linking of Green Line routes 709, 710 and 711 with the 724 and 725 to form cross-London routes, as London Transport had always wanted. Many long-established garage loyalties were broken too. A few notable examples may be given from a long list: the removal of Catford from route 12 which thereby lost its official allocation of oil-engined STLs; the transfer of route 28 from Battersea to Chelverton Road, bringing 2RT2s to the route; and the removal of the venerable Palmers Green allocation from the 29. A number of Country Bus changes also derived from the new agreement. Routes 310 exchanged its Hertford North operation with routes 395/A; route 321 was shortened to run Luton to Maples Cross, Uxbridge being covered by a new 351 from St Albans; and route 339 was extended from Ongar to Epping, in place of route 392. There was also a scheme of changes in the Dartford area under which route 423 lost its Longfield to Hook Green section to route 489A from Gravesend and was extended to Crockenhill at the other end and the 477 lost its Dartford to Denton section.

Tram route 31, which had been something of a 'Cinderella' since its brutal curtailment in 1939, was given a little more status from 12th November 1947, when it was extended to run from Wandsworth to Islington Green, daily. A Wandsworth allocation was restored at the same time, at the expense of route 28 being transferred to Clapham. One more wartime cut was restored on this day, route 72 being extended in Monday-Saturday off-peak hours from New Cross to Savoy Street. The Sunday operation of route 31 beyond Westminster did not survive beyond 7th November 1948 and the following Wednesday saw a reduction in the number of trams allocated to Holloway because London Transport were having difficulty in finding enough drivers at that depot.

Drivers were required to have had six months' driving experience before they were allowed to drive through Kingsway Subway but Holloway ran only Subway routes. Before the war when Holloway ran other tram routes, there was no problem but now the only way experience could be gained was by spending six months at a south London depot. Not surprisingly, this was unpopular and it became increasingly difficult to persuade staff to co-operate. Routes 31 and 33 both lost work at Holloway, Wandsworth and Norwood each taking two additional runnings.

The other side of the coin from the restoration of pre-war standards was the removal of special facilities which had been introduced for essential workers during the war. Even as late as 1949 some of these were still hanging on, often because a lot of overtime was being worked on peace-time production. Routes 36 and 38 had been given a

number of boosts during the war because of the number of strategic factories, not to mention Woolwich Arsenal, which they served. On 23rd February factory journeys which were still running on Sundays and some morning peak shorts were finally withdrawn.

Some improvements were squeezed out of the ever-shrinking pot, or from existing resources by the miracles of scheduling. Route 240A was an extension of Edgware to Mill Hill short-workings onward to Page Street, Bunns Lane, to serve new housing, which used the same number of buses. Similarly 'free' extensions were opened by Country Buses to Potters Lane, St Albans (355), Napsbury Lane (358) and Leith Hill (412). Route

Above C110 at Waterloo, one of the purpose-built Leyland Cubs which returned to the Inter Station service in October 1946. At first they shared the operation with two of the modified STs but assumed full responsibility at the end of May 1947 D.W.K. Jones

Above The 59 group of routes had been serving Camden Town for 65 years before they were wrenched away in November 1947 to run instead to West Hampstead, although route 59A was a relative newcomer, having started in January 1938. A frequent performer on the 59A was STL1167, seen here in Camberwell garage yard, whose distinctive body had been full-fronted when originally fitted to STF1. It still stood out from others of the class because of its well-curved front profile, which

foreshadowed the RT, and the large number of opening windows. W.J. Haynes

Right The northern end of route 53A was switched from West Hampstead to Camden Town in November 1947, severing a long established connection. LT 522 had one of the LT5/1 bodies built in 1931 with separate route number and destination displays. The bus just visible behind is LT 401, one of 54 at Plumstead which had Wilson epicyclic gearboxes and still had petrol engines. D.W.K. Jones

385 was also extended into Mill Way Estate at the cost of two STLs but the programme overall was done without increasing the peak vehicle requirement. Some plans were frustrated, proposed new routes 372 (Hertford – Welwyn Garden City), 374 (Grays – Uplands Estate), 383 (Hitchin – Weston), 479 (Dartford – Horton Kirby – Swanley) and 494 (Oxted – East Grinstead) all having to be held over until the vehicles were available.

Four of these five were to get going during 1948, route 494 on 7th January, 374 (4th February), 383 (18th February) and 372 (19th May) but

the 479 had to wait until June 1949. All but the 374, which needed no extra buses, used Cubs which were in comparatively abundant supply. Otherwise, 1948 was a pretty barren year. A few improvements were eked out, but only to the extent in the full year of 14 extra buses. Swan Road, West Drayton was served for the first time from 28th January when route 223 was extended to Mill Road at the cost of two Ts and Worple Road, Staines benefited similarly on 24th March when route 224 was diverted to Laleham. The service from Staines to Stanwell was covered by new

Left Route 383, which started in February 1949, was caught up in a welter of bad publicity because it covered roads outside the old LPTB statutory area already served by Smiths of Buntingford. Smiths took the Executive to court but lost the case as the route was run under delegated powers from the BTC. Hitchin was allocated two Weymann-bodied red Cubs for the service, one of which, C94, is seen at St Mary's Square, Hitchin, alongside Hertford's Short-bodied C21 on one of the market day shorts operated off route 329A. C94 has acquired a bumper bar, not normally carried on the Central Bus version and is reputed to have had rear wheel discs for a time. A.B. Cross

double-deck route 162. The substantial unserved area of pre-war housing at Woodside Park got its first service from 21st July without a single bus being added to the schedule. This was done by extending the 125 from North Finchley but not during Monday to Friday peak hours nor the Saturday morning peak.

The extensions of the Central Line through east London to Hainault, Woodford and Epping provided the opportunity for London Transport to redistribute some of its bus resources away from roads where the tube now ran and set up new feeders to the Underground. These changes were made in the summer programme on 5th May 1948 and included one new route covering a considerable amount of new ground. The 167, operated at first by three open staircase LTs gleaned from route 150, ran from Loughton, via Buckhurst Hill and Chigwell to Barkingside (The Old Maypole), fulfilling a need already recognised before the

The level crossing in Eagle Lane which was used by route 10A had to close at the end of 1947 so that the electrification of the line for operation by tube trains could be completed. A post-war STD on route 10A is held at the crossing while LNER class N7 0-6-2 tank engine 9639 hauls a suburban train across its path. LT Museum

43

war, while feeding three Central Line stations. The 150 was simultaneously extended to Ilford by absorbing short workings off the 25A, and the 139 was switched away from Leytonstone to run northwards to Barkingside, adding yet more to the strength of the feeder service to Gants Hill. The 147 was also extended from its wartime terminus at Wanstead Lane to Redbridge Station. This scheme alone used half the extra buses scheduled during 1948.

Most extra buses put on by Country Buses were used to improve frequencies on existing routes but they did manage

some new routes in addition to those already mentioned. Route 307 was extended in Harpenden to Westfield Estate on 19th May at no cost; the 422 was introduced on 2nd June between Leatherhead and Boxhill Holiday Camp at the cost of one T; and a spur working from Horley to Outwood was attached to the 424 at no cost in vehicles on 11th August.

These frugal changes during a period of serious inadequacy in most areas bear testament to the severity of the problem of vehicle shortages. Yet the Executive somehow had to assemble a fleet of vehicles to supply transport for competitors and officials attending the 14th Olympiad which was held in London between 29th July and 14th August, although transport for competitors was needed from 8th July to 21st August. The number of buses and coaches needed varied from a basic total of 33 up to 80 at its peak. The competitors were accommodated in newly built houses scattered around London and the events themselves took place at 13 different venues, although the main track and field events were at Wembley.

Fortunately, the really big traffic flows to and from Wembley could be carried by Underground, as it would have been well nigh impossible to find any more buses for special services and, indeed, with one exception none was run. The only extra road services were provided on trolleybus route 662, fortuitously the only direct link between central London and Wembley apart from the infrequent Green Line. There were plenty of trolleybuses available because the arrival of the new Q1s had built up a temporary surplus. Seventeen were allocated to two supplementary services, each of ten trolleybuses an hour between Paddington and Wembley and Scrubs Lane and Wembley. This proved to be extravagant and after three days the Scrubs Lane service was reduced to operating only when the main break from the stadium took place. The subordinate role of road services for this important event was well illustrated by a comparison of the extra revenues earned during the Games which was 16.6 per cent higher than 1947 on the Underground but only 1.6 per cent on road services.

The end of 1948 brought a stop to the upward trend in the numbers of passengers carried which had been evident since the end of the war. Record numbers had been carried in 1948 but a reversal of the trend began to be apparent during the year when Country Buses in particular were reporting a measurable decline in off-peak traffic. Saturday trade was also dealt a blow when the engineering industry agreed to change to a five-day working week. The records of 1948 were never to be repeated but peak demand remained at a high level and the 'battle of the queue' had to be fought for several more years.

A perennial problem on services from London Bridge into the City was to collect fares before passengers reached their destinations just across the river. One solution was to have a kerbside conductor selling tickets to the queues as shown in this photograph. The conductor is using a TIM which shows that he is from Camberwell garage and is working on the queue for routes 7A and 17 which had a heavy short distance traffic to Bank and Cheapside.
LT Museum

4   GREEN LINE RETURNS

THE NETWORK of Green Line coaches had been closed down twice because of the Second World War. First when the coaches were withdrawn without notice on 1st September 1939 to release the vehicles for use as public ambulances and then again, with rather more notice, on 30th September 1942 when drastic reductions in mileage had to be imposed to save fuel and rubber. In between, there had been a gradual restoration culminating in the establishment, from 4th and 18th December 1940, of a network of routes terminating in London which covered most pre-war country destinations. The significance of this wartime network to the post-war structure is that the Board had obviously already started to have new ideas on how the system should be designed and operated.

Despite its outward trappings of success, Green Line had always had a troubled existence because this type of short-stage medium distance service had fallen foul of the traffic authorities right from the beginning. They were thought to create congestion and were regarded as a nuisance on the roads of central London. The Road Service Licensing provisions of the 1930 Road Traffic Act gave the authorities a fresh opportunity to advance their campaign and this culminated in the formation of the Amulree Committee of Inquiry. The committee's findings were that drastic limitations should be imposed on the number of routes which could be operated and the extent to which they could penetrate central London. This had a disastrous effect on usage and profitability. London Transport had tried hard in the years between 1933 and 1939 to persuade the Traffic Commissioner to relieve the coaches of these onerous conditions, but they had made very little progress by the time war broke out and the matter remained in abeyance.

The services which were introduced in December 1940 seemed to indicate that the Board was willing to contemplate a slimmer operation and to accept the need to reduce the number of coaches penetrating the heart of the West End. Coaches were removed from Piccadilly and ten of the pre-war destinations were omitted. Of these only four were to make their way back into the post-war system. A number of services also took a shorter route through the centre, no doubt as a wartime fuel saving measure. For example, routes which had gone by a roundabout route in order to get as close to central objectives as possible, now slipped in by a less ambitious route and these changes, with modifications, became formalised after the war. This was the first indication that London Transport may have abandoned its campaign for justice, which had been led with such vigour by Ashfield and Pick before the war.

The fruits of the new thinking came to light in October 1944 when London Transport submitted proposals to the Traffic Commissioner for a thoroughly revised post-war network. Double-deck operation between 1940 and 1942 had apparently proved its worth because the new system was designed to be operated throughout by double-deckers, which were to replace the single-deck coaches as soon as the new vehicles could be obtained. This led to a number of route alterations to avoid low bridges. Frequencies were designed to take account of the higher capacity of the vehicles, which altered the balance on some routes each side of London. Some of the cross-London links were therefore altered to make them compatible and the opportunity was taken to design a system in which routes continued in a direct geographical progress across London, from the north-east to the south-west for example. The new system was to be given its own group of route numbers in the 700 series, a rather better idea than the wartime duplication of Central Bus numbers and more in keeping with the logic of the rest of the numbering system.

The Board proposed to abandon various sections of pre-war route, including most of those which had not operated during the war. These were presumably the weaker parts of the pre-war network which were by now covered, efficiently in the opinion of London Transport, by Country Bus services, many of which had been introduced to replace the coaches. The destinations not to be restored were Edenbridge, Tatsfield, Horsham, Great Bookham, West Byfleet, Farnham Common, Abbots Langley and Baldock. The Ongar route had not operated during the war but its Epping to Ongar section was to be restored as part of route 718, leaving the route through Chingford, Leyton, Clapton and Dalston unserved. Two routes which had run during the war were also down for abandonment, the most drastic being the pre-war B north of London which would have removed coaches from the route through Wembley, Harrow, Northwood, Rickmansworth, Chorleywood and Amersham. No doubt the existence of the Metropolitan Underground line over much of this route played a part in the decision. The Amersham – Aylesbury section had been covered since 1942 by bus route 359 jointly operated with Eastern National and this was considered to be adequate. Similarly, the Eastern National bus service between Hitchin and Baldock was considered sufficient cover for the pre-war coach route over those roads. This was another interesting change of tack compared with pre-war attitudes as such outrunning powers had been jealously guarded during the Board's formative years.

The former route X from Aldgate to Romford via Hackney, South Hackney and Eastern Avenue was omitted in anticipation of the opening of the Central Line extension. Presumably the expectation that the Northern Line extensions would be completed led to the omission of the Watford – Golders Green tube feeder route T, although this had in any case long been an odd man out in the system. Other sections of road, particularly the arterial roads, were either served adequately by

The Traffic Commissioner foiled the Board's plan of 1944 for the 710 to run through from Crawley to Amersham and the route started with its northern terminus at Baker Street, but London Transport got its way in November 1947 when the 709/710/711 were linked with the 724/725. T 471 is in Marylebone Road at Baker Street station on the extended route, carrying the sort of full load that was commonplace at the time. V.C. Jones

The Bishops Stortford service was planned as a matching replacement of pre-war V to Liverpool Street, with an extension to Aldgate but the direct route through Whitechapel was chosen for the final version. Seen at the post-war terminus in Aldgate lay-by, LTC 17 was one of 12 which were assigned to Country Buses from 1st July 1947 for use on Green Line services from various garages including Epping. A.B. Cross

No photograph is known to exist of a 726 in service during its first season when Watford (Leavesden Road) garage ran it with 10T10s but this posed official view of T 684c shows how they must have looked. LT Museum

bus services or were considered to have little traffic value and the routes concerned were either abandoned or diverted to serve more useful objectives. These were Baldwin's Hill (north of East Grinstead), Stoats Nest Road Coulsdon, Purley Way, the section through Feltham between Ashford and Hounslow Heath, Barnet By-Pass south of Hatfield, the section between 'The Cherry Tree' and Longcroft Green, Welwyn Garden City, the section through Hertford Heath between Hoddesdon and Hertford, Hertford Road and Southbury Road through Ponders End, Great Cambridge Road south of Southbury Road and Epping New Road. Diversions to avoid low bridges were to take coaches away from Thames Ditton and Park Street.

The volume of operation in central London was to be reduced from the pre-war total of 60 coaches an hour to 52 as a consequence of the assumption that double-deckers were to be used. Two coach routes were removed from the restricted central area zone altogether (pre-war G and P), leaving Piccadilly clear of coaches and reducing the use of

Trafalgar Square and Whitehall. The latter also lost the double-running section of the pre-war C routes, whose replacements were to run via Lambeth Bridge rather than Westminster. Another minor retrenchment was the loss of the summer extension of the Brentwood route from Aldgate to Windsor.

Some of the pre-war cross-London operations were retained intact but there were a number of radical changes. Wrotham was linked not to Aylesbury via Rickmansworth but to Whipsnade (703), which gave the latter a better central London objective than Marylebone station while not increasing cross-town movements. Tunbridge Wells was joined to Windsor (704), instead of to Chertsey and Woking, and the route from Westerham via Bromley was also to go to Windsor via Great West Road (705), rather than to Staines via Richmond and Kingston. Richmond was to be covered by a new 712 from Dorking, following the K3 south of Kingston. The rest of the D and K3 were to be absorbed into the replacement for pre-war route N (Windsor–Epping) which was to be re-routed between Staines and London via the D as far as Kingston and the K3 via Putney (718). It was also to be extended to cover the Epping to Ongar section of route W and the route through central London was also to be modified to follow route 715 between Marble Arch and Albany Street so as to serve Oxford Circus. The main road route through Bedfont (pre-war N) was to be covered by the Ascot and Sunningdale routes (701, 702) which had run via Feltham before the war. The reformed routes through Chelsham were both linked to Hemel Hempstead, from Westerham (706) and Oxted (707) but the route to Aylesbury via Watford was to get a frequent daily service numbered 708 through from East Grinstead, which had been linked previously to Dunstable and Luton. These changes gave a more frequent service north of Watford and to both northern terminals. The Caterham route, diverted via Coulsdon and Croydon, was to go to Chesham via Uxbridge (709), instead of Windsor, the Crawley route to Amersham instead of Abbots Langley (710) and Reigate to High Wycombe, instead of Watford (711). The Dorking via Epsom routes were to be linked to Dunstable (714) and Luton (713), instead of Baldock and Welwyn Garden City. The former K3 route through Kingston and Putney to London was to be diverted via Richmond and Hammersmith and linked to the Luton via Barnet route (712). This had run to King's Cross via Finchley and Highgate before the war but had been diverted during the war via Golders Green to terminate at Victoria. This proposal assumed the same route which was considered to serve better objectives. Woking was to be served by a new route 717 running via Woodham and New Haw instead of West Byfleet and linked to Welwyn Garden City, rather than Tunbridge Wells. Chertsey was to be attached to the Hitchin route north of London, again instead of Tunbridge Wells (716).

The 'East End' routes, those which had terminated at Liverpool Street and Aldgate, were treated separately from the rest as they did not penetrate the 'Amulree' restricted zone. Apart from the two which were to be omitted altogether, the routes were to be almost exactly as in 1939, including a route 724 to Grays serving the 'by-pass' sections between Rainham and Purfleet. The Bishop's Stortford route (720 – pre-war V) was to be extended from Liverpool Street to Aldgate to establish the Minories as the eastern centre for coach services. At this stage its intermediate route via Bethnal Green was apparently to be retained.

To an impartial observer these proposals might have looked like a considerable retreat from the Board's pre-war desire to increase the presence of Green Line services in central London and to be broadly in line with the Commissioner's policies. Not so the Traffic Commissioners advisers, in whom all the latent antipathy to Green Line bubbled to the surface. They looked upon the plans with deep suspicion and argued for the restoration of single-deck routes on a network exactly the same as 1939. Even the principle of linking routes to eliminate central London terminals, which ought to have been welcome to the traffic authorities, was considered to be capable of 'unlimited expansion', which was apparently anathema to them. The removal of coaches from Piccadilly was grudgingly accepted as an improvement but 'apparently the traffic is thrown onto double-deck vehicles along Millbank and past the House of Commons', the latter apparently a most heinous crime. The Commissioner's staff were convinced that using double-deckers on lower frequencies would somehow lead inevitably to a need to increase the service, particularly as '. . . Green Line services had been greatly worked up . . .' before the war and in normal circumstances that trend would have continued. The underlying tone was one of disapproval that the coaches had achieved any expansion of demand, an attitude which appeared again later in the negotiations when the need to control '. . . the troublesome business of duplication . . .' was raised. Yet they were also worried that the total seating capacity on offer would be substantially greater than in 1939 even with the reduced level of service. All of which exacerbated their fear that the larger capacity would increase time spent at stops, particularly on these services where many people carried luggage. In confidential internal minutes they accused the Board of 'juggling the figures'. Their conclusion was that if double-deckers were to be used, there should be a commensurate reduction in total service so that the same number of seats was provided '. . . instead of regarding the use of double-deckers as a justification for routeing additional services through the central area.'

Of the individual proposals, the diversion of the former H3 away from King's Cross was not accepted, on the grounds that King's Cross was an ideal distribution point and that it had been one of the most remunerative services. Perhaps

Another battle lost by the Board was the attempt to relink the Luton – King's Cross route across London and the pre-war route was recreated as the 727. The terminus was moved from the old Crestfield Street coach station to this new site in Judd Street on 29th September 1947, where TF16 is dwarfed by arch-rival Birch Bros' K151. This interesting vehicle had a Leyland Tiger TS7T 3-axle chassis which had been remounted in 1943 with this Birch-built 64-seat forward-entrance body, a layout which Birch favoured for its double-deckers. D.W.K. Jones

more to the point, the route used the coach station as a terminus, avoiding the need for on-street boarding and keeping the coaches out of the central zone. The re-linking of the Whipsnade route was also disliked despite the fact that this would not have increased the number of vehicle movements compared with pre-war, there even being a hint that they disapproved of the Board's attempt to increase demand by giving it a better in-town objective. The increased use of Park Lane, although it was the boundary of the restricted area, also attracted criticism as did the allied increase in journeys using Baker Street, Orchard Street and Oxford Street.

London Transport submitted revised proposals to the Commissioner in November 1945 which were broadly the form in which the network was eventually introduced and assumed single-deck operation in all but two cases at the outset, but still with the intention of conversion later. The route to Aylesbury via Amersham was restored to its 1939 form, linked to Wrotham as 703, but with the condition that the route north of Amersham could not be reintroduced until negotiations with Eastern National about the fate of route 359 had taken place. The Whipsnade route became a separate 726 from its pre-war Marylebone terminus. The routes to Watford were to be restored by re-routeing the 709, 710 and 711 north of London and introducing new routes 724 and 725 (High Wycombe and Chesham respectively to Oxford Circus). However, the Board claimed that the section north of Oxford Circus could not be operated until additional garage accommodation could be supplied in Watford because that used by coaches before the war had been taken up by the expanded bus network. They therefore sought a

temporary stand in Portland Place, the point at which the 724 and 725 would also have to terminate. The 721 (Brentwood) and 722 (Corbets Tey) were the two exceptions which were to be double-deck operated, the reason for this being that they were high frequency services on which significant reductions could be made in peak hour services. This would fulfil a wish which had been in the Board's mind since the mid-1930s. The Commissioner continued to doubt the claim about reduced frequencies.

The Luton via Barnet route was restored to King's Cross (727), the southern end terminating at Baker Street and numbered 714. The routes via Epsom became 712 and 713. The Epping to Ongar section of 718 was omitted, probably in anticipation of the (then believed to be) imminent extension of the Central Line and the 'by-pass' version of the London – Grays route was also omitted, the whole service to Grays and Tilbury being concentrated on the 723. The earlier proposal to extend route 720 from Liverpool Street to Aldgate was replaced by one to use the more direct route along Whitechapel Road, omitting Bethnal Green and Liverpool Street altogether.

Interestingly, presumably in deference to the Commissioner's wish that the pre-war network should be restored in its 1939 form, some of the proposals to withdraw sections of route were shown as 'deferred' introductions rather than withdrawals. Those qualifying were: between Abbots Langley and Watford, Baldock and Hitchin and Horsham and Dorking; the Bushey Heath – Apex Corner section of route T and the Epping to Bishops Stortford section of route N; and the whole of routes X (Eastern Avenue) and W (Ongar). None of these appeared subsequently but in 1950 the possibility was considered of extending route 716 from Hitchin to Baldock as a part of a general review of coach services. Nothing happened.

There was one addition to the programme which was of exceptional interest but proved to be ephemeral. This was for a cross-country route, numbered 719, from Luton to Windsor via St Albans, Watford and Uxbridge. The Traffic Commissioner approved it once he was happy about the route through Uxbridge.

The Traffic Commissioner was inclined to challenge the Board's contention that it could not accommodate the 709, 710 and 711 at Watford, not without some justification as it turned out because room was found for route 726 at Leavesden Road garage. 'Once the Board, especially Green Line, get their noses in anywhere, even though . . . temporary, they have the bad habit of [making it] permanent.' With this in mind the Commissioner suggested that either the introduction of the whole routes should be deferred until accommodation was available, or that they should go to Watford and stand on the highway or that they should go to Victoria and turn at Gillingham Street 'bus station'. There was no reason, the Commissioner said, why they should traverse busy central area streets just to terminate at Oxford Circus (!). However, the principle of terminating in central London was accepted eventually as a temporary measure, providing the terminus was at Allsop Place, Baker Street, rather than Portland Place.

A compromise was also reached for the routes serving Baker Street. The Board conceded its wish to run the 718 via Oxford Circus and accepted that Baker Street routes should run southbound via Marylebone Road and Edgware Road, the northbound route remaining as Portman Street and Baker Street. The Police had wanted the routes to run in both directions via Edgware Road. In recognising, rather grudgingly, that the 715 route through Oxford Street was a direct replacement of a pre-war route, the Commissioner's office nevertheless felt the need to remind themselves that they should 'clamp down' on the use of the stops at Selfridges as they had before the war.

The hope had been that the services could be restored in five stages starting in January with routes 720, 721 and 722 but government restrictions were not lifted until 1st February and the first stage had to be deferred. There was a possibility that it could be combined with stage two (route 715) in February but this proved too ambitious, possibly because the full complement of staff was not available at Romford.

The magical aura of Green Line at last returned to London's streets on the dull and misty morning of 6th February 1946, welcomed by one newspaper headline as 'Green Streak In The Mist', typical of the tone of the general Press acclaim. The very first wheel to turn on a public road was the 715 which left Hertford for Guildford at 5.40am. Route 720 had the honour of being the other pioneer. Both routes used restored 10T10s painted in the Lincoln green and white of the Country Bus fleet and their destination blinds

Green Line coaches returned to much acclaim on 6th February when this evocative photograph of T 581 was taken at Oxford Circus. At first, the coaches were painted in the 1939 style of Country Bus Lincoln green and white and their blinds and side route boards had white lettering out of black. The unusual kerbside position of the route number on these early blinds was believed to be an aid to recognition after dark, when the difference between a coach and a single-deck bus would have been difficult to detect on unlit country roads.

The TF class returned to the Green Line on 6th March, and to east London although not to their short-lived pre-war haunts through Ilford and Romford but to route 723 from Grays garage. Green and white TF 73c is at Aldgate parked in front of a 10T10 on the 720 and alongside the rather primitive refreshment stall for staff on layover. A.B. Cross

and side route boards had white lettering out of black. The pre-war practice of carrying the name GREEN LINE in the destination display was continued but the words were one above the other so that the number was on the right-hand side of the display, a position not adopted generally on single-deckers for another 30 or so years.

The delayed introduction of route 721 (Brentwood – Aldgate) – but not yet route 722 – took place on 6th March, together with three of the routes in the original March programme. The double-deckers proved to be brand new Daimlers; their newness being more than a little overshadowed by their austerity – albeit 'relaxed austerity' – specification, which was in sharp contrast to the relative luxury of the TFs which had just been introduced when the route was withdrawn in 1939. The Ds were also painted in green and white, with brown roofs and carried Green Line

bullseye symbols each side of the front destination blinds and on the side and rear panels between decks, in addition to the Green Line fleetname in the usual positions. Together with the wording on the destination blinds, this meant that the Green Line name appeared no fewer than nine times on each bus!

The other routes in the March programme were the 704 (Tunbridge Wells – Windsor), 709 (Caterham – Baker Street), 710 (Crawley – Baker Street) and 723 (Tilbury – Aldgate), which heralded the reappearance of the other two main Green Line vehicles, the 6Q6 which was used on routes 709 and 710, and the TF which was the type allocated to route 723. Tunbridge Wells and Windsor operated 10T10s on the 704. The whole programme, which was completed in a shorter period than planned but in a different order, may be summarised as follows:

Date started 1946	Route number	Destinations	Original stage	Garages		Vehicle type
6th February	715	Guildford – Shepherd's Bush – Oxford Circus – Hertford	February	Guildford	Hertford	10T10
	720	Bishops Stortford – Aldgate	January	Epping		10T10
6th March	704	Tunbridge Wells – Victoria – Windsor	March	Tunbridge Wells	Windsor	10T10
	709	Caterham – Baker Street	March	Godstone		6Q6
	710	Crawley – Baker Street	March	Crawley		6Q6
	721	Brentwood – Aldgate	January	Romford (London Rd)		D
	723	Tilbury – Aldgate	March	Grays		TF
8th March	716	Chertsey – Hyde Park Corner – Hitchin	March	Addlestone	Hitchin	10T10
3rd April	703	Wrotham – Victoria – Rickmansworth – Amersham	April	Swanley	Amersham	10T10
	711	Reigate – Baker Street	April	Reigate		6Q6
	718	Windsor – Kingston – Victoria – Woodford – Epping	April	Windsor	Epping	10T10
	722	Corbets Tey – Aldgate	January	Romford (London Rd)		D
	724	High Wycombe – Oxford Circus	April	High Wycombe		6Q6
1st May	708	East Grinstead – Victoria – Hemel Hempstead	April	East Grinstead	Two Waters	10T10
	714	Dorking – Kingston – Hyde Park Corner – Baker Street	July	Dorking		TF
	717	Woking – Hyde Park Corner – Welwyn Garden City	March	Addlestone	Hatfield	10T10
	727	Luton – Barnet – King's Cross	July	Luton		TF
29th May	705	Sevenoaks – Westerham – Bromley – Victoria – Windsor	July	Dunton Green	Windsor	10T10
	712/713	Dorking – Epsom – Victoria – St Albans – Luton/Dunstable	April	Dorking	St Albans	TF
	726	Marylebone Station – Whipsnade Zoo (Summer only)	April	Watford (Leavesden Rd)	Romford (London Rd)	10T10
19th June	702	Gravesend – Victoria – Sunningdale	July	Northfleet	Staines	10T10
	725	Chesham – Uxbridge – Oxford Circus	July	Amersham		6Q6
22nd June	701	Gravesend – Victoria – Ascot	July	Northfleet	Staines	10T10
26th June	706/707	Westerham/Oxted – Victoria – Aylesbury	July	Chelsham	Tring	10T10

GREEN LINE

(Route map showing the completed Green Line coach system in its original form, August 1946)

Route terminals and destinations shown on the map include:

716 HITCHIN · 713 DUNSTABLE · 712 727 LUTON · 720 BISHOPS STORTFORD · 706 707 AYLESBURY · 726 WHIPSNADE · 708 HEMEL HEMPSTEAD · 725 CHESHAM · 703 AMERSHAM · 724 HIGH WYCOMBE · 717 WELWYN GARDEN CITY · 715 HERTFORD · 718 EPPING · 721 BRENTWOOD · 722 UPMINSTER (Corbets Tey) · 723 TILBURY · 705 WINDSOR · 704 718 · ASCOT 701 · SUNNINGDALE 702 · CHERTSEY 716 · WOKING 717 · GUILDFORD 715 · 702 GRAVESEND 701 · WROTHAM 703 · SEVENOAKS 705 · WESTERHAM 706 · OXTED 707 · CATERHAM 709 · REIGATE 711 · DORKING 712 713 714 · CRAWLEY 710 · EAST GRINSTEAD 708 · TUNBRIDGE WELLS 704

Intermediate points include: Little Wymondley, Stevenage, Knebworth, Woolmer Green, Welwyn, Kinsbourne Green, Harpenden, Markyate, Redbourn, Lemsford, Stanborough, Hatfield, Stonehouse Corner, St. Albans, London Colney, Kings Langley, Shenley, South Mimms, Potters Bar, Ware Station, Great Amwell, Hoddesdon, Broxbourne, Wormley, Cheshunt, Waltham Cross, Turkey Street, Enfield, Sawbridgeworth, Harlow, Potter Street, Thornwood, Epping Forest, Loughton, Buckhurst Hill, Woodford Wells, Woodford, Gidea Park, Harold Park, Romford, Hornchurch, Dagenham, Rainham, Wennington, Aveley, Grays, Northfleet, Greenhithe, Swanley, Farningham, Kingsdown, Hildenborough, Tonbridge, Southborough, etc.

CENTRAL AREA MAP

Kilburn · KINGS X · MARYLEBONE · BAKER ST · OXFORD CIRCUS · ALDGATE · PICCADILLY CIRCUS · MARBLE ARCH · Shepherds Bush · Hyde Pk Cnr · Trafalgar Sq · VICTORIA · Eccleston Bge · Hammersmith · Walham Green · Stockwell · Clapham Common · Putney · Vauxhall · Kennington · Brixton · Elephant

The map published in August 1946 showed the completed system in its original form. LT Museum

Below This Coach Stop in Park Lane at Marble Arch shows that the practice of showing destinations on the flags of principal stops was continued at first, although it now took the form of a single plate rather than the individual inserted slats which had been used pre-war. A Green Line 10T10 can be seen in the distance about to overtake an ST in a typically quiet roadscape. LT Museum

COACH STOP
703 AMERSHAM
706 707 AYLESBURY
708 HEMEL HEMPSTEAD
712 LUTON
713 DUNSTABLE
716 HITCHIN
717 WELWYN GARDEN Cᵗʸ
718 EPPING
QUEUE THIS SIDE
712. 713. 716. 717. 718

There were a few changes compared with the programme produced in November 1945 which may have been made for reasons of schedule efficiency. The 705 was extended to Sevenoaks, from which route D had been withdrawn in 1938, and the northern terminals of 706/707 and 708 were exchanged. The planned route 719, which should have started in July, did not appear and did not do so subsequently. No reason has been discovered for this.

The arrangements for picking up and setting down Green Line passengers were at first similar to pre-war practice. Inside the Metropolitan Police District boarding was allowed only at defined coach stops but alighting was permitted at any bus or coach stop. Outside the Metropolitan area both boarding and alighting was allowed at any bus or coach stop. This approach was now somewhat out of date as the old free-and-easy approach to stopping had changed significantly after 1942 with the general introduction of fixed stops to save fuel and rubber. Any return to the former arrangement was now considered unthinkable by the Board and it is not therefore

53

		WEEKDAYS AND SUNDAY—continued											(TT.6511)		
ALDGATE *Minories Coach Station*	12 30	1 0	....	1 30	2 0	....	2 30	3 0	....	3 30	4 0	..	4 30	5 0	5 30
Whitechapel *London Hospital*	12 35	1 5	....	1 35	2 5	....	2 35	3 5	....	3 35	4 5	..	4 35	5 5	5 35
Bow Road Station, *Underground*	12 41	1 11	....	1 41	2 11	....	2 41	3 11	....	3 41	4 11	..	4 41	5 11	5 41
Stratford *Broadway*	12 47	1 17	....	1 47	2 17	....	2 47	3 17	....	3 47	4 17	..	4 47	5 17	5 47
Leytonstone *Thatched House*	12 51	1 21	....	1 51	2 21	....	2 51	3 21	....	3 51	4 21	..	4 51	5 21	5 51
Wanstead *The George*	12 58	1 28	....	1 58	2 28	....	2 58	3 28	....	3 58	4 28	..	4 58	5 28	5 58
Woodford *The Castle*	1 7	1 37	....	2 7	2 37	....	3 7	3 37	....	4 7	4 37	..	5 7	5 37	6 7
Buckhurst Hill *Bald Stag*	1 11	1 41	....	2 11	2 41	....	3 11	3 41	....	4 11	4 41	..	5 11	5 41	6 11
Loughton *The Crown*	1 16	1 46	....	2 16	2 46	....	3 16	3 46	....	4 16	4 46	..	5 16	5 46	6 16
Epping Forest *Wake Arms*	1 23	1 53	....	2 23	2 53	....	3 23	3 53	....	4 23	4 53	..	5 23	5 53	6 23
Epping *Church*	1 30	2 0	....	2 30	3 0	....	3 30	4 0	....	4 30	5 0	..	5 30	6 0	6 30
Thornwood *Carpenters Arms*	1 35	2 5	....	2 35	3 5	....	3 35	4 5	....	4 35	5 5	..	5 35	6 5	6 35
Potter Street *Red Lion*	1 42	2 12	....	2 42	3 12	....	3 42	4 12	....	4 42	5 12	..	5 42	6 12	6 42
Harlow *Post Office*	1 47	2 17	....	2 47	3 17	....	3 47	4 17	....	4 47	5 17	..	5 47	6 17	6 47
Sawbridgeworth *White Lion*	1 54	2 24	....	2 54	3 24	....	3 54	4 24	....	4 54	5 24	..	5 54	6 24	6 54
BISHOPS STORTFORD *Bricklayers Arms*	2 9	2 39	....	3 9	3 39	....	4 9	4 39	....	5 9	5 39	..	6 9	6 39	7 9

BOARDING REGULATIONS — FROM LONDON

Between Aldgate *Minories Coach Station* and Epping Forest *Wake Arms* passengers may board at coach stops only as under

Aldgate *Station, Underground*	Leytonstone *Thatched House*	Woodford *Castle*
Whitechapel *London Hospital*	Leytonstone *Harrow Green*	Woodford *Horse and Well*
Stepney Green Station, *U-D*	Leytonstone *Station, LMS*	Buckhurst Hill *Bald Faced Stag*
Mile End Station, *U-D, Burdett Road*	Leytonstone *Green Man*	Buckhurst Hill *Roebuck Lane*
Bow Road Station, *Underground*	Wanstead *George*	Loughton *The Crescent*
Bow Road *Bow Church*	Snaresbrook *Eagle*	Loughton *Crown*
Stratford *High Street, Warton Road*	Snaresbrook *Clarendon Road*	Loughton *Traps Hill*
Stratford *Broadway*	Woodford *Gates Corner*	Loughton *London Transport Garage*
Leytonstone *Maryland Point*	Woodford *Cricketers*	Goldings Hill *Baldwins Hill*

Between Epping Forest *Wake Arms* and Bishops Stortford passengers may board at any bus or coach stop on request.

BISHOPS STORTFORD - LONDON *Aldgate*   **GREEN LINE COACH 720**

		WEEKDAYS AND SUNDAY—continued											(TT.6511)		
BISHOPS STORTFORD *Bricklayers Arms*	12 0	12 30	1 0	....	1 30	2 0	2 30	..	3 0	3 30	4 0	....	4 30	5 0	5 30
Sawbridgeworth *White Lion*	12 15	12 45	1 15	....	1 45	2 15	2 45	..	3 15	3 45	4 15	....	4 45	5 15	5 45
Harlow *Post Office*	12 22	12 52	1 22	....	1 52	2 22	2 52	..	3 22	3 52	4 22	....	4 52	5 22	5 52
Potter Street *Red Lion*	12 27	12 57	1 27	....	1 57	2 27	2 57	..	3 27	3 57	4 27	....	4 57	5 27	5 57
Thornwood *Carpenters Arms*	12 34	1 4	1 34	....	2 4	2 34	3 4	..	3 34	4 4	4 34	....	5 4	5 34	6 4
Epping *Church*	12 41	1 9	1 39	....	2 9	2 39	3 9	..	3 39	4 9	4 39	....	5 9	5 39	6 9
Epping Forest *Wake Arms*	12 46	1 16	1 46	....	2 16	2 46	3 16	..	3 46	4 16	4 46	....	5 16	5 46	6 16
Loughton *Crown*	12 53	1 23	1 53	....	2 23	2 53	3 23	..	3 53	4 23	4 53	....	5 23	5 53	6 23
Buckhurst Hill *Bald Faced Stag*	12 58	1 28	1 58	....	2 28	2 58	3 28	..	3 58	4 28	4 58	....	5 28	5 58	6 28
Woodford *The Castle*	1 2	1 32	2 2	....	2 32	3 2	3 32	..	4 2	4 32	5 2	....	5 32	6 2	6 32
Wanstead *The George*	1 11	1 41	2 11	....	2 41	3 11	3 41	..	4 11	4 41	5 11	....	5 41	6 11	6 41
Leytonstone *Thatched House*	1 18	1 48	2 18	....	2 48	3 18	3 48	..	4 18	4 48	5 18	....	5 48	6 18	6 48
Stratford *Broadway*	1 22	1 52	2 22	....	2 52	3 22	3 52	..	4 22	4 52	5 22	....	5 52	6 22	6 52
Bow Road Station, *Underground*	1 28	1 58	2 28	....	2 58	3 28	3 58	..	4 28	4 58	5 28	....	5 58	6 28	6 58
Whitechapel *London Hospital*	1 34	2 4	2 34	....	3 4	3 34	4 4	..	4 34	5 4	5 34	....	6 4	6 34	7 4
ALDGATE *Minories Coach Station*	1 39	2 9	2 39	....	3 9	3 39	4 9	..	4 39	5 9	5 39	....	6 9	6 39	7 9

BOARDING REGULATIONS — TO LONDON

Between Bishops Stortford and Epping Forest *Wake Arms* passengers may board at any bus or coach stop on request.
Between Epping Forest *Wake Arms* and Aldgate *Minories Coach Station* passengers may board at coach stops only as under

Goldings Hill *Baldwins Hill*	Woodford *Cricketers*	Leytonstone *Maryland Point*
Loughton *London Transport Garage*	Woodford *Gates Corner*	Stratford *Broadway*
Loughton *Traps Hill*	Snaresbrook *Clarendon Road*	Stratford *High Street, Warton Road*
Loughton *Crown*	Snaresbrook *Eagle*	Bow Road Station, *Underground*
Loughton *The Crescent*	Wanstead *Green Man*	Mile End Station, *U-D, Burdett Road*
Buckhurst Hill *Roebuck Lane*	Leytonstone *Green Man*	Stepney Green Station, *Underground*
Buckhurst Hill *Bald Faced Stag*	Leytonstone *Station, LMS*	Whitechapel *London Hospital*
Woodford *Horse and Well*	Leytonstone *Harrow Green*	Aldgate *Station, Underground*
Woodford *Castle*	Leytonstone *Thatched House*	

The timetable leaflet issued for the introduction of route 720 on 6th February 1946 shows the restrictions on boarding within the Metropolitan Police Area and the more relaxed arrangements which applied outside during the early post-war years.

surprising that from 30th September 1946 within the Metropolitan Police area both boarding and alighting could take place only at defined stops. The deleterious effect of this was offset to some extent by the addition of 65 stops to the system. These arrangements were extended to stops outside the Metropolitan area from 11th May 1947, after which Green Line coaches stopped only at Coach Stops everywhere on the network.

Compared with other London Transport services, Green Line fares became relatively more expensive than pre-war. Whereas other fares had increased by roughly 10 per cent since 1939, coach fares were set at a level 16.66 per cent higher and only single fares were allowed. The aim of this was to bring them broadly into line with the equivalent monthly return fares on Main Line railways, public policy being to prevent road services from attracting traffic away from the railways. This was why Green Line fares were increased at the same time as railway fares on 1st July 1946 to 33.33 per cent above pre-war, whereas other London Transport fares remained unchanged. The minimum fare within London was set at 1s 6d, 50 per cent higher than pre-war. Weekly tickets were reintroduced from 30th September 1946 and on the following day Cheap Day Returns to and from central London were issued

on Tuesdays, Wednesdays and Thursdays for use outside peak hours. Their issue was extended to cover Mondays and Fridays from 4th June 1948 and then to weekends, with restriction on travel from London during the evening peak also removed, from 11th June 1949. The major revision of London Transport fares on 1st October 1950 saw considerable reductions in Green Line rates, which were brought more into line with suburban railway charges, including the lowering of the London minimum to the pre-war level of one shilling. After that, coach fares rose in line with buses.

Once the network had been introduced very little change was made to it during its first six years. An attempt was made during the winter of 1946/47 to provide the missing Watford service. This was done by putting short-workings on route 708 between Watford and London, operated from Watford (Leavesden Road) garage, but this seems to have been as much as anything to find work for the crews off 726 during the winter close-down of that service. Presumably this slipped by the Traffic Commissioner who might have been expected to insist on the extension of the routes from Baker Street! The shorts were withdrawn on 17th February 1947 but that was not quite the end of the story because Country Buses had plans at about this time to introduce a supplementary service on route 706 between London and Berkhamsted. To provide the resources for this, Central Buses were asked for the return of four of the 1/7T7/1s then on loan to them, but they were not prepared to release them and the plan was never implemented. As part of the big upheaval associated with the introduction of the new scheduling agreement on 12th November 1947, routes 709, 710 and 711 were extended to the destinations which London Transport had wanted in 1944, absorbing the 724 and 725, and the idea of reintroducing the Watford services was dropped for good. When route 726 came back for the summer of 1947 it was allocated to Romford (London Road), which had shared the operation before the war, and operated officially by STLs, five of which had been allocated to Romford in August 1946. These, in common with all vehicles used on the 726 were required to carry a First Aid kit and lifting gear because the route was licensed as an express carriage. Leavesden Road never again ran coaches.

A coach service to Tatsfield was restored from 9th June 1948 when route 706 was diverted to make a double run. Another town which lost its service in the post-war network, Chingford, regained a service from 10th May 1950, when the 718 was re-routed north of Walthamstow, following strong local protests. It did not follow the route of the pre-war W through the deserted glades of Epping Forest to the Wake Arms but bus route 145 from Chingford via Whitehall Road to rejoin its own route at Woodford.

Another desire expressed in the 1944 plans which was eventually fulfilled, although in a considerably modified form, was the linking of the Luton – King's Cross route across London to Dorking. Route 714 was extended from Baker Street to Luton via King's Cross on 30th September 1951 in anticipation of the proposed closure on expiry of its lease, of King's Cross coach station, which had moved to Judd Street on 29th September 1947.

Green Line did not start to make its contribution to the post-war expansion of services until 4th July 1951 when the first new route, 723A, was introduced between Aldgate and Grays to serve the Aveley LCC Estate. It was extended to Tilbury Civic Square via Dock Road on 30th April 1952, to cover the 723 which was diverted via Chadwell St Mary and extended to Tilbury Ferry following the transfer of services in Grays and Tilbury from Eastern National to London Transport. The other estate newly served during the period under review was Sheerwater, which route 717 was diverted to serve from 3rd December 1952. This set the scene for the great expansion which was to take place during the 1950s, the very thing that had haunted the Commissioner's office when the post-war plans were being reviewed.

Centre right From 1947 onwards route 726 was operated exclusively by Romford (London Road) garage, usually with Daimlers but sometimes with STLs. On Easter Monday 1949 an expectant queue waits to board D148 for Whipsnade Zoo in Allsop Place, which had replaced Marylebone as the London terminus in 1948. By this time D148 had been repainted in the post-war coach livery of two shades of green. A.B. Cross

Right The thirst for travel in the absence of widespread car ownership gave Green Line an important role in the late 1940s when heavy demands were made on services particularly on Bank Holidays. Easter Monday 1949 was a typical example, a fine day when long queues formed on Eccleston Bridge and a constant succession of reliefs flowed past, particularly on the Windsor routes which were always most popular and often ran every few minutes. STL1011, originally a forward-entrance STL6 but now with a rear-entrance STL14 body, has just deposited its load from Windsor and prepares for its return journey. A.B. Cross

5   CENTRAL LONDON IN 1946

Although this view of Cannon Street was taken from the Dome of St Paul's Cathedral in 1950 the landscape would have been the same in 1946 as nothing had yet been built to cover the devastation caused by the 1940 blitz, much of it inflicted in one relentless overnight raid at the end of December 1940.
Imperial War Museum

THIS CHAPTER is devoted to a walk around London to provide an introduction to the routes, service levels and types of vehicle that could be encountered in mid-1946, the first full year of peace. Since the earliest days of bus operation there had been a basic core of bus routes which served the purpose of bringing people into town from the suburbs, many of them continuing right across from one side to the other, and this was still the case in 1946. The tram and trolleybus routes which terminated on the edge of the central area were also long trunk services reaching out to the extremities of the system.

The walk will not stray far outside the area contained by what was then known as the Inner Circle (later the Circle Line) as the structure of routes ensured that this area was served by a representative cross-section of the double-deck

motor bus types, trams and trolleybuses then owned by the Board. The London through which the walk passes was a war-torn city. Although little rebuilding had occurred, bombed buildings had been cleared and their sites made tidy. Where a building in a terrace had been bombed, the party walls had been rendered to make the adjoining houses damp-proof and, quite often, massive wooden buttresses could be seen against walls which had not originally been external. The completely devastated sites, of which there were large contiguous areas in some parts, particularly the City, were made safe by building brick walls along their boundaries, inviting nature to move into the resulting exposed basements with yellow ragwort, pink willow herb and mauve buddleia. Buildings which remained intact showed signs of six years of neglect or repaired bomb damage, a common sight being shop windows reduced to a picturelike display in the middle of hardboard or wooden fillings which had replaced the lost plate glass. Such was the London through which the equally war-weary fleet threaded its way in 1946.

The excursion starts at Oxford Circus which on weekdays was traversed by no fewer than 18 bus routes with a peak hour maximum frequency, even in those straitened times, of 337 in each direction. Then as now the routes were divided into three main groups: those which came along Oxford Street from the east and continued along it to the west; those which came up Regent Street from the south and turned west to continue along Oxford Street; and those which, having come up Regent Street, continued northwards. There were two exceptions: route 113 which was the only route with its terminus at Oxford Circus; and route 137, which uniquely travelled between Oxford Street and Hampstead Road via Great Portland Street. Route 53A was also an oddity, although included in the third main category, because it turned westward immediately north of Oxford Circus to reach Baker Street via Wigmore Street.

In the first group, which had the highest number of hourly peak movements across the circus (117), there were seven weekday routes. The 7 was worked from Middle Row garage officially with STs but often with some admixture of petrol STLs of the original General 60-seater design and the later 'sloping body' type. All three types sang out the characteristic high-pitched notes of the AEC crash gearbox, a sound not dissimilar from that to be found on AEC products almost to the end of production by that company. Route 8, once the home of LGOC's very first STLs, was by now worked from Clay Hall and Willesden with standard oil-engined STLs, whose musical attributes, influenced by their preselective gearboxes were softer and not too dissimilar from the sound of an AEC Routemaster. Two routes which were stocked predominantly with oil-engined LTs were the 17 (London Bridge – Shepherd's Bush – Park Royal in peak hours) worked by Hammersmith (R) and the 73, one of the most frequent crossing the circus with a peak flow of thirty buses an hour and needing ninety-two buses from Mortlake and Tottenham. Some STs could also be seen on the 73. The 23 (Marylebone – Becontree Heath) was worked by Barking using Guy Arab IIs with every type of bodywork to be found in the class, the bark of their 5-cylinder Gardner engines adding their own unique touch to the chorus. The 25B and its peak hour variant 25C to North Woolwich were worked from Forest Gate and needed 82 standard STLs between them.

The second group was almost as large with 109 peak buses an hour on six routes plus another 33 short workings terminating at Oxford Circus. Two of the routes were worked exclusively by standard STLs (at least officially), the 6 shared between Hackney and Willesden garages and the 60 worked from Clay Hall and Cricklewood. Until

June 1946, when they were moved to Edgware, those at Cricklewood included short-wheelbase STL 1260–1263 which carried bodies from the former DST class, except for STL 1262 which had lost its Dodson body in a V1 attack in 1944 and now carried a standard ST version. The 12 was a complicated and frequent route needing a total of 95 buses of three types from five garages. Catford supplied standard STL oilers, which contrasted with Croydon's STs and the large quantity of standard LTs supplied by Elmers End, Nunhead and Shepherd's Bush. Croydon would often turn out a petrol-engined STL, and sometimes this would be one of the many Tillings still allocated to their family home. Route 13 provided the first

Left Middle Row's all-petrol fleet included a large number of STLs which were its normal contribution to route 15, then as now one of the more important trunk routes crossing Oxford Circus. Like all petrol-engined STLs, STL 375, a 6STL3/2, had a crash gearbox and in appearance was much as it had been when new, although the roof ventilator shows this to have been one of the first 25 STL3-type bodies to be built. It shares the stand at Ladbroke Grove with an STL 1.
A.B. Cross

Below Terminating buses on several routes could be found lurking near Oxford Circus in Great Castle Street, Princes Street and Margaret Street, officially a turning point but invariably treated as a stand. This was the furthest point reached on route 12 by Croydon's buses, on this occasion represented by no less a bus than ST 1 which at this stage of its life carried a standard ST2 body with rounded cab.

glimpse of the famous pre-war STDs, with their familiar but subtly different looks and their own special deep-throated roar rising above all the AEC sounds. The 13 was also worked by Cricklewood who supplied STs. The 15 was worked with an interesting cross-section of the 'obsolete fleet', oil-engined LTs and the occasional ST from Upton Park and petrol-engined STLs from Middle Row. Finally, the 88, the second route with a total peak movement of thirty an hour, was worked predominantly by Merton with the second of the wartime types to be seen here, Daimlers, many of them brand new. It also had a small Hammersmith allocation of LTs.

The third group had a peak flow of 54 an hour on through services and another 33 terminators on routes 12 and 88. It included the closely-knit group of routes, 3, 59A and 159, all worked by standard STLs but each with its own speciality. Those supplied by Chalk Farm for the 3 were

mostly of the sloping-bodied STL18 type, while those from Streatham on route 159 included a number of the final pre-war 15STL16 version, many in the short-lived 1945 all-over red livery. One of the Camberwell STLs which appeared from time to time on the 59A was STL1167, which carried the body from STF1 still at that time fully streamlined but in half-cab form. The fourth route was the 53A on which Plumstead and Old Kent Road both ran LTs but with a few STs from the latter. The Plumstead LTs included petrol-engined examples with pre-selective gearbox and fluid transmission, of which there were fifty-four. This combination produced one of the most distinctive and endearing bus sound effects to be found in London, particularly when idling in neutral when the warbling song of the gearbox rose above the quiet hiss of the petrol engine to provide a gentle contrast to the more sonerous beat of the 8.8 litre oilers.

Oxford Street looking towards Marble Arch in 1946 with the Cumberland Hotel on the right and one of the famous Lyons Corner Houses on the corner of Old Quebec Street. Nearest the camera an STL11 type in the new red and cream livery prepares to tackle a sizeable queue, while further back there is another STL11 on route 6 and one of the earlier STL5 type, with destination indicator at the bottom of the display, on route 30. Waiting at the traffic lights at Park Lane are a 2RT2 and a 6Q6, beyond them two more STLs and just disappearing into Edgware Road, an ST. *LT Museum*

The two exceptions mentioned earlier as not conforming to any of the three general traffic patterns of buses using Oxford Circus were the 113, another Hendon working with pre-war STDs, and the 137 which was shared between Camberwell, Chalk Farm and Victoria, all normally with STLs, although Victoria's share would occasionally include a wartime STD, similar in sound to the pre-war variety but with a pronounced whistle from the transmission. Also seen at Oxford Circus, so recently restored after wartime exile, were the six Green Line routes. Three made the north-south movement, the 709, 710 and 711, all using 6Q6s. The others shared the west to north movement with bus route 137; the 715, one of the two pioneers, worked 10T10s, and the 724 and 725, both with 6Q6s.

Moving westwards from Oxford Circus, the 25B and 25C take their leave at Bond Street and, in passing, it can be noted that operation of the Green Line coach stop at Selfridges was restricted to the evenings on Monday to Friday, after 2pm Saturday and all day on Sunday. This was a legacy of the punitive Amulree restrictions of 1933 which, with a few minor exceptions such as the 715, banned Green Line services from an area broadly enclosed by the modern ring road on Mondays–Fridays and on Saturdays before 2pm.

The next group of routes to be encountered was at Orchard Street where three services from Baker Street emerged and turned towards Marble Arch. Two of these, the 30 and 74, brought the first sight of 2RT2s, from Chelverton Road and

Putney respectively, the weighty resonance of their 9.6 litre pot-cavity engines contrasting with a lighter sound of the STLs supplied by Hackney for route 30. Standard STLs were also seen on the third of these routes, the 2, worked jointly by Cricklewood and Norwood. The southbound 13, 23 and 113 also entered Oxford Street from Orchard Street but turned left to go eastwards. All these routes left Oxford Street by Portman Street although Baker Street itself, being two-way in those days, was used from Portman Square northwards.

Although no Green Line routes ran southbound in Baker Street, six used it on northbound journeys, running via Marylebone Road and Edgware Road southbound. They were the 712, 713 and 714 all with the third type of coach to be met on this tour, the pioneering underfloor-engined TF, and the 716, 717 and 718 all with 10T10s.

At Marble Arch routes 6, 7, 8, 15 and 60 went their own way to Edgware Road and routes 12, 17, 88 and 715 to Bayswater Road. Routes 2, 30, 73 and 74 turned left into Park Lane. They were joined there from Edgware Road by the most frequent route encountered so far (thirty-six an hour), the 16, a Cricklewood working with STLs and a handful of STs; and the 36, a former Tilling route still worked by Catford but now shared with Camberwell, both with standard oil-engined STLs. Also speeding across from Edgware Road were the southbound halves of the Baker Street Green Line routes and four others, all worked with 10T10s, the 703, 706, 707 and 708.

Park Lane as it looked in 1946, long before the dual-carriageway arrangement was built. Two STLs dominate the road, almost deserted of other traffic. Barnaby's

59

Piccadilly Circus in 1946. Eros had been removed at the start of the war for safe keeping and was not returned to its pedestal until July 1947. In front of it, an STL passes on route 22, while at the eastern end of Piccadilly another STL can be seen on route 19. An STD on the 13 has just left Lower Regent Street in the company of a Daimler on the 88, one of the most frequent services then operating. Merton's Daimlers on this route were the most prominent utilities in the West End. Topham

No bus routes turned left from Park Lane into Piccadilly where this tour continues. At Hyde Park Corner it was possible to see the greatest concentration of 2RT2s away from their home town of Putney itself. They passed this point on four routes, the 30 and 74, already encountered, and the 14 and 96 (Putney Common – Wanstead), both of which had standard STLs from their other garages, Holloway and Forest Gate respectively. Three other routes came from Knightsbridge. The 9 was worked by Dalston with STLs and STs and Mortlake with standard STs and LTs. Among the considerable variety of LTs on route 9 it was sometimes possible to see LT 21, the only one of the class to have been fitted experimentally with an A171 7.7 litre oil engine of the type used in earlier STLs. It had been fitted with an enclosed staircase body by this time and could be distinguished from the standard type only by a trained ear. Route 19 was worked by Battersea with STLs and Holloway with STLs and STs while the 22 was worked by Hackney STLs and Victoria's utility STDs topped up with a couple of STLs.

Four routes came from Grosvenor Place into Piccadilly, the 25B and 25C already met at Oxford Circus and the 38 and 38A. The 38 was yet another major route on which the normal rolling stock was standard oil-engined LTs, in this case worked entirely by Leyton. The 38A, shared between Leyton and the tiny outpost at Loughton, serves to introduce the petrol-engined open staircase variety which both garages worked and which were the oldest buses still scheduled for all day service in the Central Area. Also to be seen at Hyde Park Corner, making its way between Knightsbridge and Grosvenor Place was route 52, so recently graced by 2RT2s but now with STLs worked by Victoria and Willesden with some STs from the latter.

Walking via Piccadilly and Haymarket, no fresh routes would be encountered until Trafalgar Square but a pause at Piccadilly Circus would enable the visitor to observe the swirl of buses of nearly every double-deck type then working in London, the only absentees being Bristols and Guys and to enjoy the variety of sound-effects.

One of the more dominant, especially on the gradient up from Lower Regent Street, was from the AEC crash gearboxes which rose through the scale to a rather hysterical high pitched scream. These could be heard on the LTs, with their powerfully baritonal sounding 8.8 litre oil engines, and STs with their quietly purring petrol engines. Contrasting with these were the STLs and most of the Daimlers, which gave out the melodious tones of the Wilson type epicyclic gearbox, something shared by the 2RT2s which emitted a deep heavy sounding beat. There was also the occasional flash of green as one of the 6Q6 coaches slipped through.

The 9 and 96 joined the routes from Regent Street to continue down Haymarket to Trafalgar Square, the others branched off to Shaftesbury Avenue. At Trafalgar Square, there were three routes from Whitehall into Strand. The 11 route, one of London's most frequent at thirty an hour, was worked from Hammersmith with LTs and Dalston with STLs. The 77 and 77A both had Daimlers from Merton with STLs from Victoria but also had occasional visits from unfrozen STDs. During the short-lived operation of Guys from Victoria the 77A had the distinction of being the only route to have had an official allocation of both Ds and Gs and was the only route to have been operated by three of the four utility types.

A unique movement between St Martin's Place into Strand was made by route 1 worked by Catford and Cricklewood STs. In passage between St Martin's Place and Whitehall came route 24, a Chalk Farm STL working, the 29, worked by standard LTs from Palmers Green and West Green and the 39 by Battersea and Chalk Farm with STLs. Also making this movement was the 134, the second route to be encountered with an allocation of open-staircase LTs (from Potters Bar). Holloway also participated with STLs.

From Trafalgar Square, the walk abandons buses briefly and follows the southbound Green Lines down Northumberland Avenue to Victoria Embankment, where trams could be sighted on their reserved riverside track. At Charing Cross Underground Station there was a peak frequency of 138 trams in each direction on 17 routes, eight of which were in pairs, each constituent working one way around the loop. Every conceivable variety of tram could be seen. The dominant type was the E/1, which contained the oldest cars still working, and could be seen on routes 2/4 (from Wimbledon) and 22/24 (Tooting loop via Vauxhall peak hours only), worked by Clapham depot with usually the later 1922 model, the 26 (Hop Exchange – Clapham Junction), worked from Wandsworth, the 36/38 (Abbey Wood – Embankment), from Abbey Wood and New Cross, the 40 (Savoy Street – Woolwich/Plumstead in peak hours) and 72 (Savoy Street – Woolwich via Lee) both worked from New Cross.

The later all-metal E/3s, just 15 or 16 years old in 1946, were the mandatory allocation for the three routes passing through Kingsway Subway, route 31 (Battersea – Westminster, and peaks to Bloomsbury) worked from Wandsworth, 33 (West Norwood – Manor House), worked from Norwood and 35 (Forest Hill – Archway) worked from Camberwell, with a small Holloway presence on each route. The more powerful contemporary of the E/3s, the four-motored HR/2s could be seen on Dog Kennel Hill routes 56/84 (Embankment – Peckham Rye) and 62 (Savoy Street – Forest Hill), both worked from Camberwell. Some of these had bodies of the same style as rehabilitated E/1 cars. The only former Underground Group company cars still in service were the Felthams (class UCC) which could be seen in abundance on the most frequent pair of routes 16/18 (Embankment – Purley), worked by Brixton Hill and Telford

Smartly turned-out open staircase LT104 working from Potters Bar garage on route 134 stops outside the National Gallery in Trafalgar Square where, just visible between the front of the bus and the gallery, the Dex Harrison shelter which won the design competition in 1946 has been erected.
A.B. Cross

Former LUT Feltham 2132 works a peak hour 18X and former Leyton Council Car 187 is making for Manor House on route 33 under the powerful protection of Thornycroft's Boadicea statue on the corner of Westminster Bridge. The substantial wooden shelter on the left was inherited from the LCC and the London Transport Tram Stop with blue roundel is on a former LCC post. Evidence of wartime neglect is only too apparent in the condition of the track in the foreground. F.W. Ivey

This view of Strand, by St Clement Danes Church, drips with atmosphere as well as rain, as Brush-bodied D93 makes for Tooting with Aldwych station yet to re-open after its wartime closure in the background. Remarkably, the delightful Whitbread Dennis lorry is still fitted with a headlamp mask and retains its white blackout markings. The Omnibus Society

Avenue depots at a maximum peak hour frequency of 28 trams an hour. The former Croydon Corporation depot at Thornton Heath also supplied cars for the 16/18, a mixture of former Croydon E1 style cars, including rehabilitated examples, similar cars formerly owned by Walthamstow Council and some E/3s.

Variety was added to this basic arrangement in substantial numbers by former East Ham and West Ham corporation cars, with their distinctive small indicator boxes, on routes 36/38, by the numerous rebuilt and rehabilitated cars of class

E/1 and M/E3 and by the appearance in peak hours on route 16/18 of the experimental LCC 'Bluebird' car number 1.

Returning to the buses at Aldwych, the route of the walk was crossed here on their way between Waterloo and Kingsway by the 68, shared by Chalk Farm, Norwood and Croydon, all with STLs, and the 68A an exclusive Norwood STL working. In the case of Croydon the recently allocated STLs were the only oil-engined examples at the garage. Two routes passed between Waterloo Bridge and Fleet Street, the 6A with its

curious morning peak only service, worked by Hackney STLs from the main route 6 allocation, and the 67 (Waterloo – Stoke Newington via Chancery Lane), a Tottenham ST working. At this point, the 1 turned off to cross Waterloo Bridge, while the 77 and 77A joined the northbound movement up Kingsway and a little further on the 67 slipped into its private domain in the narrow canyon of Chancery Lane.

At Ludgate Circus the direct crossing south to north was made only by the 63, a Nunhead working with LTs. From St Bride Street into Ludgate Circus came route 18B (Brent Station – London Bridge), a rather circuitous route at this end and unique in using Southwark Bridge, worked by Willesden, officially with STLs but often with STs too. On a Sunday this was covered by the extended 18, which brought Alperton's Guys onto the scene. The movement from Blackfriars Bridge to Ludgate Hill was made by route 4A, the only route to use the eastern side of St Paul's Churchyard, the devastated Aldersgate Street and Goswell Road, worked by Camberwell and Holloway with STLs and some STs from Holloway.

A wartime view of Ludgate Hill showing the destruction which was still apparent, if tidied up, in 1946. Photochrom Ltd

A short detour passing the bomb sites of Farringdon Street to Charterhouse Street would reveal the first sight of trolleybuses which, like the trams, were not allowed to penetrate the inner zone by more than a few hundred yards. Charterhouse Street was the effective terminus of the Holborn Circus routes with a peak flow of 70 an hour in each direction. Although the operation was intended as a loop working, there were usually several trolleybuses standing on each side of the street humming quietly to themselves while awaiting their departure time. Four of the routes worked in pairs, each going one-way around the loop. The 513/613 (Hampstead Heath – Parliament Hill Fields) were of particular interest in being worked by Holloway (later re-named Highgate), the largest of the 21 depots, with the short-wheelbase Leyland B1, B2 and B3s whose foreshortened three-axle arrangement made them look as though they were not yet fully grown. Routes 517/617 (from North Finchley via Archway), also worked by Holloway, shared in the large allocation of different types found at that location, predominantly J2, J3, L1 and L2 but with some K1, K2 and L3. The 521/621 (also from Finchley but via New Southgate) was a Finchley working on which it was possible to see C2, C3, J1 and J2 AECs, and the 543/643 (from Wood Green via Stamford Hill) were worked by Stamford Hill with K1, K2 and K3 type Leylands. Two other routes worked only one way around the loop. The

565 (peak hours only from Barking) was part of the 118-vehicle strong Barking Road group, worked by Poplar and West Ham with L3s, but also M1s and N2s. According to some sources they also saw, very occasionally, members of the E classes normally confined to West Ham's other routes; and the 659 (from Waltham Cross) was worked by Edmonton depot with K types. One unusual visitor often to be seen on the 521/621 was the class X4 experimental chassisless trolleybus, 754, the only one with a London Transport body (built at Charlton Works). This was readily identifiable by its front passenger exit enclosed by a pair of folding doors which by this time remained out of use.

Returning to Ludgate Circus, the walk continues up Ludgate Hill, passing under the railway bridge at its foot (on which the occasional steam train could be seen mingling with Southern Railway suburban EMUs), continues along St Paul's Churchyard on the south side of the cathedral and, in a bomb-flattened landscape, into Cannon Street. At Mansion House station most routes turned left, joining the sole route which used the length of Queen Victoria Street, the 76, worked by Tottenham with the earliest type of wartime Guys. The 18B continued a little further, turning off down Queen Street on its way to Southwark Bridge, where it met the trams at their truncated terminus. The 13 continued the full length of Cannon Street to meet the next group of routes which crossed London Bridge, an interesting collection which included the 17, already met at Oxford Circus.

Five routes made the swan-neck at Monument station to pass into Gracechurch Street. The 8A was worked by Clay Hall and Willesden on a joint schedule with route 8 using STLs from both. Route 10 (Abridge – Victoria) was another route which, like the 76, crossed two Thames bridges, London and Lambeth. It was one of two routes on which Leyton's outside stair LTs could be seen at this point, the other being route 35. The 10 was also run by Victoria with STLs and unfrozen STDs and the 35 was shared with Camberwell which supplied STLs. Standard LTs were represented by Upton Park's share of route 40 whose other buses were Camberwell STLs, while other members of the 'obsolete fleet' could be found on route 47 where petrol STLs, including Pickup, Tilling and Chiswick examples and some STs, were Bromley's contribution while STs and oil-engined STLs came from Dalston.

Routes which bore to the left up King William Street to the Bank were the 21 worked by Sidcup and Old Kent Road, both with LTs, the 43 worked by Muswell Hill, also with LTs and the 133. On the 133 it was possible to see nearly every type of pre-war STL, those from Croydon garage being petrol-engined examples of Tilling, Pickup and LGOC design and those from Streatham oilers which included some 15STL16s, the last pre-war design.

By following the route of the 10 and 40 through Fenchurch Street, another important group of trolleybus routes was to be found terminating in the Minories 'lay-by' at Aldgate, just on the Inner Circle boundary. Routes 567 (Barking Broadway – Aldgate, and Sunday to Smithfield) and 569 (North Woolwich – Aldgate peak hours only) were part of the group of trunk routes radiating out along Barking Road which had been operating only six years, having been the last of the tram to trolleybus conversions. Like the 565 encountered at Holborn, they were worked by Poplar and West Ham with predominantly L3s, but also M1s and N2s and occasionally members of the E classes. The other routes were the 653 (Aldgate – Tottenham Court Road), worked by Holloway with a bewildering variety of trolleybus types, the most numerous being J2, J3, L1 and L2 but with some K1, K2 and L3 and routes 661 (Leyton – Aldgate via Leytonstone) and 663 (Ilford – Aldgate) both worked by Bow with the elegant N1 and N2. One speciality seen from time to time on the 653 was the experimental Kingsway Subway trolleybus, class X5 number 1379, with its distinctive double-sided platform and straight staircase.

Sharing the lay-by terminus were four Green Line routes, two single-deck, the 720 an Epping working with 10T10s, and the 723 worked by Grays using TFs; and two double-deck, the 721 and 722 both worked by Romford (London Road) with utility Daimlers.

Most of the motor bus routes at Aldgate have already been seen but there were two newcomers that ran just inside the Inner Circle. Route 42 was once a major north-south trunk route, but was now a six-bus operation worked by Camberwell with STs, while the 78 was worked by Nunhead with LTs and Dalston with STLs. Route 78 continued northwards to Liverpool Street where two more trolleybus routes were to be found. The 557 (from Chingford Mount) was a Walthamstow operation on which E1, K1 and K2 could be seen, and 649 (from Ponders End, and Waltham Cross on Sundays), was worked by Edmonton and Stamford Hill with K type Leylands.

Holloway depot provided a considerable variety of trolleybus types on route 653 at Aldgate, among them J2 class AECs like 984, which had Birmingham Railway Carriage & Wagon Co. bodies dating from 1938. In the background is one of Romford's Daimlers on route 721. A.B. Cross

Aldgate lay-by was always busy with trolleybuses, parts of four of which can be seen here, the one on the left being one of the many AEC/MCCW chassisless L3 class vehicles which operated on the Barking Road routes. It was also the terminus for route 42 and short workings on other routes, particularly the 15, both illustrated here. Camberwell's STL 342, on the left, was one of the first STLs to be fitted with an oil engine when new, being part of the batch of 11 which were fitted experimentally with the newly developed 7.7 litre AEC oil engine. It was still carrying its original type of STL3/1 body which is clearly a derivative of the STL1 type fitted to Middle Row's STL 46 on the right.
A.B. Cross

There were two other trolleybus terminals within the Inner Circle. At Bloomsbury, where buses, trolleybuses and trams could be seen side by side in Theobalds Road, and at Tottenham Court Road. Any visitor to Bloomsbury would have been bound to spend a lot of time observing the comings and goings of the E/3 tramcars climbing out of or diving into the Kingsway Subway at an average of one every two minutes in each direction. A system of signals ensured that only one car was on each track on the slope at one time but there were also traffic signals because the trams had to cross two lanes of motor traffic at the junction with Southampton Row. One of the heart-stopping sights was of a tram held at the top of the slope, standing at a giddy angle while the driver pulled his screw brakes on as tight as possible.

While enjoying these comings and goings, the visitor could also watch trolleybuses across the road making their way to the Red Lion Square terminus via Parton Street, a narrow road which disappeared without trace when the Drake Street/Procter Street gyratory was built in the 1960s. These were routes 555 (to Leyton via Shoreditch, and on Sundays to Woodford) and the 581 (to Woodford via Islington), both worked by Hackney (later Clapton), with Leyton sharing the 581, using all-Leyland K1 and K2s; and the 665 (Bloomsbury – Barking) another constituent of

the massive Barking Road group sharing the same allocation of trolleybuses as the others already met.

The Tottenham Court Road terminus was just south of Euston Road, under which ran the Inner Circle. Of the three services to be seen there, the 653 has already been encountered at its other extremity, Aldgate, a roundabout journey of 64 minutes. The 627 (to Edmonton Town Hall, and on Sunday to Ponders End), was another predominantly Holloway working with the same varied allocation as the 653, with a smaller Edmonton presence, working K and P1 type Leylands and some evening peak workings from Wood Green using H1s. The H1 was particularly associated with Wood Green and was the normal rolling stock on the third route, the 629 (to Enfield).

Five motor bus routes which entered the area inside the Inner Circle have not been mentioned so far. One of these, the 27A could be seen at the Euston Road junction worked by STLs from Holloway and Twickenham. The other four could be found at Kensington Church which could be reached by riding on the 27A. They were the 28 shared between Middle Row, with petrol STLs and a few STs, and Battersea with standard STLs, its long time companion the 31, worked by Chalk Farm and Battersea had standard STLs. Willesden worked STLs on the 46 (Alperton – Waterloo), as did Merton officially on the 49, which also had a smaller input from Hammersmith with STs. Merton's contribution more often than not included Daimlers, which they seemed to regard as interchangeable with STLs.

Resuming from the end of the walk at Liverpool Street, the other principal central London hub at the Bank of England could be reached with a short stroll down Leadenhall Street. Here, the six-way junction was controlled by Police traffic signals operated by a constable from a box at the side of the road. It was criss-crossed by 598 buses on 18 routes during a typical peak hour, an average of one every six seconds. Even on a Sunday the number reached 288 an hour during the afternoon. A notable absentee from this mass of buses was the Green Line coach, which was banned under the 1933 Amulree rules.

One of the things that were special about London buses in this period, which was very visible at Bank, was the extensive use still made of three-axle double-deckers. That they were still very much in evidence in central London can be inferred from the fact that the garages mentioned in this chapter as working the core routes include 16 out of the 20 then operating double-deck LTs in significant numbers. Of the remaining four, buses from Hanwell and Hornchurch did not visit the centre of town and Seven Kings LTs could be seen only at night on route 298. Although the 23, Barking's only weekday route to work into town was scheduled for operation with Guys, Barking still had about forty LTs. These could be seen in town, sometimes on the 23 during the week but invariably on route 9 on Sundays when it was extended to Becontree Heath. The Sunday replacement for the 23, the unsung route 163, was also worked by LTs, but from Upton Park.

Former Leyton Council E/3 car 173 breasts the summit of the Kingsway Subway slope, flanked by two elegant gas lamp standards, before crossing traffic running between Vernon Place and Theobalds Road and the southbound flow from Southampton Row. On the left in front of the lamp standard is the signal which controlled the release of trams onto the slope.
C. Carter

6 INDUSTRIAL RELATIONS

Above An army lorry engaged in strike-breaking on route 6 in Bishopsgate is about to be overtaken by Willesden STL744 on the same route which is terminating at 'HACKNEY'. This would normally have meant Hackney Garage but in this special case probably means it is turning somewhere short of that point to avoid passing a garage on strike. D.W.K. Jones

Right More accustomed to bumping about over poor ground in a battle zone, this lorry offered a harsh contrast to the smooth running trolleybuses usually found on route 581. The scene is Upper Street Islington, where the tracks for tram routes 33 and 35 can be seen behind the lorry. D.W.K. Jones

THE RETURN TO peace time conditions was a slow and arduous process and the pace at which improvements were made to working conditions was never fast enough to satisfy a war-weary staff who made their feelings abundantly clear at each stage, usually against the policy and wishes of their own Trade Union. The history of labour relations with road services staff in this period started in a spectacular fashion with the summer schedules for Central Buses, Trams and Trolleybuses planned for introduction on 19th April 1944. Although these included service increases throughout the week, the arrangement of the duty schedules was not acceptable to platform staff. Above all, they did not like spells of duty which ran from midday until 4pm, spanning lunch time and disrupting meal patterns to the claimed detriment of their health. They also objected to new running times which were being reduced to take account of low levels of road traffic, claiming that they would have to 'drive like madmen' to keep to the new timings. Other matters which troubled them were service levels, which they thought were still inadequate and the continuation of the emergency measures which allowed large numbers of standing passengers. Their concern over inadequacy was expressed more explicitly at the end of the dispute which arose over these schedules. They were unhappy that so many buses were run in the evenings at weekends, when they were least needed by essential workers, while during the week evening buses were cut to save petrol, leaving workers '. . . waiting hopelessly at the end of queues while we are carrying cinema crowds . . .'

The first outward sign of discontent came on Saturday 15th April 1944, when there was a sudden unofficial strike of trolleybus staff at Hackney depot. They were joined the same evening by staff at Bow, Leyton, Poplar, Walthamstow and West Ham, removing services from a total of 15 routes in east and north-east London. The weekend had been chosen so as not to interfere with the journeys of essential war workers but the Transport & General Workers' Union stepped in anyway on the Sunday to call for a return to work the following day, which is what happened. On the day the summer schedules started, staff at Hackney and Stamford Hill trolleybus depots and Hackney and Mortlake bus garages withdrew their labour, leaving routes 6, 6A, 9, 22, 30, 37, 73, 543, 643, 555, 581, 647, 649, 677 and 683 with either a reduced service or none at all. At some stage the staff at Nunhead working on route 37 also withdrew. Despite another call from the Union to call off the strike, on 20th April it spread to Hammersmith and Victoria bus garages but the staff at Stamford Hill went back.

The disruption to essential movement was considered so serious that the Government took the unprecedented step of calling in the Army to act as drivers. Ninety army lorries seating between 16 and 30 passengers were put into service on that morning with drivers supplied by the RASC, 50 substituting for buses and 40 for trolleybuses. There were no conductors and passengers were carried free of charge. They ran on bus routes 6, between Leyton Town Hall and Liverpool Street, 9 (Mortlake – Brook Green), 30 (Hackney Wick – Islington) and 73 (East Sheen – Brook Green). The parts of trolleybus routes covered were Leyton to Bloomsbury via both 555 and 581, and West India Dock to Smithfield (677). Later in the day real buses began to appear on routes from Mortlake garage and later still Hammersmith, driven by soldiers from the RASC. These carried soldier conductors but no fares were charged because King's Regulations governing the conduct of army personnel expressly forbade the acceptance of money from members of the public. Nevertheless many grateful passengers gave tips and the more canny soldiers positioned themselves strategically on the platform to encourage the idea.

The staff at Hounslow garage were strongly opposed to the use of troops but undertook to continue working while there was no army presence in the area. Hounslow buses on route 33 were curtailed at Twickenham to avoid entering the area served by army buses, which worked well until

buses driven by soldiers began to arrive in Hounslow that evening. The staff walked out at 5.30 pm but at a subsequent meeting agreed to return the following day if the army kept out of Hounslow. Troops arrived at the garage the following morning to run the buses and Hounslow formally joined the strike. Hanwell bus garage joined on 21st April but Mortlake and Nunhead resumed normal working. Staff at Victoria offered to take buses out to carry essential workers in peak hours, without payment, but this was not acceptable to the management. By midday on 21st April the use of soldiers had enabled full normal services to be provided on all routes operated by Hackney, Hammersmith, Hanwell and Victoria garages with some buses from Hounslow. By this time lorries had been taken off motor bus services but continued to operate on trolleybus routes as the soldiers could not drive trolleybuses.

Below Passengers queue at Liverpool Street station for a ride on a lorry on route 6 with two London Transport inspectors supervising and a soldier/conductor in the act of boarding the vehicle. D.W.K. Jones

Bottom There is a longer queue for this lorry, which has some protection from the weather, but the attention of some passengers has been caught by something overhead – a marauding enemy aircraft perhaps? Another lorry is across the road about to turn around, a Tilling STL on route 47 edges into the left of the picture and an LT on route 78 can be seen in Middlesex Street. D.W.K. Jones

Meanwhile, the Trade Union had issued a statement on 20th April calling on staff to return to work in accordance with Union policy and resolve the matter in a constitutional manner. They also issued an appeal to the public to give all possible assistance to those members who were still at work. Although this had no immediate effect, there were various garage and depot meetings during the day on Friday and there was a full resumption of work on Saturday morning. This was slightly marred by a brief walkout on Saturday morning by staff at Hounslow trolleybus depot, who had made a similar offer to the one by Victoria garage, which was also not accepted. The introduction of army lorries onto route 657 caused the strike to collapse and normal operation resumed on Sunday morning, 23rd April, after which operation by the army ceased.

The grievances about schedules were eventually resolved by negotiation but the discontent about the standing passenger regulations did not go away. It bubbled away in the background before coming to the fore at the end of 1945. The emergency regulations at that time allowed standing passengers at all times, the only relaxation being that between 7.30pm and midnight the number permitted on full size buses was reduced from twelve to eight. On small saloons the numbers varied between nine and twelve and on single-deckers with perimeter seating, up to 20 could be carried. Following an approach from the Transport & General Workers' Union, London Transport asked the Regional Traffic Commissioner to consider some easement. The Commissioner agreed to reduce the maximum number permitted to stand in off-peak hours from twelve to eight and the new rules were applied from 10th November. A Delegate Conference of the Union held on 9th November would not accept the new arrangements and resolved instead to refuse standing passengers altogether in the off-peak.

The negotiations which followed resulted in an agreement to return to the pre-war arrangements by stages linked to the gradual improvement in services. The off-peak limit was reduced to five from 17th November, and from 7th January 1946 off-peak standing was abolished except after 10.30pm when five remained the limit. The peak hour figure was reduced to eight on 13th February and was planned to come down to the pre-war limit of five on 20th May but the staff, with Union support, applied the new rule from 15th May. On Central Buses, the carriage of 20 standing on specially adapted single-deckers came to an end in the Kingston area on 31st October 1945 and over the rest of the system on 9th January 1946, the large standing area now being reserved for a mere five passengers.

The feelings of impatience which underscored these disputes were present throughout this period when staff and passengers alike were looking to a quick return to peace-time standards and many small disputes arose from this basic cause.

One of the worst examples was a series of Saturday strikes by staff at Alperton and Hanwell bus garages, the cause again being new schedules. Although these included some improvements, others known to be needed were left to be done when resources became available. The strikes were severely criticised by a Delegate Conference which condemned the unofficial action and pointed out that such actions could only make worse staff/passenger relations which were already at a low point. Such a condemnation, not from the Union hierarchy but from their own colleagues at other garages well illustrates how bad things had got.

Relations between staff and passengers had indeed deteriorated. Staff coming back from war service had been changed by their experiences. Many found it difficult to adjust to civilian life and others who had shouldered major responsibilities were disinclined to accept the servile role which many passengers seemed to expect of them. Passengers in their turn expected the high standards which they remembered, perhaps in a slightly rosy haze, from before the war. The situation became serious enough for the Board to embark on a major campaign under the title 'Courtesy Aids Service'. This was launched on 19th March 1946 in a series of posters displayed on vehicles and London Transport properties, aimed primarily at staff but also at passengers. Items were carried in Traffic Circulars stating how many letters of complaint and commendation had been received each fortnight and one letter from each category was published. The letters of complaint did not reveal the identity of the culprits but a named photograph of those concerned accompanied the commendations. A leaflet was produced containing 17 panels each with a piece of advice for a particular section of the workforce and the slogan was carried on most publicity while the campaign was running.

Pay and conditions of service were a significant cause of unrest in the aftermath of war. One of the reasons many men did not return to London Transport from war service was that they were able to find better paid employment with more regular hours of work in other industries. Transport workers had lost their pre-eminent position in the scale of wages during the war when the flourishing manufacturing industry had been able to offer substantial increases. The security of the job which had been so important during the years of high unemployment, was also now rated much lower because most employment appeared to be secure. The wage award made to platform staff in 1946 amounted to between 7s and 10s a week and consolidated the various special 'war-advance' payments. The payments above 7s were to those staff in grades where differential rates were reduced. This gave an increase of up to £1 15s, 42 per cent above 1939 but still way behind the relative position before the war. The nub of the problem from the Board's point of view was that income had not been allowed to keep pace, the only fare increase in this period having raised about 10 per cent extra revenue. Unless it could be allowed to make up the difference by increasing fares, the Board was in no position to meet the aspirations of its staff to re-establish their relative position in the pecking order.

The less attractive nature of the job made recruitment much more difficult. Although at any one time during 1946 as many as 1,700 new staff were in training, recruitment was not keeping pace with the needs of increasing services. Despite this the Board diligently observed its statutory obligation under the 'Re-instatement of Civil Employment Act' of 1944, to dispense with the services of women, and the number of women conductors had been reduced from 10,000 to 4,000 by 1946. The Act was intended to ensure justice for those who wanted to return from war service to their civilian jobs after the war but its application in this case was questioned by the women who pointed out that many of the men replacing women were new to the service and not former employees. When the first dismissals were due at Windsor on 15th January 1946, the women challenged the policy but they did not have the support of the Trade Union and in the end had to give way. Nevertheless, the sustained recruitment drive did not have the results needed and the Trade Union had a change of heart when they began to realise that the introduction of a 44-hour week might be in jeopardy because of the shortage of manpower. In January 1947 they made a formal request for the policy to be suspended, the Board agreed and on 1st February announced that no more 'girls' would be dismissed and that the policy would be reviewed later in the year. In March the Board decided that women should again be taken on in 'men's jobs' where recruitment of men was not possible, and a recruitment drive was started. Two other changes were made to try to boost recruitment: the minimum age for conductors was reduced from 25 to 21; and the pre-war practice was resumed of recruiting drivers directly, rather than from the grade of conductor. The matter was left in this kind of limbo for three years

The question of Trade Union membership also became an issue in 1946. The Board had recognised certain Trade Unions as representative of staff for the purpose of negotiating pay and conditions since its formation in 1933 but there had been no pressure on staff to join any Union. The

recognised Union for bus staff was the Transport & General Workers' Union, to which the overwhelming majority of staff belonged. In 1946 the Union informed the Board that they would no longer work with staff who were not members of the Union. The Board decided that this could hamper its ability to do its job and that its best interests would be served by agreeing to an all-Union staff. On the understanding that all non-members

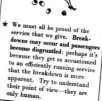

would be given the opportunity to join the T&GWU and with an undertaking from the Union that it would respect the observance of all collective agreements, the Board agreed to dismiss any employee who was not in the appropriate Trade Union. Eighty per cent of the non-members joined the Union.

At the end of 1946 the Transport & General Workers' Union submitted a claim for improved conditions of service and a reduction in the working week. It was an important and far-reaching application which sought to secure some of the improvements which had been denied in 1937. There were prolonged negotiations and in the end the Board and Union agreed to seek mediation by the Minister of Labour and National Service. He appointed a Committee of Investigation whose recommendations were the basis of the subsequent agreement under which common

Part of the leaflet issued by London Transport aimed at changing the behaviour and attitude of staff under the banner 'Courtesy Aids Service'.
Ken Glazier collection

conditions of service were applied for the first time to all three road services departments. The big prize for the staff was that the guaranteed working week was reduced from 48 to 44 hours, with no alteration to pay. Hours actually worked remained about the same for Central Buses, but the hours for Trams and Trolleybuses and Country Buses and Coaches were reduced to come into line. Staff were also granted one day's paid leave for each of the six bank holidays on which they were required to work, in addition to the existing annual allowance of two weeks. The new agreement applied from 24th June 1947 but the substantial changes to schedules could not be introduced immediately and special compensatory payments were made in the meantime. Two thousand additional staff were needed to work the revised rosters and it was agreed that, until they could be recruited, the gap would be filled by overtime and rest day working.

On 6th July there was a partial unofficial strike of Central Bus, Tram and Trolleybus staff who were protesting that the agreement did not include payment at time-and-a-half for working on Saturday. Further threatened strike action was avoided by the insistence of the Union that its members should honour agreements freely entered into. The introduction of the new schedules should have taken place on 29th October but there were many aspects of the new duty schedules which the staff did not like, particularly on Country Buses, and the Union asked for their introduction to be deferred while the grievances were examined. They were put into operation on 12th November. Some Central Bus staff refused to work the new schedules on the day but this final fling did not last long. The resulting schedules caused considerable upheaval in allocations of routes to garages, prompting some route alterations. These are discussed in Chapter 9.

The discontent about payments for Saturday working continued to rumble on until, on 1st October 1948, the T&GWU finally submitted a formal claim for time-and-a-half to be paid to staff working after 1pm on Saturdays. The claim was rejected because the Executive regarded Saturdays as being part of the standard 44 hour week. A Delegate Conference on 28th December asked the Executive to see representatives of the staff and two meetings with Lord Latham took place on 30th and 31st December but these did not change anything. On 1st January 1949, which happened to be a Saturday, staff took their own initiative and went on strike. Unusually, the strongest action was taken by tram and trolleybus staff, with 27 of the 29 depots out of action all day. Nine Central Bus garages also struck for the whole day and another 37 of the 52 joined in from 1pm. Country Bus support was more patchy, only 11 of the 30 garages taking part from 1pm.

The Executive reacted strongly, apparently with the tacit support of the Trade Union, by issuing notices announcing that staff would be paid only for time worked, which meant being paid at a flat hourly rate without enhancements. Staff were also warned that anybody taking similar action in future would be considered to have terminated their employment. There was a meeting between the Minister of Labour and National Service and the Union on 4th January, followed by a Delegate Conference the following day at which it was agreed to refer the dispute to arbitration. An Arbitration Tribunal was set up, chaired by John Cameron, and reported in March. They found that no case had been made for special payments for working after 1pm as part of a normal working week but they recognised that the irregular hours of transport workers removed opportunities for leisure which were increasing elsewhere. They therefore recommended a temporary compensatory payment of 7d to 9d on the hourly rate, which was equivalent to time-and-a-quarter. This payment, which became known as 'The Cameron Award', was intended to apply only until enough manpower was available to make it possible to roster more Saturdays off. The cost of applying the award was estimated by London Transport to be £375,000 a year, which was equal to half the increase in operating costs incurred in 1949.

Meanwhile the old problem of standing passengers became the subject of another dispute. In 1948 there had been a public outcry against the restrictions on standing passengers when services were under such severe strain and inadequate to meet demand. The Minister of Transport therefore amended the regulations from 10th May 1948 to allow eight passengers to be carried during peak hours or at other times if undue hardship would otherwise be caused. Notices giving the new rules were posted on all vehicles but the Executive, instead of giving precise instructions to staff, merely drew their attention to the revised notices. Although this was unpopular it was accepted as inevitable, until the availability of vehicles began to improve during 1949, when attitudes began to harden again. A Delegate Conference passed a resolution that there should be a reduction to five standing from 18th May, followed by a complete ban in 1950. The negotiations which followed led to an agreement to reduce to five from 28th August 1949 and the total ban did not take place.

Since the policy of dismissing women conductors had been suspended in 1946, London Transport had struggled without success to recruit and retain enough staff to overcome the persistent staff shortage, even to the extent of recruiting in the 'provinces' and setting up hostel accommodation. In March 1950 it admitted defeat and decided to start recruiting women conductors again. Perhaps anticipating claims that it was looking for cheap labour, it took the precaution at the same time of removing the condition of

This oblique item in the Traffic Circular was how London Transport informed staff of the important changes to the standing passenger regulations.

Standing Passengers   88
In connection with the revised arrangements relative to standing passengers in buses, the attention of conductors is drawn to the notices which will be exhibited on buses with effect on and from Monday, 10th May.

employment which decreed that women could earn only 90 per cent of a man's wage for their first year of service. The new policy was very unpopular and came at a time when platform staff were already at odds with their own union because it was refusing to put in a claim for an extra £1 a week. The recruitment of women was opposed unanimously at a delegate conference and the policy was suspended while talks took place. These ended in agreement with the T&GWU and the first recruits reported for training on 28th August. There was an immediate unofficial ban on overtime and rest day working by staff at Watford (High Street) who were joined during the next few days by Luton, Watford (Leavesden Road), Two Waters, Tring and Leatherhead. Central Buses joined in on 7th September when staff at Mortlake and Riverside refused to work with women conductors. Hendon came out on strike on 13th September and by 16th September 16 garages were on strike. Tram and trolleybus staff did not feel so strongly but three east London trolleybus depots joined the strike on 15th, followed by Highgate on 16th September. The Trade Union refused to support the action and the Minister of Labour even went so far as to claim that it was a communist plot.

Most Central Bus garages were back to normal on 17th and 18th September and later in the month 150 women were assigned to garages where recruitment of men was 'impossible'. Country Bus garages were less compliant. Two Waters and Tring resumed on 17th September but the others did not; they were joined by Chelsham at the end of the month and remained in dispute until 1st December. Even when the dispute was over, the majority of individuals refused to volunteer for overtime and the effect on services continued. Reduced services were introduced on routes operated by the two Watford garages and Luton from 8th November and were restored at High Street from 1st December but six coaches and drivers were hired to cover gaps in Luton's services from 11th December and similar action was later taken at Watford.

Staff shortages in the Central Bus area were especially acute in north-west London where a lot of industry offering better pay and conditions was concentrated and the arrival of the new women conductors made little difference. On 2nd May 1951, therefore, coinciding with the opening of the new Peckham garage, a mass of route re-allocations was instituted, aimed at moving work from the north-west to the east and south-east, where recruitment had always been easier.

One other item of labour relations which was of great importance during these years was the way in which the post-war vehicle replacement programme was conducted. Lord Ashfield had foreseen at an early stage that this would be one of the most controversial topics affecting staff relations in the immediate post-war years and directed that a joint management/Trade Union committee should be set up to oversee it. The Bus

Allocation Advisory Committee started its work in 1946, its main job being to agree in what order routes should be converted and to solve any other related problems that might be encountered. Representatives from the Transport & General Workers' Union sat alongside senior managers from the two bus operating departments, the schedules allocation team and the Rolling Stock department and the co-operative work of this team undoubtedly ensured the smooth running of the replacement programme. More on this subject can be found in Chapter 7.

Although there had been a number of strikes and bans of various kinds in the early post-war years, the period is characterised by a steady improvement in working conditions and by the absence of official strike action by the Trade Union who assiduously withheld support from any unofficial action. The Union was constantly reminding its members that they should honour freely negotiated agreements. Apart from the usual ups and downs of day to day operations, there were no more serious disputes until the staff shortages of the mid-1950s began to create new grounds for serious grievance.

Above At the end of 1950 there was an unofficial ban on overtime at a number of Country Bus garages in protest against the decision to resume the recruitment of women conductors. Staff at both Watford (High Street) and Luton garages, who worked route 321, took part and London Transport hired coaches, complete with crews, to cover deficiencies in the service. This Leyland Tiger PS1 owned by 'Bunty Coaches' is on route 321 at Watford in the company of a Craven RT and, across the road, an 18STL20. D.W.K. Jones

Below The unfrozen STDs should have run until at least 1954 but the drivers at Victoria took against them and they were withdrawn prematurely in March 1951. STD 102 is seen in reduced circumstances as a training bus in the yard at the side of Edgware garage. D.W.K. Jones

7 THE AILING FLEET

AT THE BEGINNING of 1947 London Transport should have been in possession of 500 of its new RT, with a steady flow of deliveries continuing to reach a total by the end of that year of about 1,000. There were also 77 new trolleybuses on order, most of which were intended to replace the 16 year old 'Diddlers' at Fulwell. Delivery of these should have started in November 1946, after which they should have been arriving at the rate of three a week. That is what the contracts called for but the start of production had been delayed by shortages of fuel and power which had kept factories working well below capacity, disrupting not only the supply of materials for new buses but also spare parts for the existing fleet. None of the new trolleybuses had appeared by the beginning of 1947 and it was to be another year before the first was received.

AEC had come close to meeting its obligations for the supply of motor bus chassis by delivering the first on 26th March 1946, albeit nearly four months late, and then supplying them at a steady rate, reaching a total of 148 during the year. A revised estimate allowing for this late start had been that 110 completed vehicles should have arrived by the end of 1946. As well as the power

problems, the two body manufacturers were also faced with a national shortage of qualified tradesmen and took much longer to get started, although they were party to the estimate of 110 for 1946. Even as late as November 1946, when deliveries for that year were already out of the question and no work had been laid down in the factories, the suppliers were optimistically forecasting that 511 would be built in 1947. In the event it was not until May 1947 that the first complete bus was received and then the rate of delivery remained well below the number for which the contract provided. The stockpile of chassis became so large that storage space ran out and AEC had to be asked first to slow down and then suspend deliveries between March and June 1947. Meanwhile nine operators outside London put RT type chassis into service with bodywork of the manufacturers' standard designs.

This shortfall left the Board with a badly impoverished fleet and a severe shortage of materials and spare parts to keep it going. In January 1947 London Transport had a total fleet of motor buses comprising 5,925 double deck and 1,116 single-deck of which 5,824 double-deckers and 967 single-deckers were licensed. There was a policy to keep Country Buses fully stocked because nearly all its services worked to published timetables on relatively low frequencies, so all but three of the unlicensed double-deckers were in the Central Bus fleet giving them 5,041 buses to supply a peak vehicle requirement of 4,536. This left a margin of 11 per cent spare, tight at the best of times but in the circumstances of 1947 precarious, especially as 14 of those 'spare' buses were earmarked for private hire work and 43 as driver trainers. Most of the unlicensed vehicles were effectively no longer available for service as there were 19 open staircase LTs and STs which had been condemned and withdrawn for disposal, 29 Tilling STs, deemed unfit and eight STs fit only for use as trainers. Otherwise, there were three

downs and few ups during the next three years and it is worth keeping this example in mind as the story unfolds.

During the war years when Chiswick Works was occupied by London Aircraft Production, most body overhauls had been carried out at Chiswick Tram Depot, with about 40 per cent handled at Reigate, Alperton and Elmers End garages, and the interval between them had been increased from between 15 and 20 months to two years. When the demands of war production began to ease in 1944, Chiswick started to do a few overhauls. With the departure of London Aircraft Production the works was gradually able to resume its pre-war role but the construction of new bodies was not possible in the immediate

One of the garages which carried out overhauls during the war was Reigate, which continued to do so until as late as 1948. In this interior view there are two STLs, two STs, two mainly obscured 10T10s and three 4Q4s, one of which, on the right, is a 1/4Q4/1 still carrying the clips for a side route board fitted when it was converted for Green Line operation in 1936.
D.W.K. Jones

STs still on loan outside London and 42 buses being overhauled. The single-deck position was happier, the majority of those unlicensed still being in the hands of the American Red Cross and the Home Office or being overhauled.

Those are the bald theoretical figures but an examination of what happened on one day in January 1947 is a better illustration of the struggle confronting garages day after day for the first five years of peace. In theory Central Buses had 5,470 single- and double-deck buses for its total peak output of 4,889, an apparently reasonable margin of 581 spares to cover unexpected problems. In fact, 64 were scheduled for an all-day dock, 55 were being overhauled, 46 were at Chiswick for repair, another 46 were awaiting accident repairs at garages, 35 were undergoing body repairs and repainting at garages and 138 were mechanically defective at garages. The most telling statistic, though, is the 126 vehicles standing idle awaiting materials, a stark measure of the shortages which were being experienced. Of the remainder, 39 were trainers, leaving just 32 buses over the entire fleet to cover emergencies, less than one for each garage. Bad though this was, the availability of buses for service was to go through many worse

post-war period because all available factory effort had to be devoted to maintaining the existing fleet. By the time such production might again have been possible, circumstances had changed and the British Transport Commission, who preferred to maximise use of the ECW factory, held the statutory authority. Overhauling at Alperton ceased in October 1945, at Elmers End in May 1946 and at Chiswick Tram Depot in October of the same year but Reigate continued with this work until 1948.

Once it became apparent that the preferred solution of replacing the life-expired fleet with new vehicles as quickly as possible was not available, London Transport decided that their bodywork should be thoroughly overhauled, rather than patching and 'making-do' which was considered an unsatisfactory waste of labour. It had been the practice pre-war only to remove body panels when decayed timber was suspected but it was now necessary to strip all panels and this was exposing conditions which in many cases required a complete rebuild. The amount of material this called for was no less than two-and-a-half times what had been needed when the fleet was in good condition which in turn lengthened the time

spent by a bus going through overhaul. Even with overhauls being given only every two years, the number which Chiswick should have been handling in a week was 50 but with the greater amount of work and a depleted skilled workforce, the actual number had dropped to the alarming level of nine.

London Transport had already turned to others for help with renovating bodies in 1944 when 21 undertakings, a mixture of repair companies and bus operators with spare workshop capacity, were employed to work on a number of STs, LTs and STLs. This approach was now adopted on a larger scale and contracts were eventually let with six companies who renovated the handsome total of 1,106 buses between November 1945 and October 1949, nearly six a week. The largest number was handled by Mann Egerton of Norwich who renovated 511 STLs, all but two of the class

ST 530 was a unique example of rebuilding. It was damaged while on wartime loan to Central SMT and its subsequent repairs left it with this utility-style upper deck, including crude looking sliding vents.
Capital Transport collection

The gleaming new looking finish of STL 523 at Palmers Green, a 1/16STL18 dating originally from 1934, is a perfect illustration of the high standard achieved in its renovation programme by Mann Egerton. It is painted, as were all the refurbished STL 18 and 18/1s, in a variant of the pre-war scheme of red on the main panels and white around the windows but with brown roof. Standard STLs were painted in the contemporary red and cream livery.
D.A. Thompson/LTPS

put out to contractors, 262 LTs and 29 STs. The total of 802 gave an average of nearly five a week, although, at its peak, production from Norwich reached six or seven a week. The other two main contractors were: Marshalls Flying School of Cambridge which took care of 154 in all, 74 double-deck and 60 single-deck LTs, 18 1T1s and just two STs; and Berkeley Caravans Ltd of Biggleswade who did 134; 96 STs and 38 LTs. Smaller contracts were let with Express Motor Body Works of Enfield, who did ten LTs in the summer of 1945 and Samlesbury of Preston, who did six at the end of 1947. The two odd STLs were renovated in 1948 by Portsmouth Aviation Ltd, well known for rebuilding buses for operators outside London.

The work was intended to have a four year life and the vehicles chosen were therefore those which would have to be kept going for a number of years, the only petrol-engined vehicles to be treated being the STs and the single-deckers. The quality of workmanship, particularly from Mann Egerton, was high and the STLs emerged from Norwich looking like new buses. They were rewarded with contracts for 130 new single-deckers in 1948 and 1949. Marshalls' work on the single-deck LTs and 1T1s was also remarkable in turning out bodies which were virtually new, although still with the original 1931 profile.

These projects and the parallel work being done at Chiswick and Reigate did not run without hitch. Allocation of material was strictly controlled by the government and sheet steel and timber were always in short supply. Various stratagems were employed to conquer this problem, even to the extent of cheating on the control regulations and the programme was undeniably successful. Even so, there was still a large number of oil-engined STLs which could not be included

Above Marshalls wrought a remarkable transformation in the 78 single-deckers they renovated at Cambridge, producing what looked like a brand new bus built in an out-of-date body style. Elmers End's LT1131 has just turned out of Beckenham Lane and is picking up at Bromley College, with Bromley's RT 242 about to join it. LT1131 was a 1LTL1/3, the code given after renovation to the type with a rear indicator box.
The Omnibus Society

Left The hangar in Cambridge used by Marshalls for the repair and refurbishment of London Transport buses. There are nine buses, all LTs, in various stages of preparation, including examples of all main enclosed staircase body types among the eight double-deckers. The single-decker on the left was one of 60 which were given heavier treatment than the double-deckers because they had to be kept in service for up to four years longer.
Cambridgeshire Libraries

Below T46 was one of the 18 rebuilt by Marshalls in a similar style to the LTLs, with similar striking effect, The serene backdrop of the Wyrardisbury River and the presence of a lowbridge STL in the background proclaim this to be the stand at Staines West station, where a multitude of Central and Country routes jostled for space over the years. The renovated Ts were important for route 218 as they were the only vehicles suitable to cross Walton Bridge on which there was a weight restriction. D.W.K. Jones

but which had to be kept running until at least 1950. To give these an extra couple of years' life a method was devised in 1948 of bolstering the bodywork by means of strengthening straps. These were the same width as a window pillar and ran from cantrail to skirt, bolted onto the pillars needing support. These were usually on the outside of the body but in some cases they were installed on the inside too. The result was unsightly but this simple idea bought a crucial extra two years of life for a significant number of buses.

Similar supply problems plagued the maintenance of the chassis too. Mechanical components had been called upon to perform for much longer during the war than would normally have been expected, their increased life being achieved by patching and making-do, but many had now reached the point where no more life could be squeezed out of them. The rate at which this

could be put right was held back by the availability of spare parts and although supplies were running at one-third above pre-war levels in 1946, this fell far short of the amount needed to remove the backlog of work. Just how serious this was can be gauged from the effect on the output of overhauled engines from Chiswick in December 1946. There were 329 engines which should have been despatched to garages but were not ready, of which 56 were standing on the shop floor having been completed except for one small vital but unavailable part. The catch in this was that if more material had been available, there would not have been enough staff to work on it because there was a national shortage of skilled labour.

Like the rubber tyred fleet, the trams emerged from the war in a battered and run-down state, suffering from arrears of maintenance and shortages of essential spare parts and materials every bit as serious. However, the trams had to cope with an additional problem because the tracks on which they ran were also in a parlous condition. They too had been subject to substantial bomb damage, neglect and shortages of steel for replacing worn out rails. The type of maintenance carried out had also been at a minimum, for example the practice of welding all joints had been all but abandoned, partly to reduce the work-load but also because working at night during the blackout was not possible. There were many places where the track was not properly supported because the road around and beneath had broken up and the condition of many junctions and crossovers was unstable.

Apart from the general shortage of skilled staff, the Permanent Way Department had its own unique problem because it had planned its manpower requirements between 1936 and 1939 on the basis that the trams would have gone by 1943 and the department would cease to exist.

Few new men had been trained in those years and the number available when events suddenly turned sour was at the minimum level needed to keep the system going for another three years. Such younger men as there were had been called up for military service and the department was left with an ageing and inadequate workforce many of whom, exhausted by the demands of wartime working, left as soon as the wartime regulations preventing them from doing so were lifted. Attempts to recruit returning servicemen proved difficult because this heavy type of work and the fact that working at night was essential were no longer attractive in the post-war world of full employment and regular hours. At the beginning of 1947, there was a shortage of 127 which had barely changed for nearly six months during which a paltry eight new recruits had been taken on and even they were reluctant recruits who really wanted to be drivers or conductors.

The trams themselves were in an equally distressed state, having spent the past six years working well beyond the normal limits of endurance, without benefit of proper overhaul and with the minimum of maintenance. By pre-war standards, their appearance and general condition were a disgrace, a quality they shared with the bus fleet. There were 894 trams in the fleet at the beginning of 1947, of which 850 were licensed and the remainder awaiting disposal. In theory that should have been ample to cover a peak output of 733 but on one sample day in December 1946, 110 cars were out of service for repair or renovation, leaving a margin of only seven spare serviceable cars spread between nine depots. The tramway network, concentrated as so much of it was in south-east and inner south London, had been right in the thick of the enemy bombardment and the fleet had suffered disproportionate damage as a result. Consequently, the resources of the Central Repair Depot at Charlton, already depleted by its commitment to the production of munitions and aircraft parts, had been drawn away from routine maintenance and parts which would have been replaced were called upon to keep going well beyond their normal lifespan. In trying to recover the backlog once it was able to return to full normal activities, Charlton was faced with the familiar problems of supply shortages and lack of skilled staff to do the work.

When the Board set out its priorities for restoring pre-war standards it had decided to give immediate priority to the replacement of the obsolete motor buses and announced that the replacement of the remaining trams would not be started until at least 1950. This was something of a compliment to the trams. The great majority were significantly older than the 'obsolete' buses and even the youngest were as old as

The ageing bodywork of some trams was given a little more life by installing diagonal struts across the ends of the lower deck to give extra support. These can be seen on E/1 car 1824 at Tooting Broadway running from the underframe at each end, above the middle of the truck, to the end panel between the lower deck and the platform. 1824 was a comparative youngster among the E1s, being one of the 1922-series with more powerful 60 hp motors which were a common sight on Clapham's routes. C. Carter

most of them, but London Transport were obviously confident that they were robust enough to be kept going for another five years, whereas it was clear that the buses were deteriorating fast. This set the permanent way and rolling stock departments the daunting task, while coping with all the problems already described, of bringing the cars and track up to a standard which would keep them going for up to another five years.

Despite the shortfall in RT deliveries, 1946 was actually quite a good year for new buses, 233 double-deck and 60 single-deck being received, compared with 1947 when the total of new RTs reached only 182. There was an absolute gap in deliveries of double-deckers for five months after the arrival of the last STD on 3rd December 1946 and by the time RT 402 was taken into stock there was an outright shortage of fit buses amounting to 62. Bad though this seemed at the time, during the following three years the situation was to get far worse as the battle to keep buses in a roadworthy condition failed to come up to even the relaxed standards then being employed by the vehicle inspectorate. In fact the rate at which buses were condemned began to rise sharply in June 1947 and the bus shortage had already risen to 131 by the beginning of July. It remained in three figures until November 1949, the worst month being December 1948 when it reached 260. This was also one of only two times when a shortage was allowed to occur in the Country Bus fleet. These numbers refer to the buses that should have been available for the daily run-out but were not. There were many others which were nominally fit but failed on run-out and the notorious expression 'no bus available', once an unthinkable event, became part of day-to-day business. As many as 425 buses fell into this category on a single day and this did not include the scores of other buses which failed while in service, making the sight of broken down buses at the side of the road all too common.

The White Knight which had been expected to ride to the rescue of the dilapidated fleet was the 3RT3. Planning for the post-war bus replacement programme had started in April 1944 when an agreement was entered into with AEC for the supply of chassis and spare parts in the period up to 30th September 1950. Agreements were subsequently signed with the Board's chosen manufacturers of the bodies, Park Royal Coach Works Ltd, as it was at that time called, and Metropolitan-Cammell-Weymann Motor Bodies Ltd. The latter was a sales organisation for the Metropolitan-Cammell Carriage and Wagon Co, Birmingham, and Weymann Motor Bodies Ltd of Addlestone. It was the Addlestone company which was to be the Board's supplier, although provision was made for MCCW to help out if necessary. As soon as the Government signalled that peacetime production was to resume, formal contracts were made with a view to delivery of chassis beginning in December 1945 and of completed vehicles from July 1946.

When it became clear at the end of 1946 that this programme was slipping badly, with diminishing hope that lost time could be recovered, the Board looked for additional suppliers. After negotiations with five possible companies, only one of which had supplied bodies to London Transport in the past, contracts were placed with Saunders Engineering and Shipyard Co. of Beaumaris, Anglesey for 250 and Cravens Ltd of Sheffield for 120, all for delivery in 1948. These extra orders exhausted AEC's capacity to supply chassis and the Board turned to Leyland Motors Ltd with whom a contract was signed at the beginning of 1947. They were to supply 1,000 7ft 6in wide chassis (RTL) and 500 8ft wide buses, complete with bodies (RTW). The body contract for the RTLs was placed with Metro-Cammell and deliveries were planned to start early in 1948.

One of the reasons for the delay in getting bodybuilding under way was the method of construction which London Transport had decided to adopt. Based on their wartime experience of building aircraft, the Board had decided to go for jig-built bodies finished to fine tolerances, so maximising the scope for interchange of bodies between chassis. The resulting product though superficially similar to the 2RT2 was in fact substantially different and bore a closer resemblance to the prototype RT 1 in having metal framework and a self-supporting rear platform. It also differed mechanically, notably in having a new engine, the A204, which had toroidal cavity pistons rather than the pot cavity type used on the 2RT2s. The effect this had on the sound of the vehicle running was remarkable. Instead of the deep, heavy throb of the 2RT, the new buses produced little more than a quiet purr, their gearboxes not yet worn enough to produce the distinctive musical sounds of later years. One of

In one of the stranger episodes of the early post-war period the eight Bluebird LTs which still had Gardner engines were transferred in April 1947 to Country Buses because Central Bus drivers apparently did not like them. They were restricted to a limited number of services because of their extra length and were allocated to Grays garage at first for route 370 and later 371A. Later all but two were fitted with AEC engines and most of those went back to Central Buses. The snout-like projection of the bonnet which can be seen on LT 1420 was the main recognition feature of these buses, which they retained even after having AEC engines substituted.
D.W.K. Jones

the loudest sounds produced was the 'plop' of the gear engaging as the driver depressed the change pedal.

Delivery of 3RT3s began on 28th April 1947, Weymann being first off the mark with RT 402. Park Royal Vehicles Ltd, as it had now become, delivered RT 152 on 12th May but then neither manufacturer sent any more until late June. After that deliveries flowed steadily at about six or seven a week but this was still well below the maximum of 11 or 12 called for in the contracts and far behind the number needed to catch up the shortfall. The replacement plan prepared in 1946 gave priority to the withdrawal of the open-staircase LTs at Leyton, Loughton and Potters Bar and the Tilling STLs at Bromley and Croydon. The largest concentration of the LTs was at Leyton which therefore received the first RTs. Deliveries were concentrated at that garage until

October, interrupted only by a handful that were sent to Croydon to replace the post-war STDs, which in turn went to Loughton to replace open-staircase LTs there. Seventy-seven went to Leyton and the first route on which they appeared was the 10, followed by the 35 and the 144, rather than the sort of premier central London route on which one might have expected the Board to flaunt them. This illustrates how the early replacement programmes concentrated on sending the new buses as direct replacements for the oldest, even when this meant their being relegated to some fairly minor suburban routes. Even so, both routes 38 and 38A were to have participated, despite the 38 being operated by the later oil-engined version of the LT, the intention being to have a complete allocation of modern buses, including the STDs from Loughton on the 38A. This was in line with the policy agreed with the Trade Union that on routes with split allocations, RTs should only 'run against' oil-engined STLs and STDs. The staff specifically asked for the change of plan at Leyton, for reasons unknown, and it left the 38/A with a mixture of RT, STD and LT and the 144 a similar mixture of RT and LT.

The remaining open-back LTs were at Potters Bar, which was the next to get RTs for route 134. This was far from being the end of these pioneering Renowns because anything that was serviceable and could pass the Body Committee's inspection was retained in service. Their last big scheduled operation, requiring 19 buses at its peak, was to run the replacement service for the LNER suburban trains between Ilford and Woodford which were withdrawn on 29th November in preparation for the extension of the Central Line. These ran, in diminishing numbers, until October 1948, but as late as 5th May 1948 three were allocated to new route 167, an allocation which survived into 1949. Apart from this, many were to be found in the next two years working as backups at garages all over the fleet, and the last five were still in service in the Special Events fleet in January 1950. The next type due for replacement was the Tilling STL with allocations of RTs to Croydon for route 197 and Bromley for the 47. In practice it was STs and 'General' STLs which were replaced, the staff at Bromley having asked, rather surprisingly, to keep the Tillings rather than the Generals. In fact, the vehicles which were being withdrawn and scrapped were a mixture of all types of LT, ST and petrol-engined STL, the criterion determining their fate being solely the condition of their bodies. But for the wishes of the Bromley staff, some of the displaced Tilling STLs would have been sent to Country Buses, where nine were already operating. The plan was to replace Tilling STs at the request of the Country Bus staff, who were unhappy with their open staircases.

The LPTB handed over its responsibilities to the new London Transport Executive on 1st January 1948, one of the five Executives set up by the British Transport Commission which had been

The sleek modern lines of the 3RT3s in their gleaming new paint were a stunning sight when they first began to mingle with the rest of the tired and elderly fleet. Park Royal's first, RT 152, was in original condition without an offside route number plate when photographed in Newington Causeway on the Sunday bifurcation of route 10 to Elephant & Castle. J.L. Smith

Few buses were withdrawn immediately the 3RT3s began to arrive but one which was transferred to training duties in August 1947 was ST 1039, which then carried on as a trainer until December 1949. D.W.K. Jones

formed to take responsibility for the newly nationalised railways and London Transport. The business of the undertaking continued in much the same vein, the same vehicle policies were followed and the same problems of shortages and late delivery of new buses were to plague the undertaking. Hopes of taking delivery of 1,500 new double-deckers during 1948 had already been dashed when the Government imposed restrictions on home market production so that exports could be boosted. After allowing for this and other known delays, the Executive was expecting 1,040 new RT family vehicles during the year, including the first 80 of the Leylands, and 100 of a planned 130 new single-deckers. Only 755 double deckers and 34 single-deckers were received and by December the worst level of bus shortage in the whole post-war period was being experienced. Most serious was the late start made by both Saunders and Cravens who should have supplied 130 and 70 respectively but only managed one and three. By diverting part of Park Royal's production from AECs to Leylands, the target for RTLs was almost met, but there should also have been 40 RTWs and none of the eight-footers arrived until March 1949. Metro-Cammell should have delivered 40 bodies but was having serious problems in meeting its commitments and in the end had to admit that it could not produce the RT3 type body. A compromise was reached under which 600 of its order was transferred to Park Royal and the remainder was to be built in a mod-

ified form using their own methods of construction, but the first RTL from Birmingham did not arrive until August 1949, ten months late. Despite a strike of vehicle builders which had closed the Park Royal and Weymann factories for three weeks in April and caused a loss of about 90 RTs, those two builders came within ten of meeting their commitments.

The Executive foresaw that when the log-jam was released there would be more bodies being built than chassis available and decided to take desperate measures. A scheme was devised under which 300 STL chassis would be radically modified so that they could be fitted with standard RT bodywork from the main production run. These became the ill-starred SRT class. A production line to carry out this work was set up during 1948 at the unused railway depot at Aldenham. The first 125 were based on the latest and best of the pre-war STLs, the 15STL dating from 1939, and the first five were withdrawn for modification in October 1948. The bodies from these were transferred to the batch of chassis carrying the metal-framed Park Royal bodywork dating from 1937, which was now in irreparably poor condition and had to be scrapped. The class ran into problems almost from the start and only 160 of the planned 300 were built, the last 35 being taken from the 4/9STLs dating from 1937/1938.

The long delayed delivery of the new trolleybuses which had been ordered in 1946, began during February and the first went into service at

Above left Their displacement from mainstream operations did not spell the end for the open staircase LTs as many were found other scheduled work or were spread around the fleet to help cover vehicle shortages, five surviving into 1950. LT 46, which has one of the square cab LT2-type bodies originally fitted to LT 2–50, is on the bus service which replaced the LNER steam trains between Ilford and Woodford while work on the electrification for the Central Line was completed. The Omnibus Society

Above The classic London open staircase is demonstrated by LT 125 at the Chislehurst War Memorial stand on route 161 while helping out at Sidcup garage. F.G. Reynolds

The Q1s were the ultimate trolleybus design for London, sleek, beautifully proportioned and stately. The smooth quiet running of their BUT chassis and 120 bhp Metrovick motors was a huge contrast to the vintage tram-like sounds of the Diddlers which they replaced. Still pristine, 1794 is at Wimbledon Town Hall. *The Omnibus Society*

eral design of the chassis was similar to the pre-war 664T, although they were assembled at the Leyland factory in Ham. The motors were supplied by Metrovick and produced 120 bhp, substantially more than the pre-war 95 bhp, and the control equipment was by English Electric. The MCW bodywork was a clear derivative of the late pre-war designs on the L3 and P1 classes but were made to look sleeker by having five bays rather than six. They were superb vehicles offering a smoothness and quietness of ride which remains unrivalled to this day and likely to remain so until the modern much noisier forms of control can be tamed.

Delivery of the Q1s was spread over a period of 13 months but enough were in service by 29th September for the whole of routes 601–605 and the last of the A1 and A2 classes were withdrawn. Many of the Diddlers continued to be active as trainers and could be seen at many depots around the fleet for a couple more years. Two of the experimental trolleybuses were re-allocated to Hounslow for route 657, centre-entrance 61 (X1) and 2-axle 63 (X3). The experimental 3-axle vehicle, number 62, was regarded as being close enough to standard to be allocated to Holloway. Subsequent deliveries of Q1s were allocated to route 667, from which they displaced C1s which were re-allocated to Stonebridge Park. By March 1949 the trolleybus fleet totalled its maximum of 1,764.

At the beginning of 1948 deliveries of RTs from Park Royal and Weymann had reached their contracted level of 11 a week and rapid progress was being made on spreading the benefits of the new buses. After Bromley, it was the turn of Middle Row garage, which then operated an all petrol fleet of STs and STLs, for route 15 and 28. The special interest in this case was that Chelverton Road also operated route 28 which therefore

Fulwell during March. When first authorised by the Ministry of Supply in 1945 they were to have been 7ft 6in wide Metro-Cammell bodied AECs built to the latest pre-war standard design, but two important changes had occurred in the meantime. In 1946 the Construction and Use Regulations had been modified to allow buses and trolleybuses to be built to a width of eight feet and the Board had been able to persuade the Police and Licensing Authority to allow their use on the suburban routes around Kingston and on route 667 between Hampton Court and Hammersmith. The other change was that AEC and Leyland, recognising the diminished market for trolleybuses, had set up a jointly owned company called British United Traction to manufacture and sell trolleybuses on their behalf. In fact, the BUT 941Ts were effectively AEC products and the gen-

Among the various types of petrol-engined STL which could be found on route 47 before the arrival of the RTs were the Pickup STLs, so called because they had been acquired from Chas. H. Pickup in 1934. They originally had 6-bay open top Park Royal bodies but had been fitted with standard Chiswick-built upper decks to suit 5-bay bodywork soon after acquisition, which is why the upper- and lower-deck pillars do not line up in this view of STL 557 at Shoreditch Church. *Gavin Martin*

Right Former LUT trolleybus 61 and the two experimental trolleybuses built for London Transport in 1934 were displaced from Fulwell by the arrival of the Q1s and were transferred elsewhere for further service. X3 class number 63, London's only 4-wheeler, is at the Duke of Cambridge, Malden, before it moved from Fulwell to Hounslow (later renamed Isleworth). The stop flag is one of the LUT type with the word 'TRAMWAYS' on the bar of the bullseye and a prominently displayed Fare Stage number. F.G. Reynolds

became the first route to have an official allocation of both 2RT2s and 3RT3s. The allocation to route 15 also brought the type for the first time in any quantity into the heart of the West End.

The new buses continued to spread, first to Turnham Green (route 91), Cricklewood (113 and 240) and Upton Park (routes 15 and 129), the allocation to Upton Park being the first where oil-engined LTs were displaced. Route 240 at Cricklewood was operated by oil-engined STLs whose replacement appeared to be out of line with the policy of concentrating on the oldest vehicles, although it was STs which were actually displaced from the garage. The most likely reason for this was that the number of garages to which the first 520 3RT3s could be allocated was limited at this time to 12, the number of servicing kits then available, and the choice of route may have been because of its hilly nature. Another constraint which was to affect the later spread of allocations, was that the overall height of the RT3 was 14ft 3½ins, nearly four inches higher than the STL but there were 35 Central Bus and eight Country Bus garages which did not have that much headroom. A programme was initiated to raise their roofs to the required level but this took time and some were not ready for several years. This project also included work to make the garages suitable for 8-foot wide buses, mainly by altering washing machines and fuelling bays. The remainder of this first RT programme brought in Holloway, Seven Kings, Willesden and Catford garages.

There was one RT missing from those delivered to garages in May 1948, RT 657. This was because its body and registration number had been appropriated for use on the prototype Leyland, RTL 501. The high number came about because it was the intention at the time to number the 8-footers in the same series but by the time the production run started this decision had been rescinded. The new chassis was based on Leyland's standard PD2 model Titan but with so many differences that it was in effect a different model. Leyland themselves always referred to it as the 7RT, London Transport's classification. The chassis profile, air-operated pre-selective

Below Cricklewood received its first RTs in February and March 1948 for routes 1, 13 and 240. Two can be seen on route 13 in this general view of Golders Green bus station with a Hendon STD sandwiched between them, the one nearer the camera being RT 377. Also in view are a Massey-bodied Guy and part of an STL on route 102 by the Hippodrome, Park Royal-bodied STL 2102 on route 2 and a 2RT2 and a 3RT3 on route 28 on the left. Note that the white spot originally introduced for the wartime blackout was still being applied to new buses. LT Museum

Two early post-war AECs which would have felt at ease in many a fleet outside London but which stood out as oddities in the London Transport fleet, Mann Egerton-bodied T 772 and Weymann STL 2690, share a corner of the yard of Watford High Street garage. T 772 is a Two Waters bus on double-deck route 302 waiting to make one of the rare works journeys to Apsley (Shendish Lodge), which is just about readable in the cramped display needed to fit the masked indicator box. Gavin Martin collection

The interior of a 15T13, showing the neat but conservative finish achieved by Mann Egerton using the same green and cream colour scheme as on the RT fleet. The moquette on the seats was also the usual post-war pattern but, surprisingly on a bus built as late as 1948, London Transport has accepted non-standard chairs without toprails, although on the otherwise identical bodies supplied for the TDs, the standard type was installed. LT Museum

gearbox, fluid flywheel, air brakes and automatic lubrication system were identical to those on the AEC RT, with which it also shared the low bonnet line. Its radiator shell, although in the classic Leyland shape, had the same profile and dimensions as the AEC making it quite different from the standard design. Nevertheless, the front end of the chassis, with the characteristic square dumbirons, enforced a small change in the design of the RT3 body, evident in the upward slope taken by the bottom line of the dash panel. Before the RTL went into production, this amendment was made to the standard body design. RTL 501 was the only 7RT3. It was licensed on 16th June 1948 and went into service experimentally at Turnham Green, the nearest garage to Chiswick Works, where it ran alongside RTs on the 91. Although

the new 9.8 litre O.600 Leyland engine was comparable in performance to the AEC A204 of the RT, the RTL was never wholly satisfactory in service. The steering, which was surprisingly of Leyland's standard design, was much heavier than the RT which made the type perennially unpopular with drivers and there was a tendency for the engine to 'hunt' when idling, setting up violent vibrations through the body.

It had always been the intention that Country Buses should not receive any of the first 515 new RTs because the green fleet was considered to be in better shape than Central Buses. The delay in deliveries set back hopes for a start early in 1948 but the programme for the next 525 included 227 for Country Buses, mainly from Weymann but including the first 27 of the expected Cravens. Meanwhile the country department had not been entirely bereft of new buses. Despite the undoubted surplus of single deckers in the fleet, the Board had been persuaded in 1947 to place an order for 30 AEC Regal III 0962s with Mann Egerton bodywork to help with the expansion of services. Mann Egerton had acquitted itself well in the renovation programme and their work was well liked by London Transport but they won the contract against competition from a number of bigger companies because they were able to offer quicker delivery. Unfortunately they, like everybody else, suffered from material shortages and government restrictions and missed their target by five months.

These were the closest London Transport ever got to having the single-deck version of the RT which had been included in the first post-war replacement plan of 1942. However, the model was based on the standard specification as offered to operators outside London and they had non-standard bodies. They were included in the T class whose oldest members were by now 19 years old, a decision comparable to classifying the RTs as STs. Numbered T 769–796 (coded 15T13) they went into service between March and September at Two Waters and Watford (Leavesden Road). They were painted anachronistically in the 1939 Lincoln green and white style, although with green roofs, but this suited rather well the simple classical lines of their Mann Egerton bodies.

Those who doubted the claim that the Ts were essential for service expansion were proved right in July when Country Buses announced a review of the single-deck fleet. They had apparently found that the mechanical condition of the country single-deck fleet had so improved that they could afford to lend 25 older vehicles to Central Buses. There were to have been thirteen 5Q5s, leaving only two still painted green, and twelve 4Q4s but only seven of these were released and the absence of the other five became a bone of contention between the two departments for the rest of the year. There was in fact a constant battle between Central and Country, throughout the years when the 'obsolete fleet' was being replaced, to claim what each considered to be their fair share of what was available, especially in the allocation of new RTs.

All the Qs were painted red, the 5Q5s going to Sidcup for route 228 and the 4Q4s to West Green for route 233. Seven 5Q5s from West Green also went to Sidcup where the buses displaced were single-deck LTs. Alleged problems with sightlines in the grounds of Alexandra Palace led after a few weeks to the exchange of West Green's 4Q4s with a like number of 5Q5s from Dalston. This boost in the Central Bus fleet enabled the sixty LTs and eighteen 1T1s which were included in the renovation contract with Marshalls, mentioned earlier, to be released progressively between July 1948 and October 1949.

Delivery of the 15T13s was completed on 30th August and after a pause of five weeks, the new TD class Leyland single-deckers for Central Buses began to flow. They did not have platform doors and were fitted with housings for trafficator equipment but were otherwise uniform with the Ts. The chassis were identical to the 1TD1s, except for having a cast aluminium radiator shell, and therefore had synchromesh rather than preselective gearboxes as fitted to the Ts. The first went into service during October at Hornchurch on route 250 and they were eventually dispersed among nine garages. Their arrival allowed a start to be made on scrapping the Ts and LTs in worst condition and, from February 1949, the return of the 4Q4s to Country Buses.

Meanwhile, the delivery of RTs had continued uninterrupted, with Central Buses sending further supplies to Holloway, followed by Dalston and Mortlake. During the deliveries to Dalston, starting at RT 752, the first important modification was made to the RT3 body, making it fully

interchangeable with the RTL but including a number of other changes, such as a route number plate under the canopy and housing for semaphore trafficators. These were a stepping stone to the standard design without roof box (RT3/1) which was to appear on RT 852 later in the year, on which the number under the canopy became an illuminated blind.

Among these deliveries was RT 778 which had been earmarked for use in an experiment with Miller RV7 direct selection gearbox, continuing work that had started before the war. It was sent to Turnham Green in September 1948 where it was joined over the next ten months by RT 902, 2207, 2208, and 2273. These experiments led eventually to the adoption of this type of gearbox in the Routemaster.

Weymann delivered the first two green RTs on 15th July 1948 and the first four (RT 597–600) went into service at Tring on 21st July. Between then and January 1949, 200 entered the country fleet, to be joined after September by the first 27 Cravens which took until April 1949 to be com-

'Courtesy Aids Service' posters appeared on all publicity, and on buses, coaches, trams and trolleybuses in the position then reserved for traffic notices, the panel ahead of the platform, as here on Tilling STL 84. The bus is in Newington Butts, with the Elephant & Castle pub behind it, waiting at the Police-controlled traffic lights before crossing into Newington Causeway.
Capital Transport collection

Mud-spattered from its journeys through the Essex and Hertfordshire countryside but still evidently new, TD 43 was one of 14 supplied to Enfield garage for routes 205 and 242 at the end of 1948. It is at the western terminus of the route, Potters Bar garage, which was no doubt operationally convenient but at the wrong end of the High Street to serve the town properly.
D.W.K. Jones

The last 100 Park Royal and 50 Weymann roof-box RTs embodied major modifications which later caused them to be recoded RT10 but when they were new they were still classified RT3. They were made suitable for mounting on RTL chassis, had a route number plate under the canopy, a stepping-stone towards the illuminated display which was to become standard, and were provided with housings for semaphore trafficators. These changed the appearance in several ways, the deep valance on the canopy was removed, a smaller nearside driver's mirror was fitted and the bottom of the dash panel had a slight upward curve to clear the bulkier Leyland dumbiron. RT779 is at Law Courts in Strand, accompanied by STL2518, a 15STL16.
C.F. Klapper/Omnibus Society

pleted. The 12 garages which benefited, some with more than one delivery, were, in order of first receipt, Tring, Two Waters, Leatherhead, Grays, Watford High Street, Hertford, Northfleet, Windsor, St Albans, Epping, Reigate and Hatfield. Weymann changed to the revised RT3 design at RT 962 and the RT3/1 non-roofbox design at RT 1012.

Delivery of RTs to Central Buses continued apace for the rest of the year and new buses were arriving at the rate of 17 or 18 a week by December. Among them were the first 43 RTLs, the first of which had been received on 24th November, three Cravens and one Saunders RT. At the end of 1948 900 3RTs and 34 RTLs were licensed, already 15 per cent of the double-deck fleet, and the red ones were scattered among 21 garages in all parts of London, ensuring that the RT was becoming a common sight throughout the metropolis. For all that, the fleet was still in a dire state as the number of buses condemned by the vehicle inspectors persistently exceeded the number of new buses being licensed. This guaranteed that the shortage of fit buses remained at a high

level throughout the year, reaching its worst point in October when there was a net loss of 15 buses, bringing the total shortage up to 262. The average daily 'no bus available' was 323 at that time but this was as much to do with knife-edge maintenance standards as to bus shortages; it had been at a much higher level earlier in the year.

The operation of single-deckers and hired coaches had continued to supply some relief to these problems but London Transport carried on its dogged search for other sources of help. Ideally, this would have been some government action to release supplies of materials to accelerate the building of new buses but the Executive's constant badgering of ministers eventually had a surprising result. An arrangement was made with the newly nationalised Tilling Group for 200 (later reduced to 190) standard Bristols to be placed on loan to London and the first of these started work in December 1948. Later deals brought in three Daimlers from Maidstone and 17 pre-war Regents from Leeds. A separate account of this episode is given in Chapter 8.

Despite all these problems, London Transport had to deal during the year not only with the usual peaks in vehicle demand represented by major events, particularly the Derby, but also with the special requirements of the Olympic Games. These were held between 29th July and 14th August but in addition to the extra service buses needed to carry the crowds, London Transport also had responsibility for supplying transport for the competitors and this commitment started on 9th July. To be ready to meet these commitments and those of other big events

Two STs with very different provenances on routes 301 and 302, which were swept away by the Country Area's first RTs in July 1948. ST 1094 was a former East Surrey bus with Ransomes Sims & Jefferies bodywork, and ST 884 a former Tilling. Apparently somebody had taken the trouble to cut one side from a standard blind to fit it into the narrow box of the Tilling, with the result that part of the place name has been lost. D.W.K. Jones

Right The RT3/1 introduced the body design which was to be the standard for all subsequent RT family vehicles, except for those from the Saunders factory. Epping was one of only a handful of garages whose double-deckers were solely STs after the war and the whole lot were replaced by new RTs at the end of 1948. RT 1024, on the stand at Epping garage after switching between trips from the 396 to the 339, gives a good demonstration of why Country Buses soon abandoned the offside route number plates. The chore of changing the plates in these circumstances, common practice on Country Buses, apparently being too much for the average conductor.
The Omnibus Society

such as the Derby and Wimbledon Tennis, London Transport established a 'Special Events Fleet' in March 1948. It comprised vehicles which were no longer up to the strains of normal service operation but were still fit enough for less strenuous low mileage duties. Its constitution varied as older vehicles finally expired and others newly qualified for the status of semi-retirement, but there were always LTs, STs and petrol-engined STLs. Once established it remained in being until the obsolete fleet had been replaced and was finally stood down on 23rd February 1950

The Derby meeting was a headache every year between 1947 and 1949, although in 1948 the Government decreed that the Derby itself should be run on the Saturday to avoid essential workers staying away from work. This was some help but the special services needed no fewer than 228 buses and the Special Events Fleet could spare only 23. Even using every trick they could, the two departments could muster only 156 between them. To achieve this they had to resort to using training buses, which were not fit for normal service but which the Ministry was prepared to authorise for this special use, open-staircase LTs released from the Eastern Region replacement service, Inter-Station Cubs and ordinary bus Cubs.

The Olympic Games required a commitment over a much longer period and the vehicles used were a mixed lot of 21 single-deckers, mostly CRs and 12 LTC Private Hire coaches. These were supplemented before the games by ten double-deckers from the Special Events Fleet and during the games by 40 double-deckers which were simply withdrawn from normal service. The heavy reliance on CRs proved a mixed blessing as they were not the most reliable of buses in any case but they were hit particularly hard by an intense heat wave at the end of July which had a disastrous effect on them.

During 1948 some relief to Chiswick's capacity problems began to become available as some work was transferred to temporary facilities which had been set up in the unused Northern Line depot buildings at Aldenham. Accident repairs had been transferred by the beginning of 1948 and the depot gradually took over responsibility for the overhaul of, first lowbridge buses, then the TFs and the whole of the service vehicle fleet. The acceptance, preparation and licensing of new buses also moved to Aldenham which then became the base for the manufacture of ancillary items of equipment such as fare-tables and blinds. The largest project allotted to Aldenham at this time was to carry out the conversion work on STL chassis to create the SRT class. The first post-war RTs became due for overhaul in 1950 and this became Aldenham's principal task from then onwards.

In connection with the new arrangements at Aldenham, six 3RT3s were withdrawn in the autumn of 1948 and fitted with new RT3/1 bodies by Park Royal. Their own bodies had been damaged in accidents and were used to form a spares float, which remained in existence only until the beginning of 1950. They were RT 279, 290, 367, 392, 486 and 593.

London Transport ended 1948 in the deepest crisis it had experienced but 1949 was to be a remarkable year during which 1,618 new double-deckers and the balance of 76 TDs were taken

The Leyland contribution to the post-war replacement programme began to appear, belatedly, at the end of 1948 and West Green was the second garage, after Sidcup, to receive an allocation. RTL 44 is alongside Weymann-bodied G 377 in Victoria Station forecourt on 20th August 1949.
A.B. Cross

STL 2574 in The Pavement, Clapham Common, shortly before it was withdrawn. Its chassis was used to create SRT 78 and its handsome STL 16 body was used to replace the rotting Park Royal structure on STL 2124 which then remained in service until the very end of STL operation in September 1954. *A.B. Cross*

condition of the fleet. To these must be added the 200 buses which were borrowed, the balance of 180 Tilling Bristols, three Daimlers from Maidstone Corporation and 17 pre-war AEC Regents from Leeds, all of which made a helpful contribution. In January there was a shortage of 250 double deckers, offset by a surplus of 70 single-deckers, and shortages persisted through most of the year, but there was a gradual if bumpy trend of improvement. There were some high monthly shortages which interrupted the trend, the worst being July when 199 was reached but this was during the period of enforced withdrawal of the SRTs. In November, for the first time since 1947, the number of new buses exceeded the number withdrawn and, finally, in December the momentous day arrived when there was a small surplus of fit buses available for service. John Burnell, the Central Bus Operating Manager, reporting on the number of 'NBAs' allowed himself the restrained comment '. . . we have reached the stage where fear of heavy losses on that account has passed.'

At the beginning of 1949 there were still some important routes in the heart of London being operated by vehicles classified as 'obsolete fleet' (STs, LTs and petrol-engined STLs). They were present in considerable numbers in such thoroughfares as Oxford Street, where at least 70 buses an hour in each direction in the peak were of these types, and Regent Street (52 an hour). Between them routes 7/A, 11, 17, 38, 53A, 73 and 159 used 416 of the 1148 obsolete buses still scheduled for service (36 per cent!), the largest allocation being to route 12, with a peak requirement of 104 STs and LTs. All this was to change at seemingly breakneck speed in the following 12 months.

into stock, although this fell some way short of the Executive's aspirations. They had been allocated 1,500 new chassis for delivery in 1949 but the bodybuilders were expected to be able to supply 1,700 bodies and the balance was to have been made up with 200 SRTs. The target for new buses was almost reached, the actual figure being 1,473 RT, RTL and RTW but, partly because production was suspended while mechanical problems were rectified, only 145 SRTs were built. Even so, the injection of an average of 31 new double-deckers a week, gradually rising throughout the year to a record 50 a week in December, transformed the

Petrol-engined STL 379 on route 7, one of eight important central London routes still worked by 'obsolete' types at the start of 1949. The STL3 body was one of the same type as it had carried when new in 1934, its characteristics including the small aperture for the route number display, a square cab and the prominent moulding between the side panels. *D.W.K. Jones*

After two interruptions in December 1948 when the first batches of RTLs were built, production of RTs at Park Royal ceased altogether on 16th December and did not resume until the end of May 1949. They made way for a continuous run of 229 Leylands to be bodied (RTL 24–252), after which production alternated between the two chassis makes, with SRT production being interspersed, giving totals of 85 RT, 436 RTL and 145 SRT. At first this meant that the supply of red RTs dried up completely, as Weymann and Cravens were busy with Country Buses while Saunders did not manage to produce its second RT until February. When the first allocations of RTLs to Sidcup and West Green were finished, they began to go to Hammersmith (R) for route 17 which brought them into the West End, and Barking for the 87, replacing mainly LTs.

During February Park Royal and Weymann started to produce bodies with the new code RT8. These had revised body mountings to allow them also to be mounted on SRT chassis, although the bodies supplied on the SRTs were coded RT9 as they had a different arrangement of floor traps in the lower saloon. This was the last change of significance to the standard RT body during the production run.

Weymann returned to the production of red RTs in February, enabling the long delayed completion of Muswell Hill's allocation for route 43, but Cravens continued to paint its output green until the end of April. Production at Saunders finally got into its stride in March and these very close imitations of the RT3 began to appear in small numbers sprinkled among their more numerous siblings at whichever garage was receiving a new allocation at the time. The very distinctive Cravens version was similarly spread around in small numbers, in contrast to the decision of Country Buses to concentrate them at Watford and Windsor. Meanwhile the unique RTC 1 had been completed at Chiswick in January and SRT 1 had arrived at the beginning of February. SRT 1 was sent to Camberwell for training in March and the class first went into service during April, on route 35 from Camberwell and 34 from Palmers Green. March also saw the addition of RTW 1 to the fleet. It was sent to Tottenham for training but the next two did not arrive until the beginning of May and it was not until 11th May that the first two went into service. This left one manufacturer still to show its face but it was not until August that the first

Metro-Cammell bodied RTL left Birmingham and there was then nearly a month before any more came. The 'Met-Cams' as they became known were almost identical in outward appearance to the RT8, but were structurally quite different as MCCW had used their own standard, well-respected, method of all-metal construction. RTL 551 was licensed at Tottenham in August and by December Met-Cams were being added at the rate of five or six a week. With six body-builders now making their full contribution and three sources of supply for chassis, the combined rate of delivery after August was prodigious.

A little sideshow to the mainstream events was the appearance of RTC 1. It was not a new vehicle but RT 97, last seen in service at Romford as part of the Pay As You Board experiments in 1946, which had been heavily modified. As mentioned in Chapter 4 it had been London Transport's intention to use double-deckers for all its Green Line services as soon as vehicles could be made available. In early post-war fleet plans 386 vehi-

Below Gleaming new SRT 2 parked in the yard at Camberwell garage alongside hired coaches while in use as a type trainer before it went into service, all too briefly, on route 35. D.W.K. Jones

Right The Metro-Cammell bodied RTLs, which began to arrive in August 1949, were distinguishable from the standard RT8s only by the minor detail of an inverted gutter-like scroll above the central cream band. Beneath this gloss of standardisation they were very different, as their structure was based on the company's own design of metal framing giving them a sturdiness which was to ensure they had long lives. RTL 682 was one of seven which were used to replace borrowed Tilling Bristols at Hammersmith. It was photographed at Sutton Green while working on the Sunday extension of route 88 to Belmont. D.W.K. Jones

cles were set aside for this purpose, as many as a hundred of them being for expansion of services, with delivery starting in the second half of 1948. They were shown as modified RTs but RTC 1 was intended as a possible prototype for a vehicle which would live up to the higher standards needed for coach operation. Pressure on workshop time and shortage of materials prolonged the development and it was not ready until January 1949. Its specification included saloon heating, fluorescent lighting, experimental seats to so-called 'airline standards', which in those days was a compliment, and platform doors. The radiator was moved to a position under the stairs which enabled a novel sloping bonnet and wing assembly to be designed, incorporating a full width grille. It was launched with great brio and went into service on route 715 from Hertford garage and then spent time on routes 711 from Reigate, 708 (Two Waters) and 704 (Windsor) before returning to Hertford in July. Its shortcomings soon became apparent. Although its suspension had been designed to overcome the hard bouncing quality of the RT, it still had a tendency to cause the body to sway at speed and to pitch when accelerating. It was also mechanically unreliable. Passengers did not like the quality of ride, neither were they happy that there were no overhead luggage racks in the saloon. RTC 1 was withdrawn from Green Line service in December 1949 and relegated to bus duties at Leatherhead, where it remained until March 1953.

The SRTs were to have a hardly more auspicious career. By agreement between management and Trade Union, they were defined as rebodied STLs and not part of the post-war replacement fleet, but were to be allocated to garages which were not expected to receive new buses in the foreseeable future. When they first went into service they therefore took over from STLs which were then re-deployed elsewhere, first at Camberwell and Palmers Green, then at Victoria (route 10) and one solitary example to Chalk Farm for route 24. Although the SRTs were barely distinguishable from a standard 3RT8, the only recognition features being the STL-type front wheel centres and their registration numbers, they were still mechanically an STL but weighing half a ton more. They produced a spiritless performance from their 7.7 litre engines but, more importantly, had inadequate brakes which led to experimental modifications to SRT 1, 4 and 16. Tests in Lyonsdown Road, East Barnet which had been demanded by the Trade Union, revealed serious shortcomings and all but the three which had been modified were taken out of service on 18th June. They were fitted with larger servos and did not start to go back into service until the end of July when Forest Gate received four for route 96. The staff there objected to them being used on routes with mixed allocations and they were taken away again. After that they went onto routes with a single allocation, a large number to Cricklewood for route 16, Chalk Farm for route 24, Twickenham for routes 90 and 90B and Harrow Weald for route 114. Camberwell's were moved to routes 5, 5A and 42. Production ended at SRT 160 in January 1950, ostensibly because the supply of new chassis had now reached a satisfactory level.

Although the RTWs made their due contribution to replacing obsolete buses, they were in a category of their own because the Police were adamantly opposed to their use in central London where they thought the extra width would cause congestion. They were therefore confined to suburban services where the Police presumably thought the roads were more suitable and congestion less likely. The first route chosen for them, route 41 which then as now used almost exclusively narrow inner suburban roads, barely seemed to qualify. Subsequent allocations in 1949 went to Alperton for route 187, which also had long sections of narrow roads with awkward corners; Shepherd's Bush and Hanwell (HW) for the 105, although not between Southall and Hayes on Sundays; Leyton, West Green and Enfield for the 144 and 144A; Palmers Green (112); Putney Bridge for the 85; and Harrow Weald and Edgware (140, 142 and 158).

RTs and RTLs meantime continued to gain ground all over London, adding another ten Central Bus garages which, with the four operating only RTWs brought the total running RT family buses up to 36. There had also been a little more expansion in the Country Bus fleet against strong opposition from Central Buses whose problems were still unarguably greater. Brian Harbour, the Operating Manager, had made a case for an additional 27 RTs to be painted green in the summer of 1949 and this had been agreed on the basis that 31 STs and 25 STL6s were gradually being withdrawn as unfit. When Weymann started to produce them in June, however, the urgency had mysteriously gone out of the matter and the buses were put on loan to Central Buses for one month. They were included in the new allocations going at that time to Mortlake, for route 73, and Middle Row for routes 7 and 7A, and passers-by in

Above Leyland delivered RTW1 to Chiswick in March 1949 but the main flow of deliveries did not start until May. In the meantime it was shown off to the press, which is the occasion of this photograph showing it in sparkling new condition on the sort of road the Police considered suitable for such monsters. Just as they had produced a good imitation of the STL design for the STDs in 1937, so Leyland designed a very good imitation of a wide version of the standard RT8 body which then formed the basis of their own 'Farington' body for the market outside London. One of the features unique to the RT6 body was the use of rubber mountings for the indicator glasses, which can be seen clearly here. C.F. Klapper

Below Green RT 2254 at work on route 9 from Mortlake garage during its one month-long sojourn in Central Bus service. A.B. Cross

Oxford Street and elsewhere were suddenly treated to the sight of these gleaming new buses in their fetching Lincoln green and cream livery, unblemished by advertisements. When they went to their rightful owners, they enabled Northfleet to replace STLs on route 480.

The extent of the transformation wrought in the London bus scene during 1949 can be judged by looking at the number of buses in the 'obsolete fleet' that were scheduled for service at the beginning and end of the year. On 1st January there were still 1,193 of all three types scheduled on Monday-Friday, 635 LTs, 458 STs and 100 STLs and most of the sub-types were present in this total. By 31st December, there were just 117, 50 LTs, 66 STs and a solitary STL. The order of withdrawal of the oldsters was governed by the combined efforts of the Bodywork Inspection Committee and the Ministry of Transport's vehicle examiners. Garage engineering staff lived in fear of a visit from the examiners who often left a trail of buses bearing their death warrant, the white painted inscription 'PSV71', the code for

the prohibition order, meaning that the vehicle was condemned. For this reason, even as its size shrank, the composition of the old fleet remained very varied, although by the end of the year some of them could be found only in the Special Events fleet.

Up to this time the oil-engined STLs had been left unmolested, other than those which had been appropriated for the SRT programme, but in January 1949 the first two were withdrawn. One of these was the short wheelbase STL 1263 which bore the body of a former DST and was therefore non-standard in two respects but the other was STL 1837 which carried one of the later STL14 roof-box bodies. This signalled the start of the gradual departure of the oilers, at a fairly slow pace at first but gradually building up to reach 15 in December. The grim reaper of bodywork was no respecter of age or type in the STL fleet either and vehicles of all and any type ended up in the breaker's yard. The green forward-entrance STLs, whose condition Brian Harbour had cited to justify the allocation of additional RTs, did indeed begin to go in February with the withdrawal of STL 1002 and nine, mostly the Chiswick-built STL6 version, had gone by the end of the year. Nevertheless the bulk of withdrawals was from the ST, LT and petrol STL fleet.

The random nature of disposals caused quite a lot of movement in the remaining fleet, as vehicles were shipped around to keep the balance as fair as possible. In most cases where RT family vehicles nominally replaced oil-engined STLs, it was usually the STs allocated to cover shortages which were removed from garages, but towards the end of its first RT conversion programme Country Buses replaced large numbers of STLs which were then re-deployed. Partial allocations of STs on otherwise STL routes 331 (Hertford), 353 (Amersham) and 405 (Reigate), were removed in favour of STLs while at Grays, the mixed allocation of RT and ST on routes 371/A became RT and STL. The influx of oil-engined STLs at Grays also precipitated the departure of the last three of the Bluebird LTs, originally Gardner-engined but by now fitted with AEC units, which had been running there since April 1947. LT 1425 captured some minor fame by being sent to Reigate for the Chiswick staff bus duty, on which it replaced two STs and became one of the last of the class to be withdrawn.

Central Buses also used re-deployed STLs increasingly to replace STs and LTs, often where these types were a minority allocation to an STL

Potters Bar garage relinquished the last of its petrol-engined buses with the arrival of new RTs for route 84 starting in September 1949. An endearing idiosyncrasy of the petrol fleet when the outside temperature rose was that drivers would unhook the bonnet side to increase the ventilation of the engine above what could penetrate its many vents as can be seen on STL 361. This bus ran almost until the end of petrol STL operation, being withdrawn from Turnham Green in December 1949. F.W. Ivey

route. Kingston and Turnham Green got STLs in August to replace most but not all of their remaining STs and petrol STLs, but these were themselves ousted when RTs went to Kingston in October and RTLs to Turnham Green between October and December. Almost at the end of LT operation, in December, STLs were drafted in to Muswell Hill and Old Kent Road to replace LTs on routes 251A and 159 and Alperton, replacing STs on the 18. Central Buses was by now beginning to have a surplus of STLs and some of these were transferred to Country Buses

A number of 'lasts' began to build up as the year went on. The last eight Tilling STs still in normal service at Alperton, Dalston, Middle Row, Old Kent Road, Tottenham and Willesden were withdrawn in March. Although the Tillings had not been scheduled for regular service since the early war years, they had been of stalwart help in keeping services going in the post-war years and their disappearance took away one of London's most characterful vehicle types. A few were kept in the Special Events fleet for a time and one, ST 887, was still active at the end of the year. The last of the 'Pickup' STLs still carrying its original body as rebuilt in 1934 and the last complete vehicle acquired from a London Independent still running, STL 556, was withdrawn in April. The last three open-staircase LTs still in normal service from Barking, Leyton and Upton Park were withdrawn on 26th April, although they were

Above For a class that was already in decline and without a specific role, the Tilling STs were surprisingly pervasive in the post-war period but their time came at last in March 1949 when the last eight still in normal service were withdrawn. ST 920, seen at Brook Green Hammersmith in June 1948 had already gone five months earlier but was not scrapped until April 1949.
Capital Transport collection

Below The original General STLs remained on the scene in diminishing numbers until STL 43 was one of the last of the obsolete fleet to run in service in January 1950. One of those that hung on longest was

Turnham Green's STL 185 seen here two months before it was scrapped in October 1949, wearing the mainly red 1945 livery style which was applied to some of this sub-class. It was one of the later examples and had been put into service by London Transport just after the Board was formed in July 1933.
A.B. Cross

batch of Green Line Regals, T 120, also went in April, although by this time it had a later forward-entrance body. Similarly modified T 391, which was the last of the coaches acquired from Bucks Expresses by the LGOC in 1932, went in June and the last Tilling, T 308, in October.

As the condition of the fleet improved, London Transport began to review the various temporary measures which had been used to keep services going. The first on the list was the use of CRs as peak hour reliefs. John Burnell, the Operating Manager of Central Buses said in February that he could no longer justify the expense of using 20-seaters with conductors and suggested that they should be allowed to 'fade away' as they became mechanically defective. Only a month before it had been decided to overhaul the CRs and the first 12 were to have been repainted green for Country Buses to use in their route development programme. CR 14 had already been painted green and two more were done later in the year (CR 10 and 19) but Burnell's intervention caused this idea to collapse. The first two CRs were withdrawn in March and others followed rapidly until only five were left in service at

transferred to the Special Events fleet for the rest of the year and made appearances at Epsom Races, Wimbledon Tennis and occasionally on Bank Holidays. They were by now unique for town operation anywhere in Britain and their withdrawal ended the reign of the open staircase after nearly one hundred years. The last two 'Bluebird' STs ran in July and the last three Tilling STLs at Bromley in October. In the single-deck fleet, the sole survivor of the original 1930

Now that the obsolete fleet was no more, it was the turn of the standard STLs to give way to the new order. Most prominent in this trio at Cricket Green, Mitcham in March 1950 is STL 1717, a 4/9STL14, about to set out on a peak hour shortworking to Streatham Common. The parallel stripes of darker tar in the road surface mark where the tram track had been filled in after the closure of this short branch from Fair Green in December 1933. A.B. Cross

the end of the year. These five, two more of which were later repainted green, remained in service until 1952/1953 but none of the others were disposed of until 1951.

The coach hire scheme, another uneconomic operation, was also reviewed in January and this led to the gradual running down of the number of coaches on hire until the last 58 coaches finished on 19th August. In a sense their role had been taken over to a large extent by the borrowed double-deckers, which had continued to arrive during the contraction of the scheme and were still in service at the end of the year. In practice, their work was covered by a variety of London Transport's own vehicles.

From June 1949 onwards, Central Buses began to increase the frequencies of some of its services. Increasingly, as fewer and fewer routes had official allocations of obsolete buses, the extra vehicles needed for the improved services were gleaned from displaced STs and occasionally LTs.

3. "Remember what London Transport were up against a year or two ago on their bus services? The buses they had to hire from other parts of the country? In two years they've put on the roads 2,500 of their latest 'RT' type. I'll bet the public notice the difference in smoother rides, quicker journeys, cleaner vehicles and fewer queues . . ."

This rather pedestrian cartoon appeared in the British Transport Commission's staff newspaper as part of its review of 1949 to mark the completion of the first and most important phase of the post-war vehicle replacement programme.

Below The face of the scrapyard at Rainham changed early in 1950, as withdrawn STLs began to pile up. The Renown closest to the camera is LT 822, which was withdrawn on 12th January 1950. D.W.K. Jones

95

Above Guy Motors of Wolverhampton tried to break into the London bus market in 1949 with a version of the Arab whose specification came close to that of the RT but had left it too late as the future composition of the fleet was all but settled by then. G 436 was intended as a first step towards a fully compatible chassis able to carry a standard RT body and as such was fitted with a standard Park Royal body. It is posed at Guy's Fallings Park works dressed for route 21, presumably because the display was near the top of the Old Kent Road blind. It was never allocated to this route. A curiosity which this body shared with the experimental Regent IV, also from Park Royal, was the absence of a destination blind aperture.
Industrial Photographic

Right Looking thoroughly run-down and with the ghost of the wartime white spot still visible on the back of its former DST body, short wheelbase STL 1260 was photographed at Edgware garage in the chilly mist of Christmas Eve 1949. It was the last of its type and was withdrawn in January 1950.
A.B. Cross

This meant that the number of places where these types could be seen actually increased for a time. The last three examples of this took place as late as 14th December.

There were 139 obsolete double-deckers still licensed for service on 1st January 1950 but by the end of the month none was running in normal service. There were 85 STs, 53 LTs and STL 43. The STs could be found at no fewer than 20 Central Bus and four Country Bus garages, the only official allocations being at Tottenham for route 67 and Two Waters for the 316. In contrast 41 of the LTs were at Upton Park where route 40 was

the last to have an official allocation of the type, the others being at Seven Kings, Plumstead and Leyton. They drained away quickly as new buses continued to pour in and by 11th January there were only nine LTs left, all at Upton Park, and these had gone the next day. These last few were replaced by surplus STLs, as were those at the other garages, but Upton Park was the only one also to receive new buses, a batch of RTWs for routes 129 and 145. Their RTs were transferred to route 40 which therefore claimed the melancholy distinction of being the last route on which LTs were replaced by RTs. STL 43 which was at Bromley was withdrawn the same day.

The STs kept going a little longer but in much diminished numbers. Their last official allocation at Tottenham gave way on 18th January to STLs displaced at Enfield by new RTLs, the 316 at Two Waters having succumbed to unfrozen STLs earlier in the month, and the last five Central Bus examples at Barking, Camberwell and Norwood, were delicensed on 26th January. The last four in Country Bus service at Northfleet, St Albans and Watford kept going for one more day and were delicensed on 27th January. The Special Events fleet of five open-staircase LTs, two Bluebird LTs, four standard and one Tilling ST was withdrawn on 25th February, after which only the few still in use as trainers remained. This brought to an end the first and most crucial stage of the post-war replacement programme. The next big task was the replacement of the trams and the way was now clear for that scheme to start rolling on 1st October 1950.

One of the subjects discussed during the planning of the tram conversion had been the possibility that the three routes split in 1937 should be reconnected as through motor bus routes. One of the benefits would have been that it would then not be necessary to buy new trolley-buses to replace the ageing B1 and B2 classes. Route 612 was added to the scheme, enabling 16 trolleybuses to be withdrawn but the 626 and 628 were left out because, at the time, there were still plenty of motor buses in need of replacement. A decision had to be made about what to do instead, bearing in mind that at that time the future of the trolleybus system had not been settled. The decision came during March 1950 and it went way beyond the immediate question of vehicle replacement. The Executive decided to buy 50 more Q1s, far more than was necessary to replace the B classes but sufficient to complete the allocations at Fulwell and Isleworth. The idea was that these 125 trolleybuses could form a sustainable self-contained network which could continue until the Q1s were life-expired, even if it were decided to replace the rest of the trolleybuses by motor buses. The new Q1s were delivered during 1952 and 1953 but any hope that they might still be running in 1972 or later was dashed when they were sold to operators in Spain within ten years of delivery.

The 12 months from 1st January 1950 was to

witness a record intake of 1,930 new motor buses, an average of more than six on each working day right through the year, culminating in a net increase of 673 in the size of the double-deck fleet. It was also to be a record year for the withdrawal of oil-engined STLs, a grand total of 930 standards and six unfrozens being cast aside. Two hundred of the new buses were set aside to replace the hired buses, which were returned during the year and 282 were used for new and increased services. The remaining 228 were earmarked for tram replacement.

One of the new buses was a distinct oddity, a Guy Arab III with a Meadows 10.35 litre engine and a standard Park Royal body. Numbered G436, although bearing little resemblance to the 435 utilities, it was taken into stock in December 1949 and put into service on route 173 from Old Kent Road garage in January 1950. It was an attempt by Guy Motors Ltd, rather too late in the day for its own good, to become one of London Transport's chassis suppliers and to this end the specification included an air-operated preselective gearbox and fluid flywheel and a low bonnet line. A second chassis was planned, this time with its frame built to the same profile as the RT so that a standard RT body could be fitted. For whatever reason, this ambitious idea did not come to anything even though it was supported enthusiastically by the highly respected Chief Mechanical Engineer Bill Durrant. However, it must have been obvious from the start that so much production had already been committed to AEC and Leyland that Guy's contribution would have been too small to fit comfortably into a highly standardised fleet.

Also among the buses licensed in January was a small maverick batch (RT 2116–2121) which had newly re-painted roofbox bodies. These came

Northern Counties-bodied G256 was typical of the double-deck complement at Hornchurch garage in 1950, a fact which caused discontent among drivers leading eventually to a change of policy and the earlier-than-planned withdrawal of the class. A.B. Cross

from the accident float which had been set up in December 1948 but which had now been disbanded. RT 2116 was green, the rest red. At this time, such high numbered buses carrying roofbox bodies looked very strange. The following month an old number was married to a new chassis when RT 657, which had been left out to make way for RTL 501 in 1948, at last appeared complete with an RT8 body and current registration KLB712.

Now started the relentless onslaught on the oil-engined STLs which was to leave only 903 still licensed at the end of the year. Among those which went in January was STL 1260, the last of

Hornchurch staff were expected to be content with 11 TDs as their share of the post-war fleet modernisation but the Executive did not help its own case by allocating five 9T9s for operation on route 252 at about the time the row regarding the Guys blew up. Although similar in overall design to the later 10T10s, the 9T9s could be recognised immediately by the treatment of the wings and mudguards, the presence of a bumper bar and the internal sliding door, all clearly shown on T418 on the South Street stand at Romford station. D.W.K. Jones

the curious short-wheelbase examples with a former DST body and the first three of the unfrozen STLs which, although they had more recent chassis were nearly all fitted with pre-war bodies of various types. New buses in January went to ten garages, including one (Battersea) which had not had any until then. This pattern was repeated through the year but slowed down markedly in August and September and again in November and December as buses were stockpiled for the first two stages of the tram conversion. At year end, all but six Central Bus and five Country Bus garages had at least some RT family buses allocated. In the Central Area, the exceptions included Hendon which was still happily carrying on with the pre-war STDs and Loughton which had exclusively the post-war variety. Merton and Sutton with their predominantly Daimler fleets were not expecting to join the club for two or three years and seemed happy with that arrangement but at Hornchurch, where by now there was a double-deck allocation consisting entirely of wartime Guys, the staff were distinctly unhappy. The other central garage was Streatham which had been one of the last to have its roof raised. In the Country Area two of the garages, Hitchin and Tunbridge Wells had no double deckers, which left only Addlestone, Dartford and Luton waiting to taste the fruits of modernity. A lot happened before that point was reached.

The discontent at Hornchurch about their Guys was an early indication that the staff were not prepared to tolerate their continued use until their planned withdrawal date of 1952. Barking garage complained at about the same time that the Guys on route 23 were having to run against modern buses on many other routes but they were given short shrift, being reminded that the garage already had a good allocation of new buses. Enfield complained about having to use Guys on route 144B on Sundays, because the route was

During the operability trials at Notting Hill Gate, an RTW on route 27A turns from Kensington Mall into Church Street while RTW 243, an Edgware bus temporarily on loan to Willesden, demonstrates that it can overtake a parked cycle without crossing the centre line. LT Museum

not approved for RTWs. In this case expensive arrangements were made to transfer spare RTLs in from Tottenham every week. Enfield also managed to rid themselves of the Guys running on route 102 alongside Palmers Green's STLs by the simple expedient of swapping Guys for STLs from Upton Park's route 101. In April 1950 the Trade Union was told of a slippage in the replacement programme which meant that the unfrozen STDs and Guys would have to keep running until 1953. In desperation the Union suggested that the Guys should be used for tram conversion but needless to say nothing came of that. Instead, London Transport decided to start replacing the STs in the training fleet with Guys, 18 being replaced in November 1950. The Festival of Britain was used as the catalyst to replace the remainder of the Guys on the 76, which passed in front of the main entrance to the South Bank exhibition, by new RTLs, these being replaced later by RTWs. Then in February 1951 the staff at Victoria made it clear that they were no longer prepared to drive unfrozen STDs and these were withdrawn and transferred to staff bus duties. They were replaced by some STLs and post-war STDs transferred from Leyton, where they were replaced by RTs and STLs. Following a review of the situation, the Executive changed its policy to allow the replacement of Guys out of sequence, replacing them where necessary with STLs which should have gone first. The entire fleet of wartime Guys had gone by Christmas Day 1952.

With the most serious problems in the double-deck fleet out of the way, the state of the single-deck fleet began to get more attention during 1950. There were still substantial numbers of 'obsolete' buses running and many of these would have to be kept going until the new RF started to arrive in 1951. The 98 LTs and 26 1T1s were therefore fitted with oil engines recovered from scrapped STLs in a programme stretching from January to October 1950. These included 38 LTs and eight Ts which had not been rebuilt by Marshalls. To cover the absence of these buses at the peak of the programme, Central Buses borrowed five 9T9s from the Country Area and allocated them to Hornchurch garage. Later, fourteen 4Q4s were borrowed to enable the last eleven 1/7T7/1s to be withdrawn by May. In all 26 Qs were involved in the comings and goings but the number settled at 14 in September. All but one of the Qs was painted red and they were put into Kingston garage to work routes 215 and 219.

Another group of 'obsolete' buses, still working hard were the eight lowbridge STs and these were also being fitted with oil engines. When this work started in June 1949 there was no clear plan for the replacement of these buses and they were put into a condition which would keep them running for several years. Two other types which still had petrol engines were the Inter-Station Cubs, which never lost them, and the LTCs, which were also given secondhand oil engines at the beginning of 1950. The Cubs were withdrawn on 21st November 1950; the last petrol-engined vehicles in passenger service with London Transport.

Above The RLHs added another level of strangeness to the Country Bus fleet when the first 20 arrived in 1950. Built to the specification of Midland General they had no standard London Transport features, other than details such as interior colours and moquette. The single aperture indicator displays on the side and front only were not standard to Midland General either and the reason for the decision to go unnecessarily for a smaller display has yet to be explained. A.B. Cross

Country Buses was expecting to receive 246 new buses during the year and the first 36 came in February. The remainder were split into two more batches and delivery was not completed until 1951, because Weymann were instructed to return to the red livery to provide enough buses for the first stage of the tram conversion. The batch starting at RT 3115 marked the point at which Weymann switched to the new livery with only one central cream band and was also to take London Transport through another landmark with the reintroduction of full blind displays during Godstone's deliveries, starting with RT 3137. All new buses, red and green, should have changed to the new arrangement from 21st April

but the Central Bus change was delayed because there were to be large exchanges of vehicles between garages during imminent trials of RTWs along various narrow inner London streets. The changeover to full blinds on red buses therefore coincided with the first stage of tram conversion on 1st October. The livery change, on the other hand, took place at the same time on Park Royal and Leyland bodies but was delayed for another three months by Metro-Cammell and Saunders. Cravens did not change as their last RT was delivered in April.

The remarkable group of trials in which the entire allocation of buses on routes passing through particular bottlenecks was changed over to RTW, started with a five-day operation on all routes through Notting Hill Gate between 15th and 19th May. This was followed by two more covering routes through Shaftesbury Avenue, from 19th June to 2nd July, and Threadneedle Street from 3rd to 7th July. Although the police were reluctant to admit it and took their time in doing so, the trials proved conclusively that the use of 8-footers in central London was practicable. From then operation of 8-footers was allowed but still restricted to routes for which authority had been sought and granted. Unfortunately this came too late to have any worthwhile impact on the design of the RT and it was to be another eleven years before wider buses were to appear in any quantity. The only immediate effect was that towards the end of RTW deliveries they began to be allocated to inner London routes, first to route 74 in August and then at the very end of the year to route 31. The Executive did not wait long to start putting applications to the Licensing Authority and, starting in May 1951, a mass transfer of RTWs onto central London routes took place, the suburban garages getting RTs or RTLs in exchange.

The fate of the lowbridge STs and the 'Godstone' STLs seemed to be sealed in June when the first RLHs arrived. These had not figured in London Transport's planning until a late stage because they were part of an order diverted from the Balfour Beatty group company Midland General, which had recently been acquired by the BTC. As such, they were standard AEC Regent III 9612Es, differing in detail from the 3RT, with 'provincial' standard Weymann bodywork. Their arrival finally scotched London Transport's intention, under their post-war vehicle replacement plan, to develop a low height version of the RT which could have been used to replace the lowbridge and tunnel buses.

The first six RLHs replaced the STs on route

Left In common with all the austerity types, the lowbridge STL 19 bodies had a comparatively short life with London Transport, being withdrawn when the second batch of RLHs was received in 1952. STL 2232 had a 4/9STL chassis dating from 1937 and saw subsequent service with Hants & Sussex, Kemps of Woodcote and Chiltern Queens before being scrapped in 1960. A.B. Cross

336 and the rest were shared between Addlestone (436/461) and Godstone (410). Some of Addlestone's STL19s were also transferred into Godstone to complete the replacement of the 'Godstone' STLs but none of the displaced buses was taken out of stock. Instead, Country Buses used the STLs to restore the through working across Woking, which had been lost when the STL19s took over in 1943, and they were re-licensed in September. They were allocated to Addlestone and Guildford garages, where they stayed until replaced by the second batch of RLHs in 1952. The expansion of lowbridge operation put the available fleet at full stretch once more and this also gave the STs a reprieve until the end

of 1952. They were used mostly as spares but they did have a small official allocation on route 230 between July 1951 and October 1952.

Thirty-six of the RTs allotted to the Country Bus department (RT 3224–3259) were earmarked to replace the unsatisfactory Daimlers on the Romford Green Line routes and were licensed at the beginning of August. The only concession to their status as Green Line 'coaches' was their livery, Lincoln green for the main body panels and light green for the relief band. They were also fitted with metal 'Green Line' bullseyes between the decks on each side. Their blinds were interesting too, as they had amber lettering on a green background, an almost indecipherable combina-

tion, which was eventually replaced by a more conventional black on amber version. The Daimlers were supposed to stay with Country Buses and plans were formulated for their allocation to Watford (Leavesden Road) for works route 377, Watford (High Street) for routes 332 and 344, Northfleet for routes 495 and 496 and Dunton Green for route 431. The Country Bus engineering department was not happy about this because the Daimlers were oddities in the green fleet and while this did not matter when they were all together at Romford, it was likely to cause difficulties if they were split up among a number of garages. There then ensued yet another dispute between the two operating departments, Country Buses arguing for the Daimlers to go to Central Buses in exchange for a like number of STLs and Central Buses resisting with all their might, while the Daimlers languished unused. The problem was resolved unexpectedly when the staff at Merton asked for the Ds to be sent to them and this is what happened, concentrating the entire 181 at Merton garage.

The pace of change experienced in 1949 and 1950 was never repeated and the number of new buses taken in during 1951 was substantially down on the record 1950 figure. Leyland finished its RTW contract at the end of 1950, Saunders their second contract for 50 RTs in February 1951 and Metro-Cammell delivered its last RTL in March. The years of struggle with the double-deck fleet over, London Transport now concentrated on removing the last of its 'obsolete fleet', the ageing but much loved trams and simultaneously the renewal of the single-deck bus fleet.

Single-deckers had taken a back seat during the early post-war years, but this had not always been the intention. Had London Transport's plans for putting double-deckers onto the Green Line gone through, RTs would have replaced close on 300 of the oldest single-deckers, indirectly. This would have been enough to clear out everything built before 1936, leaving the rest to be replaced sometime after 1950 by which time the new generation of underfloor-engined single-deckers would be ready. The main replacement programme followed this plan almost exactly but the change of policy on Green Line left the oldest single-deckers to carry on for four or five years longer than intended, other than those which were released by the TDs and 15T13s.

The prototype AEC Regal IV, always known by its registration UMP227, was completed by AEC in 1949 and had gone into trial service with London Transport in May 1950, on route 355 at St Albans. This eventually led to orders for 700 of the type, all but 25 of which were built to the newly authorised maximum length of 30 feet. To maintain maximum flexibility in the fleet, however, they were all 7 ft 6 in wide. Whereas in the first post-war vehicle plan, the first new single-deckers were to have gone to Central Buses, the change of policy on Green Line meant that the coaches now took priority and were to receive the first 263 30-footers. The 25 short-wheelbase vehicles (RF 1–25) were delivered between April and June 1951 as Private Hire coaches and they were joined by fifteen 8-footers with ECW coach bodies (RFW). These were in addition to the main 700 and had been ordered to meet a British Transport Commission directive to London Transport to operate contract carriage services beyond their statutory boundary for a distance up to 100 miles from 55 Broadway. Delivery of the Green Line version began, slowly at first, on 14th September 1951 and the whole coach fleet had been replaced by October 1952.

Meanwhile, the prospect of having to wait until 1952 for relief from their problems was not popular with Central Bus drivers, who were only too aware that their department was home to all the oldest vehicles, while Country Buses and Coaches had a much younger fleet. This led to a continuing series of complaints and arguments, such as the demand that the 9T9s on loan from Country Buses and the 11T11s should be replaced. In January 1951, there was a nod towards meeting the request when the first of six 10T10s was transferred to Central Buses, nominally to replace 5Q5s, which had a similar layout to the RF, for use on familiarisation training. Serious relief had to await the delivery of the Green Line RFs but it came at last in the form of 40 10T10s which were stripped of their special coach features, such as linoleum floor coverings and ash trays, and painted red. Seven went to Loughton between August and November to replace the unloved 11T11s, others going to Hornchurch and Uxbridge, where the 9T9s were ejected, and in small numbers to various other garages. This released twenty-three 11T11s and fourteen 9T9s for scrap.

One final argument developed before Central Buses could embark on its own programme. For many years the staff at Muswell Hill garage had been disgruntled about the condition of buses on route 210, an arduous route with a number of steep gradients, not least the 1 in 9 of Highgate Hill. Although Muswell Hill had been among the first garages to get new buses in 1946 and then had some of the second batch of TDs later, few of these were allocated officially to the 210, which had to carry on with LTs. Matters were made worse in 1949 when the LTs were fitted with oil engines because in that form they were less lively and their performance on hills allegedly even

more lacklustre. A few TDs were allocated to relieve the tension but the majority of buses remained LTs and the discontent did not subside. Things came to a head again in 1952 when London Transport decided to withdraw the 6Q6 coaches, rather than redeploy them, because they said they were having difficulty in getting spare parts and claimed that they were not universally popular with drivers. The Trade Union had objected to this plan when it had been promulgated in March 1951 and they renewed their complaint when the 6Q6s went into store early in 1952. This time the Executive listened and 24 of the 6Q6s in best condition were allocated to Muswell Hill at the end of March, to tide the 210 over until the RFs began to arrive in September

Above Green Line RF 141 in Clarence Street Kingston soon after going into service. All the 30-footers had an identical basic body design with minor differences related to the type of work they were doing. A.B. Cross

Below The 10T10s looked good in the red Central Bus colours and brought a brief touch of luxury to the scene when they were used to bridge the gap until red RFs were available. T 539 was one of the last of the 40 which were repainted and is seen at Ealing while working from Southall garage on route 211. The Omnibus Society

The need for help in the battle of the queue is only too evident in this scene at London Bridge station, where not much more than half of the queue will be able to board Lewis Cronshaw's Duple-bodied Daimler coach on route 13. The bus stop post and the design of the flag both date from LGOC days and have survived the blitz which caused so much damage to the former LB&SC station in the background. LT Museum

THE PROGRAMME for the restoration of services after the Second World War on all forms of London Transport was completed during 1946 and by the end of that year the total mileage being operated by all road services was about 2.6 per cent in excess of the pre-war figure. To achieve this despite the lack of availability of new vehicles and the time expired nature of much of the fleet was no mean feat. Nevertheless queues for buses, particularly at peak times, were commonplace and, in June 1946 as an emergency measure the Board pressed into service every available vehicle on peak hour services in central London, as recorded in Chapter 3. Despite this, conditions remained bad as is well illustrated by a statement made by the then Operating Manager, Central Buses to the effect that the daily average mileage lost due to 'no bus available' was as high as 28,000 miles involving 425 buses.

So during the year plans were formulated to hire coaches from independent operators to supplement resources. Negotiations were entered into with the Passenger Vehicle Operator's Association, who represented the majority of independent coach proprietors in the London area, for the practicability and terms of hiring coaches during the 1947/48 winter period. Initially the PVOA identified about 450 coaches available but only 346 of these were located in areas convenient for Central Bus operation. They were the property of about 100 different owners and their carrying capacity was summarised as 32–35 seats (250); 27–31 seats (75) and 20–26 seats (21). Eighty-three of the larger coaches were diesel engined and the remainder were petrol powered. All would be required to be passed for stage carriage work by the Licensing Authorities and the Board's engineers would need to be satisfied as to their mechanical worthiness.

The coach owners insisted that they should be driven by their own drivers and not by LPTB employees and the terms negotiated for the hire of a coach with one driver per vehicle for a 5-day (Monday to Friday) week were as follows:

	Minimum charge per day for up to 60 miles	Additional charge per mile in excess of 60 miles
32–35 seaters	£5. 15s. 0d.	2s. 0d.
27–31 seaters	£5. 5s. 0d.	1s. 10d.
20–26 seaters	£4. 10s. 0d.	1s. 7d.

These terms provided for the coach owners to garage, maintain and lubricate the vehicles and included the wages cost of the driver. The Board would provide and pay for fuel used on the Board's services and for garage runs and would provide conductors. These prices were reckoned to be below the normal 'ring' prices for private hire work at the time but there was no doubt that the average cost per mile was well above the normal running costs incurred by the Board. It was estimated that operating 346 of these coaches 60 miles daily on Monday to Friday for five months would cost £292,500 against £206,500 if a similar exercise was carried out by the Board's own vehicles. Moreover the revenue earned on these vehicles would be lower than received on a normal double deck vehicle. In the report to the Board it was stated that 'the hiring of coaches would not be a good commercial proposition, but nevertheless it is considered that the relief given to the travelling public during peak hour operation would merit the financial loss involved.' This was accepted by the Board and in due course the Ministry of Transport acquiesced to the scheme.

Meanwhile negotiations were also taking place with the Trades Unions. Union representatives were disposed to be helpful in reaching a solution to the 'no bus available' problem which was making their member's lives difficult with public complaints about matters beyond their control. The Unions were adamant however that all drivers employed on these duties should be in membership of the Transport and General Workers' Union and that the coach drivers should receive the pay and allowances of the Board's own drivers for working the same duties. The difference between £1 per day (unbelievably the coach driver's flat rate pay at the time!) and the actual gross wages earned would be refunded to the coach owner and this would be over and above the hire charge already agreed.

Between 15th and 21st October 1947 the Licensing Authorities and the Board's engineers inspected the coaches at Chiswick Works at the rate of 60 a day and initially 325 coaches were allocated for duty commencing on Monday 27th October 1947.

The basis of operation was that the coaches would cover during the peak hours for 'no bus available' requirements and any surplus vehicles would operate as extras over the heavy traffic sections of the routes. They did not carry running numbers, although D.W.K Jones recorded that Elmers End allotted running numbers and garage codes. Destination bills and route numbers were provided which were usually stuck to the windows at the front and on the sides. In one or two cases it proved possible to insert proper blinds into destination boxes but this was very rare. Conductors were to be provided from spare or such other staff as the District Superintendents and local Union officials might agree. Special ticket boxes were provided marked Coach and two

Camden Coaches of Holloway supplied eight coaches to Chalk Farm and Holloway garages, most of them Bedfords, but also this handsome pre-war Harrington-bodied Dennis Lancet loading at Friern Barnet.
D.W.K. Jones

At the other extreme were the brand new AEC Regals supplied by Venture Transport of Hendon whose six coaches operated at various times on seven routes, but most commonly on several of Cricklewood's. SME83 is on route 16 in Park Lane.
F.G. Reynolds

The Leyland Tiger was one of the most numerous chassis makes offered by participants in the scheme but the age and condition could vary considerably. This 1932 vintage Harrington-bodied TS4 on route 27A at Archway station was originally owned by Southdown Motor Services and had been acquired by Ashford Belle a few years earlier. Note the chock under the nearside wheel, a requirement for buses parked on steep slopes such as Highgate Hill.
D.A. Ruddom collection

sets were distributed, one to be used for two days and the other for three days to cover the Monday to Friday week. Fare tables were supplied with the instruction that they should be placed in the most convenient position available inside each vehicle. Route learning by the coach drivers was to be a matter for local arrangement although a memorandum suggested that an 'N.B.A.' driver might travel on the coach to give guidance. One interesting instruction issued to drivers was that they should not normally pass other buses on the route. The reason for this is not recorded but it may have been to avoid the coach, with its relatively low capacity, from being overloaded if it were following a gap in service.

Various typewritten schedules of vehicles available and allocations to garages were produced and not surprisingly in the early stages these were subject to much amendment. Some operators included in the very early lists either never actually operated or only lasted a short while. For example, Jewell's Coaches of Croydon were originally shown as having one coach to be allocated to Elmers End; this was changed to Croydon before operation began and the operator was deleted from the lists a month later. Conversely eight additional coach operators were shown starting on 24th November 1947.

Although the initial scheme was planned just for the winter of 1947/48 its usefulness to the Board was so great that further negotiations were entered into resulting in its continuation, eventually through until August 1949. An additional 200 coaches were hired in the latter part of 1948 making a nominal total of 550.

New coaches continued to be submitted to the Licensing Authorities and the Board's engineers at Chiswick Works although from 3rd February 1949 this function transferred to Aldenham. A ledger was kept by the engineers of vehicles submitted for inspection although only the second has been seen which covers the period from 19th October 1948 onwards, the last entry being dated 16th May 1949. In some ways the rejection notes are more illuminating than the acceptances. Enterprise Coaches of Kenton submitted a 33-seat Maudslay with a modern registration – SML224 – but it was rejected because the entrance was deemed to be 'too narrow'; Ideal Coaches of Barking submitted a 32-seat AEC (AGF928) on 26th October 1948 but it was 'refused examination – too dirty'. Six weeks later it returned and was accepted – it obviously took time to remove the dirt! Rose Transport of Holloway submitted a 29-seat Bedford (JXT615) on 4th January 1949 which was rejected like the Maudslay mentioned before, because the entrance was too narrow but in this case it re-appeared two weeks later and was passed. One wonders what the owner's had done to it. S.V. Twigg (County Coaches) presented a 31-seat AEC which was rejected because 'both front spring

Another common combination was the Duple-bodied Bedford OB, in this case supplied by Leighton Coach Co. of Ilford for route 148 from Seven Kings. They could also be seen on the 23 and 145 from Barking. A.B. Cross

eyes broken' and it obviously took a week to get this put right.

So what were the coaches that invaded the London Transport scene for these 22 months? The variety was endless. They went from new AECs, Maudslays and the ubiquitous Bedford OBs to aged Gilfords, Leyland Cheetahs, Tilling Stevens and even SOS models. It was a pleasure to ride from Westminster to Woolwich in the contemporary luxury of a Royal Arsenal Co-operative Society AEC Regal Mark III on route 53A; it was best described as 'an experience' to ride from Victoria to Tottenham on one of Mr Champion's Gilfords on route 76. At the time petrol engines were still common on PSVs and London Transport was no exception, however some garages were exclusively diesel and so thought had to be given to the allocation of the coaches offered for service. Even so, there were cases where allowance had to be made for a coach to return home via another garage to that to which it was allocated in order to refuel with the correct ingredient. C.J. Worsley's Sunbeam operation provided two rather rare AEC Ranger coaches – normal control vehicles with petrol engines – that usually worked from Forest Gate on the 25B but at the end of the day it was necessary for them to call into Upton Park garage to refuel. At one time five petrol coaches worked from Twickenham garage, those belonging to Garners calling at Hounslow for fuel at the end of the day and the Martindale vehicles at Kingston.

Above C.J. Worsley's Sunbeam Coaches ran two of these 1934-vintage Cravens-bodied AEC Rangers on route 25B which, being petrol-engined, had to be refuelled at Upton Park each day, although operating from Forest Gate. Charles W. Clark's Metropolitan station building of 1926 broods over this busy scene at Aldgate which includes a Forest Gate STL on route 25B and two trolleybuses leaving the Minories Lay-by. J.C.R. Downey

Left At least 12 of these Leyland Cheetahs were hired from different operators at various times, most from Smith's Luxury Coaches of Park Royal, who supplied this one to run on route 92. Two faces of substitution are shown here with T 296, an 11T11 covering on double-deck route 105, behind the coach at Greenford 'Red Lion' stand. A.B. Cross

Ansell's Coaches of Peckham presented this rare 3-axle Albion Valkyrie, built in 1937 with Cowieson 39-seat body for Young's Bus service of Paisley. The variety of bus rolling stock at the time is well represented by this assortment in Strand waiting to cross Lancaster Place. There are pre- and post-war STDs, a 'sloping-bodied' STL and, its roof box peeping over the coach's back, a 5/1-type LT. A.D. Packer

One of the documents relating to the initial setting up of the scheme states that ten double deck vehicles were offered for hire but these were refused at the time by the Board. There is no indication of what these buses were or by whom they were owned. In the event it was not until October 1948 that some double-deck vehicles entered the scene. They were from two companies – Lansdowne Luxury Coaches of Leytonstone and Safeway Coaches of Walthamstow – and they all operated on Route 25B between Victoria and Becontree Heath. They were unusual to say the least – one being an AEC Regent that originated

with Burnley Corporation with a Brush centre entrance body with dual staircases, and another a double-deck Thornycroft, quite a rare breed.

Some former LPTB vehicles reappeared in London Transport service – most notably ex-TF 1 with Castle Coaches of Lewisham, which performed on route 1 between Marylebone and Lewisham, and ex-C 1 which appeared on behalf of J.M. Motors of Holloway on route 19 between Clapham Junction and Finsbury Park and later running for Overland Lismore of Kentish Town on route 68 between Upper Norwood and Kings Cross.

All of the Central Area garages operated hired coaches at one time or another with the notable exception of Loughton. This may have been due to its location in relation to the available firms hiring or it might have been the case that in many ways the garage operated as a sub-shed of Leyton who would have made vehicles available for any 'N.B.A.' situations at Loughton. This is however pure conjecture.

Dave Ruddom remembers that at the time he was at secondary school travelling each day between Muswell Hill and Crouch End on route 212 and he recalls that Horseshoe Coaches' Bedford OB, SMF380, usually appeared about the time he wished to travel. The regular driver was a bespectacled gentleman in a cloth cap and he

Left Another former LPTB vehicle to see London service again was C 1 which JM Motors of Holloway ran on route 19. It is seen loading in Highbury, where mixed tram and trolleybus operation is evident from the presence of both conduit track and traction standards. The Cub was later sold to Overland Lismore Coaches of Kentish Town who also hired it to London Transport, but ran it on route 68. W.J. Haynes

always seemed to be rather morose but perhaps that was the effect of a dozen or so schoolboys guaranteeing a noisy descent of Muswell Hill. Other journeys that remain in his memory were an unforgettable trip on an SOS belonging to Mountain Coaches on route 9 from Charing Cross to Liverpool Street and several times travelling home from Victoria to Muswell Hill on the green liveried AEC Regal BRO420 belonging to Lee's Luxury Coaches of Barnet. It was also travelling down Whitehall on a hired coach, on which route he cannot remember, that he became very excited at seeing a brand new RT working from Potters Bar on Route 134. It was the excitement of youth at something new but now he wishes he could have had more rides on the open back LTs that were about to disappear. But that is another story.

That vision of a sparkling new RT heralds the winding up of the PVOA hired coaches scheme. During 1948 and 1949 the rate of delivery of the long awaited new RT family vehicles picked up considerably and in addition, following the acquisition of control of the Tilling Group of companies by the British Transport Commission, around 25 per cent of their new vehicles were temporarily redirected into London Transport service. The lowbridge, sunken upper deck gangway configuration of these vehicles was as equally unsuitable for London operation as many of the hired

coaches but at least there was a standardisation of unsuitability. All this meant that during 1949 the hired coaches could be phased out. Despite some disquiet among Divisional Superintendents this programme went ahead and was completed by August 1949.

It took the form of five stages – 8th April (last day of operation for 100 coaches); 27th May (l.d.o. for 149); 24th June (l.d.o. for 101); 22nd July (l.d.o. for 125) and 19th August (l.d.o. for 58). Full details of the coaches operated and periods of operation will be given in a companion book.

Some of the more antique-looking hired vehicles were the four former Trent Motor Traction SOSs owned by Mountain Transport Services of Chelsea which could be seen on routes 74 and 96 from Putney Bridge or, as here, on the 9 from Mortlake garage.
The Omnibus Society

Right TF 1 was sold to Castle Coaches of Lewisham in 1946 and then reappeared in London Transport service from Catford garage in October 1947. It was most commonly seen on route 1, as here in Lancaster Place

approaching Waterloo Bridge, but also appeared on route 36 from time to time. Its new owner has made good use of the route board clips by fixing a panel advertising the company.
Surfleet Transport Publications

Another rarity, though more at home in London, was the AEC Reliance supplied by Rayner's Coachways of Feltham, who mustered three other chassis types among the five coaches operated on various routes at Hounslow. It is in Bridge Street Staines, with one of Hounslow's new RT3/1s and a Twickenham STL on route 90. D.W.K. Jones

So ended this very interesting and varied 22 month period in the London bus scene. The only time since when anything approaching it has been seen was during the overtime ban in early 1966 when several coach companies provided services to replace temporarily withdrawn London Transport routes. This however operated on a different basis and was nothing like the widespread appearance of coaches in the PVOA scheme of 1947/49.

Astute readers will have realised that all of the foregoing is concerned with the Central Area. The scheme did extend to the Country Area but information on what happened in this sphere is very difficult to trace. The Board's Annual Report for 1947 merely states that coaches were introduced later on Country Bus routes. The only Country Buses and Coaches schedule which has been traced is one dated 19th November 1947 headed 'Programme for Operation of Hired Independent Coaches as Agreed with PSVO [sic!] Ltd'. This then details 25 vehicles to be used as follows:

Chelsham: Six vehicles from Graves of Redhill on Route 408 operating a 30 mins supplementary service in weekday peaks between Warlingham and Epsom (in anticipation of approved programme of augmentation with new single-deck vehicles). *A note also states that the Chelsham vehicles would have to be re-fuelled at Reigate since no petrol was available at either Chelsham or Godstone.*

Leatherhead: Three vehicles from Greens of Walton on Route 406 providing duplication on weekday peaks between Epsom and Kingston. One vehicle from Bookham Saloons of Bookham on Route 406 providing duplication in weekday peaks between Epsom and Kingston.

Northfleet: One vehicle from G. Atkins of Hextable on Route 480 providing duplication in weekday peaks between Dartford and Horns Cross.

Reigate: Two vehicles from Graves of Redhill on Routes 405/414 providing a 30 mins supplementary service in weekday peaks between Redhill and Coulsdon (in anticipation of approved programme of augmentation with new single-deck vehicles).

St Albans: Two vehicles from Premier of Watford on Route 330 providing duplication in weekday peaks between St Albans and Welwyn Garden City via Hatfield.

Staines: Two vehicles from Graves [this is possibly a mis-type for Greens – see Leatherhead allocation] of Walton on route 460 providing a 30 mins service on weekdays between Staines (Bridge Street) and Laleham (in anticipation of approved programme of augmentation with new single-deck vehicles). *This is a strange entry since there is no record of the 460 route (Slough – Staines via Datchet) ever working beyond Staines to Laleham. At one time journeys worked on to Ashford but these had ceased with the 12th November 1947 programme. One can only assume that, as with several cases on these Roneo produced schedules, this routeing was in error.*

Windsor: One vehicle from Try of Windsor on route 458 providing duplication in weekday peaks between Slough and Uxbridge (in anticipation of approved programme of augmentation with new single-deck vehicles).

Left Double-deckers were at first refused by London Transport for some reason but were eventually accepted from two companies, one of them being Lansdowne Luxury Coaches of Leytonstone. This AEC Regent was formerly owned by Burnley Corporation who had specified a centre entrance and two staircases for its Brush body. D.W.K. Jones

Three vehicles from Try of Windsor on route 457 operating a 30 mins supplementary service in weekday peaks between Windsor and Uxbridge (in anticipation of approved programme of augmentation with new single-deck vehicles). Four vehicles from Try of Windsor on Routes 417/441/484 providing duplication in weekday peaks between Langley and Farnham Road (George) via Slough.

Photographic evidence shows that this scheme did take effect but at the time of writing nothing further has been established as to when it ceased. Premier were still working the 330 from St Albans in March 1948 and an undated photograph exists of a Windsorian Crossley coach working on Route 353 in Windsor, a route not included in the foregoing schedule.

There were later occasions when the Country Area borrowed coaches to supplement services –

Above A number of Duple utility-bodied Bedford WTBs were hired to London Transport, this one by Cream Coaches of Hackney.
J.F. Higham

Left The forward-control Leyland Cub was not a common animal and looked a little overwhelmed when fitted with a full-blown coach body. It must have been interesting to experience the performance of this Advance Coaches example on the climb up Chingford Mount with a full load taxing its 4.7 litre engine to the limit. The Bus Stop on the left is still fitted with the departure signal lights which used to be operated by a dispatcher from the tower behind it and alongside the LT.
Omnibus Society

notably at Luton and Watford during the overtime ban described in Chapter 6 and on the 351 between St Albans and Watford and also the 396 between Epping and Bishops Stortford, none of which had any connection to this scheme.

Although the arrival of the Tilling Group Bristols helped to create the circumstances in which it was possible to phase out the hired coaches scheme, this was not the reason why they were directed to London in the first place. This went back to a decision by the Government in the spring of 1948 to reduce the number of new PSVs which they would authorise for the home market,

Right The Great West Road was not unfamiliar with the Dennis marque, as the deep throbbing beat of Lancet II engines could be heard passing through at frequent intervals on the

Aldershot and District coach services, but this Cosy Coaches example was of an earlier generation.
D.A. Ruddom collection

Above Despite their name Paddington Transport Services, who supplied this AEC Regal for route 7A, were based at Kilburn. D.W.K. Jones

Right This Harrington-bodied AEC Regal owned by Superior Coaches of Tottenham has clearly settled in as part of the daily routine at Golders Green and occupies pole position on route 102. The Guy Arab behind it is on a garage run to Ponders End and alongside is STL2413, a 4/9STL14/1, on the rarely photographed route 58. D.A. Ruddom collection

which had been responsible for most of the short-fall of 745 in RT family deliveries during that year. The Executive did all it could to persuade ministers that the production rate should be increased but without any luck, which was not surprising when the economy desperately needed the income from exports. Meanwhile, seemingly unrelated events had been taking place in the Board room of the Tilling Group. Early in 1948 the Tilling Board had reached the conclusion that the best interests of their shareholders would be served by selling the bus businesses to the British

Transport Commission. As the Commission already had a minority interest in each of the companies through shareholdings formerly held by the main line railway companies, the Tilling group became a wholly owned constituent of the BTC.

The deal was sealed in September and the Commission's Road Passenger Transport Executive lost little time in issuing a directive to Tillings to divert 25 per cent of its new buses to London. The agreement was for a total of 200 – 44 highbridge and 156 lowbridge – but this was later reduced in total to 190 and the split revised to 45 and 145. Twelve of the 19 Tilling companies were embroiled in the scheme, the largest contributors being the Eastern Counties Omnibus Co, with 38 buses, and Hants & Dorset Motor Services Ltd with 39. In both cases this represented about 12 per cent of their total double-deck fleet, making them also by far the largest proportionate contributors. Significant operators like Bristol Tramways, Lincolnshire Road Car, Thames Valley, Wilts & Dorset and the three West Yorkshire companies escaped the net. The operators who were involved were displeased, to put it mildly, at being deprived of their new buses, as they too all had old fleets in need of replacement. The widespread view was that London Transport had created its own difficulties by insisting on waiting for its standard bodies to go into production, whereas acceptance of non-standard designs until the production lines were ready could have put them about 18 months ahead on deliveries.

The Executive created a few difficulties of its own in the way it decided to allocate the vehicles, which brought it into conflict once more with the ever suspicious Metropolitan Police and the Licensing Authority. The greatest need for relief was in the Central Area and it was to that department that all but ten of the Bristols went. The ten exceptions were assigned to Country Buses where the indigenous lowbridge fleet was at full stretch and shortages frequently had to be covered by single-deckers. For the Central Area London Transport had decided that the borrowed buses should be spread as widely as possible geographically, with an allocation to each of the 27 engineering 'parent' garages and a planned maximum of seven at any one garage. In this way as many Londoners as possible would see for themselves that London Transport was making a determined effort to improve travelling conditions. The Met Police, on the other hand, had always objected to the operation of lowbridge buses within its area because the arrangement of

the upper deck with a side gangway slowed down the process of boarding and alighting unacceptably, causing delays and congestion at stops. This strict rule had been relaxed only slightly during the war to enable double-deckers to be operated on strategically important routes 127 and 230 and any attempt to widen the scope of such operations was vigorously opposed. Even in this emergency they were in no mood to co-operate, remained as stubborn as ever in their determination to keep lowbridge buses off the streets of London and were inclined at first to refuse approval altogether. When they did yield they did not bend far and produced a list of no fewer than 52 routes from which they would wish to see the lowbridge buses barred. This was eventually reduced to 16, all serving Oxford Street or Oxford Circus, but

Above An exceptionally interesting example of the little-recorded operation of coaches in the Country Area is this Dennis Arrow of Windsorian Coaches, working on route 353 at Castle Hill with a 10T10 in the background. A.B. Cross

Below These eight pristine buses were delivered to London Transport on 7th May 1949, when most of the Bristols were already at work in the Capital. The group comprises two Eastern Counties highbridge and six United Automobile Services lowbridge specimens, which were to go into service at Potters Bar, Putney Bridge, Cricklewood and Hanwell. D.W.K. Jones

each route on which the Bristols were to run had to be approved individually and the list was severely restricted. To ensure that they did not stray onto routes for which approval did not exist, their blinds carried displays only for the approved routes, although at Plumstead the 53A was included, despite being on the Police embargo list.

The allocation took some juggling by London Transport who were also constrained by several other factors, not the least being the restricted headroom of many garages, already noted in connection with the allocation of the austerity and RT family buses, which made them unsuitable for the highbridge ECW body. One route which is known to have been rejected for this reason was the 133, which had been put down as the one on which Croydon would use its highbridge Bristols. As it had short-workings turning in Streatham garage, which did not have enough headroom, it had to be deleted. The same fate befell the Sunday RT allocation on route 59, which had to be replaced by STLs when summer schedules including Streatham garage shorts were introduced in April 1949. Overhead bridges on the road also had to be taken into account as even those with a clearance acceptable for RTs were not necessarily suitable for the highbridge Bristols. An example of this, which inspired a series of warnings being issued to Croydon garage not to use their Bristols on route 12, was the railway bridge at Bingham Road station.

Another restriction which applied to all the borrowed buses was one of parking capacity in garages. The Executive's fleet contained few buses with hinged driver's cab doors, as fitted to the Bristols, most either having no door at all or the sliding variety as on the RT family and the parking arrangements at garages were planned accordingly. Many did not have the space between rows for hinged doors to be opened and these were either omitted from the list, or alternative arrangements were made for parking outside the garage shed. One other much less serious factor which seems to have been given at least a little

Top The sweet running AEC-engined Bristol K was a happy choice for Country Bus operation, where it would have been more than a match for the elderly STs running on the 336. TD893 was one of the three additional Hants & Dorset machines sent in February 1949 to Amersham, where they stayed until being returned to their owner in March 1950. D.A. Thompson

Above There were seven Brighton Hove & District highbridge K5Gs, 6401 being among the earliest of the Bristols to arrive, in January 1949. Their red and cream livery and their use of normal restricted indicator displays, although badly adjusted on this occasion at Stoke Newington Common, made them look comfortably at home in London. D.A. Thompson

Right The lower deck interior of a standard ECW lowbridge body, showing the rather austere seats then used and the gangway intruding from the upper deck, which provided a new hazard for London travellers. The extra pillar on the front bulkhead at the inner edge of the sunken gangway was a characteristic of this design. Ken Glazier collection

Above The allocation of highbridge Bristols like Eastern Counties LKH 125 to Sutton garage was no doubt dictated by its ability to accommodate their height, although this type would have been more acceptable to the police in central London rather than on routes passing through Morden. The open cab door on Crosville's lowbridge MB327 demonstrates one of the other quirks that had to be accommodated in allocating these buses. *D.W.K. Jones*

thought was the confusion that might have been caused by running green Bristols on route 87, alongside similar Eastern National buses between Romford and Gidea Park. Any doubts there might have been were obviously overcome but one simple solution which was not adopted and may not even have been considered would have been to allocate to Barking only buses supplied by Caledonian, Westcliff-on-Sea and United Auto, all of which were red.

The first five Bristols, three belonging to Eastern National and two to Western National, were delivered to London Transport, straight from the manufacturer, on 7th December 1948 and continued to arrive at roughly weekly intervals until 13th June 1949, by which time 180 had been received. Another ten came from Crosville in November 1949 not to enlarge the fleet but to release a like number for belated delivery to their rightful owners. All were Bristol Ks, 77 with AEC 95 bhp 7.7 litre engines (K6A), 113 with Gardner 5LW 85 bhp 7 litre engines. All the highbridge Bristols were K5Gs. They were delivered to Chiswick in the colours and with the legal lettering of their owning company but without fleet names and, in many cases, without fleet numbers. By chance, all the highbridge buses came from two companies, both of which used red liveries, whereas the great majority of the lowbridge ones were green, the only red ones being those mentioned earlier.

They were all fitted with holders for garage plates and running numbers and had specially made metal bullseyes attached to their radiator grilles. The destination apertures, front and back, were filled with the legend LONDON TRANSPORT flanked by two bullseyes, destination information being confined to the larger box. On all but the Brighton Hove & District vehicles, 'to and from' (so-called 'lazy') displays were carried by those in Central Bus service. Those allocated to Country Buses usually had individual readings which had to be changed for each journey and a similar arrangement was made on the Brighton buses, which had a box more compatible with the standard London restricted display. Why it was decided not to have individual displays on others operated by Central Buses is not known, but a similar decision was taken in 1951 for the STLs used as extras on normal routes during the Festival of Britain. This could suggest that there might have been a school of thought that considered such displays appropriate for special operations.

The five pioneers went into service on 6th December 1948, the two Western National K6As

Above Route 68 was unique in having an assignment from each of its three operating garages at various times. Crosville K6A MB 333, allocated to Chalk Farm, is seen at Camberwell Green with not another bus in sight, just a distant E3 tram making off down Camberwell Road on route 35. The Birmingham Guild bus stop post and early design of LT flag are worthy of note. *A.B. Cross*

Below Only 23 of the lowbridge Bristols were painted red, 18 of them coming from United Automobile Services of Darlington, whose BDO 109 is seen working from Cricklewood garage on route 2 at Golders Green. Norwood garage also ran Bristols on route 2. *D.W.K. Jones*

West Green was the only garage to have an official allocation of Bristols, a total of fifteen being allocated to routes 144 and 144A. They were all K6As, a mixture of Crosville and Hants & Dorset with a solitary Western National example. This is Hants & Dorset's TD904 when still new.

Southern National K5G 911 was joined at Nunhead by reallocated Eastern National buses when the second delivery of Crosvilles arrived in November 1949. This bus stayed at Nunhead for a year from March 1949 to March 1950.
C.F. Klapper/Omnibus Society

ated in fairly flat territory and which already had a considerable number of Gardner-engined Guys, yet the buses sent there were Hants & Dorset K6As.

Passengers had to cope with the hazards of the low ceilings on the upper deck and the protrusion of the sunken gangway into the lower. These were not only unfamiliar in London but were also encountered randomly and many a curse could be heard above the clatter of the Gardner engine as unsuspecting heads collided with rigid metal. Conductors also had to master the techniques of fare collection from a side gangway on the upper deck with half the passengers out of reach on the nearside of the bus.

All the initial allocations to Country Buses were the more powerful K6A, probably better suited to the terrain in which they were to operate and the first to enter service were five from Hants & Dorset, on 17th December. Three went to Godstone, where they operated on route 410 alongside the 'Godstone' STLs, one to Amersham for route 336 and one to Reigate, although this was swiftly reallocated to Godstone. Amersham took three more Hants & Dorset K6As in February and these were used on both routes 336 and 353, while Reigate got two more at the same time, which it used on routes 405 and 430. Country Buses were not subject to the same degree of restriction as Central Buses as most of their area was outside the fiefdom of the Metropolitan Police, but the Bristols were nevertheless supposed to be confined to those routes shown on their blind sets. This did not allow for the maverick tendency present in most garage engineers, as those at Reigate managed to fit an STL blind to one of theirs so that it could run on the 411 and there may well have been other examples of such practice.

Deliveries to Central Bus garages continued through the first half of 1949 until the last of the initial 180 was licensed on 16th June, by which time the target of 27 garages had been achieved. The 145 lowbridge type were spread around 20, 11 operating KSGs, and nine K6As, and the 45

from Plumstead garage on the 53, by this time a short suburban route between Greenwich and Plumstead Common, and the three Eastern National K5Gs from Camberwell on route 137, right through the heart of the West End and the area from which the Police wanted them banned. They were greeted with mixed feelings by passengers and staff alike. The K5Gs, in particular were noisy vehicles which suffered a lot of vibration from the five-cylinder engine and the relatively slow action of the gearbox, combined with the low power output, gave drivers a hard time. Route 137 had some severe gradients on its approach to the southern heights at Crystal Palace and the decision to give it the first of the K5Gs was an early illustration of how Central Buses apparently made no particular effort to confine them to more easily graded routes. Neither was any apparent effort made to put the K6As onto the tougher routes. In fact the very next garage to get Bristols was Barking, most of whose routes oper-

highbridge K5Gs were distributed to seven. The seven from Brighton Hove & District all went to Tottenham for routes 73 and 76 (and its adjunct the 34B). As already noted, these were unique in having a blind layout of a style showing some London influence which had been in use in Brighton since the early 1930s. This included a 'via' box suitable to carry the standard London Transport restricted display and they therefore had normal route and destination displays. They were also unique in having Brighton's standard red and cream livery, all of which in combination made them look quite at home on the streets of central London. The other 38 were all from Eastern Counties and many of them were allocated to suburban routes or to inner London routes which avoided the heart of the West End, a seemingly unnecessary snub to the Police. For example, Victoria ran theirs on routes 10, 77 and 77A, not the 137, and Putney Bridge on the 93, rather than, say, the 14 or 30.

A summary of the vehicles borrowed, the garages to which they were allocated and the routes operated is given in Appendix 3. In most cases routes operated by more than one garage had Bristols from only one of them but both routes 2 and 11 had some from each of their two garages, while route 68 took the jackpot by having them from three. Where more than one route is shown alongside a garage in the list it usually indicates that they were operated simultaneously but in a few cases the Bristols were moved from one route to another when new RT family buses were allocated, although this did not happen invariably. On route 11, for example, when Dalston received its RTs, the Bristols remained on the route until they were withdrawn, whereas at Hammersmith they moved over to route 72. When Croydon got RTs for routes 166 and 166A, the Bristols were transferred to route 68, on which they had already appeared fairly often, while the arrival of RTWs at West Green also led to some reshuffling described below. In many other cases, the arrival of the new buses coincided with the despatch of the Bristols to their owners.

The Bristols were regarded as members of the back-up fleet and, like the hired coaches and the reserve of 'obsolete' buses, were not shown as part of the official allocation. Such was the state of the fleet this had little practical effect as they were always required for service, as were all the other back-up buses. However, they did not normally run on Sundays when, the engineers were told rather quaintly, 'they may rest'. For this reason Sunday route variations were not normally shown on the blinds but, as ever there were cases where such displays were provided, probably in error, such as the North Wembley destination on route 72. There was one exception to these rules. As mentioned in Chapter 7, at the request of the Trade Union route 144 had been added to the list of routes which received RTs in Leyton's first big allocation in 1947 and the route had, ever since, been a mixture of LTs from West Green and RTs

Eastern Counties LKH 138 was one of the last four to go home on 2nd June 1950, having spent just over a year at Potters Bar. It is standing alongside post-war STL 2693 in the elegant surroundings of Holden's St Albans bus station.
D.W.K. Jones

from Leyton. This broke one of the rules of the replacement programme, that RTs should not 'run against' STs, LTs and petrol-engined STLs. As West Green was not due to receive new buses for the 144 for some time, the Trade Union asked for Bristols to replace the LTs as an interim measure. This was agreed and the arrangement was extended to include route 144A, bringing the total allocated to 15. As West Green was scheduled to operate only three fewer buses on Sundays than Mondays to Fridays this left insufficient RTLs and LTs to cover the Sunday schedules alone. West Green therefore became the exception in another respect by having eight Bristols assigned to route 144 on Sundays, the balance of its needs being met by RTLs spare from route 29. Although not recorded as an official allocation, Bristols must also have worked route 144B on Sundays, as it had a larger allocation on Sunday and there would not have been enough LTs to cover all its requirements. Routes 144 and 144A received an allocation of new RTWs in November 1949 and eight of the Bristols were transferred elsewhere. The other eight were transferred to route 144B for the few weeks until January 1950 when it in turn got new buses, RTLs, and four more of the Bristols were transferred. The remaining four spent the rest of their time at West Green on route 29 before being returned to their owners in April.

Under the terms of the agreement with Tillings, the Bristols were due to be returned at an average rate of 29 every four weeks, starting in the last four weeks of December when 35 were to go back, and finishing with a final batch of six in the second half of June. During October 1949, 'Bill' Durrant, the Chief Mechanical Engineer, made an approach to Mr Arnold of Tillings with a view to slowing down the rate of return in the early months, to ease the transition to covering

The mustardy brown of Maidstone Corporation's Brush-bodied Daimler CVG6 mingles with the reds of equally aberrant Eastern Counties Bristol K6A and Park Royal-bodied Daimler CWA6 at Morden, where the sight of a standard London bus was something to remark. D.W.K. Jones

The Brush bodies on the Maidstone CVG6s were in marked contrast to the products from the same manufacturer which could also be seen at Morden on Merton's utility Daimlers. Number 82 was one of the first two to arrive, in March 1949, and remained at Sutton until all three were returned in September 1950. D.W.K. Jones

National and Southern Vectis buses went home on 10th and 11th November. As the newcomers were K6As and the returnees KSGs, direct replacement was not practicable so there was a little reshuffle of allocations to enable Camberwell and Harrow Weald to switch from Gardner to AEC. Camberwell took seven of the new K6As, releasing three of the Eastern National buses which had to go back, the others being at Norwood (1) and Nunhead (2), while the latter also had one of the Southern Vectis vehicles. They took Camberwell's remaining four KSGs in exchange. The other Southern Vectis bus was at Harrow Weald which was allocated the remaining three Crosvilles and two Hants & Dorset K6As now redundant at West Green, while its other two K5Gs went to Willesden. Each of these two garages therefore had a temporary increase in stock but, by now, the re-allocations were beginning to coincide with the main programme of returning the Bristols which began with Western National 878 on 8th December. The last four to be returned, on 2nd June 1950, were Eastern Counties LKH 136 and 138 at Potters Bar and Putney Bridge respectively, Brighton 6406, Tottenham, and Eastern National 4034 at Nunhead.

This was not the end of the affair. London Transport was able to make up the difference between the number of Bristols originally promised and those actually received, by tapping two unlikely sources. Both were municipal operators and the first was the tiny Maidstone Corporation which had only 25 motor buses (and 19 trolleybuses) to its name. From this small resource the Corporation found it possible to lend three Brush-bodied Daimler CVG6s, the first two arriving on 29th March 1949 and the third on 24th October. This generosity of spirit is believed to have been associated with the Corporation's having problems meeting their loan charges, a factor which could explain why the CVG6s survived the other hired buses in London service by several months. They were sent to Sutton garage where they led an uneventful life running alongside the Executive's own CWA6 Daimlers, their distinctive gingery brown livery adding another shade to the spectrum of colours on the local bus

schedules exclusively with London Transport vehicles. A revised schedule was agreed, which reduced the number to be returned in December to 14, the full schedule being as follows:

Schedule:	Original	Revised (First version)	Revised (Final version)
13th period 1949	35	14	14
1st period 1950	21	10	10
2nd period 1950	33	20	20
3rd period 1950	28	35	40
4th period 1950	20	34	40
5th period 1950	37	40	40
6th period 1950	6	21	18
7th period 1950	Nil	8	Nil
Totals	180	182	182

The mysterious increase of two in the total came from another part of the revised agreement. Mr Arnold had asked for the early return (on 13th November) of six Eastern National and two Southern Vectis vehicles. In compensation an extra ten were to be diverted from Crosville, thereby increasing the total on hand by two for a short time. The Crosvilles duly arrived, five each on 4th and 8th November, and the eight Eastern

Right Leeds had pioneered the use of fluid transmission outside London in 1934 with a batch of AEC Regents similar to contemporary STLs, carrying well-proportioned bodywork by its local bodybuilder Chas. H. Roe. One of these, Leeds 133, is seen deep in Metropolitan Kent at the Downe terminus of route 146A while on loan between November 1949 and June 1950. In common with nearly all hired vehicles, double-ended destination displays were carried and London Transport's identity was established by the bullseye fixed to the radiator, while the Leeds insignia remains prominently displayed on the side.
C.F. Klapper/Omnibus Society

scene. They had indicator apertures which were the right size to take a standard London Transport display and, as they were so similar to Sutton's own stock, no restrictions were placed on their use. They therefore ran on any route the allocation man happened to choose, although they are not thought to have run often, if at all, on route 151 and their operation was normally confined to peak hours and Saturdays.

The second municipality to offer help was Leeds, who were willing to supply twenty pre-war oil-engined AEC Regents with a mechanical specification, similar to the Executive's own STLs from the same period, including 7.7 litre engines, preselective gearboxes and fluid flywheels. During negotiations, the number was reduced to 18 but one of those delivered to Chiswick was failed by the Certifying Officer, saw no service in London and was returned to Yorkshire after only five weeks, leaving 17 to be used. All but one carried 56-seat bodywork by the Corporation's favoured Leeds-based bodybuilder, Charles H. Roe Ltd, well known for its elegant and restrained designs. The exception was number 201, a Weymann product with extravagantly downward sloping front and rear windows. It had been an exhibit at the 1935 Commercial Motor Show, when this sort of 'streamline' styling was enjoying a brief vogue.

Like the Bristols, the 'Leeds STLs' – as they became known – were to have been split between three garages with allocations of six or seven each, these being Bromley, Hackney and Twickenham all of which operated STLs at the time. But during negotiations with the Trade Union, it was agreed that all 17 should go to Bromley, where they were to be allocated to routes 61, 138 and 146A which between them had a peak output of 18 buses. An internal document dated 27th September 1949, sent to the Rolling Stock Engineer at Chiswick, gave instructions for routes 47, 119 and 126 to be added to the blinds but there is no evidence that any Leeds buses ever operated on any of these routes. It is interesting to note in passing that the official allocation for routes 61, 138 and 146A remained STL while they were being operated almost exclusively by Leeds buses, adding a little credence to the idea that they were regarded as STLs in all but name.

The first Regent, Leeds 194, arrived well ahead of the others on 9th August, presumably so that Chiswick's watchful experts could give it a thorough going over before the others came. The rest came in batches between 12th and 24th Sep-

tember and the first two were licensed at Bromley on 5th October. It then took until 10th November for all the others to go into service, the longest delay being to 216 which remained at Chiswick from 14th September until 11 November. Bromley began to receive a fresh assignment of RTs during May 1950, which were placed onto routes 61, 94 and 146A. The agreed plan had been for them to go onto routes 119, 126 and 138 but this had been changed because it had been decided that these routes should have RTWs, which in turn began to arrive in June. This immediately reduced the scope for using the Leeds buses and could have been an occasion for them to be placed on one or more of the other authorised routes as none was withdrawn until 12th June, by which time the eight-footers had begun to arrive. The last three went back on 27th June and none saw any further service with their owners.

They were not the last to leave, however. The three Maidstone Daimlers continued to run at Sutton until they were sent home on 19th September 1950. Their departure home marked the end of the years of famine in the double-deck bus fleet. Only eleven days later the first stage of the south London tram 'conversion' scheme would take place, a project which had been held in abeyance while the bus fleet was restored to health.

Below The odd-man-out among the AEC Regents borrowed from Leeds City Transport was this Weymann-bodied example which had been an exhibit at the Commercial Motor Show in 1935. The exaggerated downsweep of the front windows and windscreen were in vogue at the time and a more restrained version of it even found its way into the design of RT1. It is on the stand in Sherard Road at Well Hall station, Eltham, with a new Sidcup RTL in the background on route 132. D.W.K. Jones

9   RECOVERY AT LAST

Stone Quarry Estate East
Grinstead was served for the
first time in May 1949 by a
short extension of route 424
from the town. Q7, seen in
London Road, was typical of the
rolling stock encountered on
the route in the post-war years
until the RFs arrived in 1953.
Gavin Martin collection

THE FABLED SUNLIT uplands at last came into view during 1949 as the improving health of the bus fleet, painfully slow though it was, gradually allowed resources to be devoted to new services. It was a sad irony that this coincided with the start of a decline in the total number of passengers but, important as it was as a pointer to the future, the decline was irrelevant to the needs of the moment. Services, especially at peak travel times, were by now falling so far short of meeting demand that improving service standards had to be the first priority and, for the first time since 1946, there was a significant increase in the peak vehicle requirement during the year. Central Buses added 120 double-deckers and 19 single-deckers and, although the Country Bus total remained unchanged, they did make the most of the better performance of the RTs by reducing some running times so releasing a few extra buses which could be used for service improvements.

The first half of 1949 went on much as before, with a few minor service improvements and some new routes introduced by Country Buses at almost no cost in vehicles. Perhaps one of the most significant was the short extension on 18th May of ST-operated route 316 in Hemel Hempstead to Adeyfield, an area being developed for the New Town. Others on the same day were the first service to Stone Quarry Estate, East Grinstead, an extension of route 424 at no cost, and a new Monday-Friday one-man-operated route 492 between Gravesend and West Kingsdown which needed one Cub. Two more new Cub routes started on 15th June: the 393 between Harlow and Hoddesdon, starting off through the green fields and villages which would soon be engulfed by the New Town; and the long-delayed 479 between Dartford and Swanley via Horton Kirby. On the same day another 'free' spur working was added to the 424 between Smallfield and Horne. Country Buses continued in this vein, adding an extension of the 413A to Four Elms, unserved since the takeover of West Kent in 1939 because it was outside the LPTB area, and a new route 481 from Dartford to Bow Arrow Lane (Temple Hill Estate) on 6th July.

Buses had come first to Cassiobury Park estate in north-west Watford on 5th January 1949 when route 322 was diverted through it on its way from Watford to Hemel Hempstead but the 322 was a very busy single-deck route and the need for a free-standing service was quickly apparent. This materialised on 5th October as the 332 which ran through Watford to Bushey station using one 4Q4 and its introduction coincided with some restructuring of local services. This saw the end of the 334/A (Croxley Green/Watford Met Station – Brockley Rise) most of their routes being covered by a new peak-hour only 344 (Watford Met Station – Brockley Rise) and by changes to route 385. This was diverted to run via Vicarage Road, Queens Avenue and Whippendell Road instead of Rickmansworth Road, and extended from Croxley Green station to Manor Way, all covering the former 334. At a time when services generally were being improved, these changes contained some substantial cuts which raised a tumult among the users. What they had lost were an off-peak service to Watford Met Station, a bus service along Queens Road, a large proportion of the peak service along Rickmansworth Road and one of the busiest picking-up points on route 385 at Pond Cross Roads.

Other small changes at the end of the year, all made without adding a single bus to the schedule, were a new experimental 455B from Beaconsfield to Cliveden Hospital which started on 2nd November, the extension of short-working 383s from Walsworth into Purwell Lane Estate on 9th November and the diversion of some journeys on the 469 at Knowle Hill to serve Trumps Green, another operation outside the London Transport statutory area, on 7th December.

Central Buses turned their first important corner on 22nd June 1949. That day marked the start of a series of sizeable increases in frequency on a number of routes, so resuming the restoration of standards which had been interrupted in

1947. Two buses were added to the 237 and this was followed up a week later with a total of 18 buses being added to routes 53A, 89, 103 and 175. So it went on and by the end of the year 129 extra buses (a 3 per cent increase) had been allocated for this purpose. These improvements were important and badly needed but did not carry the portentous significance of some of the contents of the winter programme, which started on 26th October and for the first time contained six new or extended routes. They were modest enough, a mere ten buses being needed, but they were a clear signal that the bad times were over and the promise made in 1946, that the development of services to 'outlying areas' would be resumed, could at last be redeemed. The routes included the first new service for Harold Hill Estate, the 86B from Romford (New Mill Inn) operated by two Guys from Hornchurch. At this early stage it covered no new ground and reached only as far as Myrtle Road in Straight Road, where there had been some pre-war building. There was also a new 120A (Hounslow Heath – Greenford 'Civil Engineer'), short-working 120s extended to serve Lady Margaret Road Southall for one extra STL; route 233 was given a long extension from Wood Green to Northumberland Park, serving some very old residential areas in Perth Road and White Hart Lane and using three extra Qs; the 234 was extended from Mitchley Avenue to Selsdon for one LT single-decker; a new single-deck 243 gave Upshire its first route (to Waltham Cross) using two TDs utilising the number vacated the same

One of several development routes started with Cubs by Country Buses, the 479, on which C 22 is seen, forged the link through the lanes south of Horton Kirby to Farningham.
L.E. Akehurst collection

Left Some journeys on route 469 were diverted to Knowle Hill in December 1949, restoring a section lost before the war because it was outside the Board's statutory area. One of the scheduled STLs was replaced with a T but the Virginia Water service continued to be double-deck and STL 1971 was working such a journey from Staines West station the following year, by which time the Godstone STLs had arrived on the Addlestone lowbridge routes. J.H. Aston

Centre left One-man operated Cubs ran in the Central Area for the last time on 19th July 1949 on routes 238 and 252. Weymann bodied C81, seen ten days earlier, was one of thirteen survivors from the original Central Bus batch which, unlike their country cousins, did not have a bumper bar. PSV Circle

day by Nunhead circular route which became 173; and the 248 was extended to Hall Lane (River Drive) from Upminster station at the cost of one TD. These set the trend for 1950 when a succession of new and extended routes was introduced.

The first of the year was new route 71 which started on 11th January 1950 and ran from Kingston to Richmond by an indirect route serving mainly pre-war housing in the pockets alongside Richmond Park (Park Road and Tudor Drive) and between the river and Ham Common (Dukes Avenue and Lock Road). Kingston was allocated five STLs. For some reason London Transport chose to give the 71 a big publicity boost, proclaiming inaccurately that it was the first new post-war route. Perhaps the leafy glades of Ham and Richmond were considered better promotion fodder than Harold Hill, Southall or Upshire. Only a week later the isolated area of established housing lying between the railway and the River Roding west of Debden got a new service in the form of single-deck route 254, whose introduction had been deferred from the December programme. To link as many areas as possible to the shops in Loughton and to at least one station, the route was in the form of a pan-handle. Starting from Buckhurst Hill station it ran through Loughton Way then in a loop passing Loughton station, High Road, Church Hill, Rectory Lane and Oakwood Hill to meet its 'handle' at Rectory Road on its way to terminate at Loughton station. This brought single-deckers back to Loughton garage after a lapse of nearly four years, the buses allocated being 11T11s.

Route 174 made its appearance in the summer programme on 3rd May, running between Romford ('Parkside Hotel') and Dagenham. It opened up new territory south of Roneo Corner through Dagenham Road, and restored the service to Oxlow Lane which had been a victim of wartime cuts. Pressure on space at Hornchurch garage was no doubt the reason why it was allocated to distant Barking, who supplied four Guys. Later in the year, on 11th October, the 174 absorbed the

Right Route 174 restored a service to Oxlow Lane as well as opening new territory in Dagenham Road when it started in May 1950. Park

Royal-bodied G135 is at New Road, Dagenham during the five months when Romford Parkside Hotel was the northern terminus. A.B. Cross

comparatively new 86B and its allocation at Hornchurch to run from Dagenham to Harold Hill (Myrtle Road), simultaneously almost doubling the service at the Harold Hill end for the price of one bus. Also in the summer programme two more isolated area of pre-war housing were served by new single-deck route 264. This ran from Hersham Green taking in Rydens Road and Ambleside Avenue south of the reservoirs at Walton-on-Thames, and the rather less promising road through Upper Halliford on its way to French Street, Sunbury. As it crossed Walton Bridge which had a severe weight limit, its allocation was restricted to 1T1s supplied by Kingston garage. The service via Upper Halliford lasted only until 10th October, after which the route ran via Sunbury village and Green Street.

The winter programme on 11th October witnessed the restoration of another pre-war service, although no extra roads were served, as well as yet another new route. The restored route was the 4 between Finsbury Park and Bermondsey ('Queen Charlotte'), which had last run in 1942, formed out of the extension of some 4A shorts from Elephant & Castle. Its six bus an hour frequency was only one-third of its pre-war level because much of its route, through Aldersgate and in Bermondsey had been so devastated during the Blitz that their populations were a fraction of pre-war. The new route was the 65A which was an extension of some shorts off the 65 from Hook to Copt Gilders Estate Chessington, achieved with the use of only one extra RT.

There was another case of a pre-war facility being restored in the first stage of the south London tram conversion on 1st October, although its withdrawal had been under rather different circumstances. New bus route 170 restored the

The old District Line station at Ealing Broadway was still in active service when Turnham Green's RT 318 made this journey to Copt Gilders estate, first served by the 65A in October 1950. *A.B. Cross*

through service from Wandsworth to Hackney which had been cut in December 1939 when an immediate conversion to trolleybus of route 31 was no longer on the cards. The 31, alone of the subway routes, had then lost its own north London section and been diverted instead to follow the 33 and 35 to Islington. Full details of this and other conversions are in Chapter 10.

The heart of Harold Hill estate was reached on 6th December when the Collier Row to Harold Wood short-workings on route 247 were extended through The Avenue, Chelmsford Road and Gooshays Drive to terminate at Hilldene Avenue and renumbered 247A. A small part of this estate, on the western and southern flanks, had been

Unlike most other new Country Bus routes at the time, the 459 was not one-man operated, although the pre-war section of the 220 to Richings Park which it effectively restored, had been. T 658 passes RT 3198, one of those allocated to High Wycombe in 1950, in Bakers Road, Uxbridge. *A.B. Cross*

built before the war but the area around the old farm, roughly where Central Park was established later, had now been covered with new LCC housing. (The farm, incidentally, was as yet still intact and working and continued in being for some years.) The 247A was joined at the roundabout on 20th February 1952, by the 174 extended from its temporary terminus at Myrtle Road via Hilldene Avenue. By this time the Guys had begun to go and both routes were operated by STLs. So too was the 246 which made its appearance on 17th October 1952 but served no new ground in the estate. It ran from Hornchurch Station to Gooshays Drive via Butts Green, Ardleigh Green and Harold Wood, coinciding with part of the pre-war Romford to Hornchurch 246 south of Slewins Lane.

Country Buses also added 33 buses to its peak vehicle requirement during 1950, mainly by way of frequency increases but including five for new or extended services. This small figure disguises the extent to which Country Buses expanded into new areas because, as in previous years, much of this was secured without committing additional buses. A substantial sweep of sparsely inhabited countryside in Surrey was the recipient of the first new service on 1st March, the 449 which ran from Dorking to Ewhurst via Ockley and Forest Green with the aid of one Cub from Dorking garage. The traffic potential of the country portion of the route can never have been all that promising so it is no surprise that London Transport went to town with a publicity campaign extolling the beautiful countryside which could be visited by the 449. In fact most of the service was concentrated between Dorking and Chart Downs Estate, the country end being served only three times a day.

The next was not a new route at all but one which had been operated privately by the Loudwater Estate company from there to Rickmansworth station. They had asked London Transport to take it over but the route could not be operated economically from either Amersham or Watford garages, so the Executive recruited the existing driver, who lived in Loudwater, and arranged for the bus, a Cub, to be outstationed in the old garage there. This was a rare distinction in London Transport shared only by the bus for route 412 which was kept at Holmbury St Mary. Takings were paid in to the booking office at Rickmansworth station and the bus went back to Leavesden Road every Friday for servicing. The route was introduced on 7th June 1950, numbered 336A and came to fame in later years as the last to be operated by the GS class.

Restoration of pre-war facilities was less common, because less necessary, on Country Buses once the Green Line network had been re-established but there was one case on 5th July which was of unusual interest because it covered ground served by Central Buses' route 220 until 1939. Route 459 ran between Uxbridge and Richings Park Estate but instead of running via Cowley Road it followed the exclusively Country bus route through Iver Heath, then ran via Swallow Street and Bangors Road South. This might have been seen as a device to transfer the work to the cheaper department without attracting comment from the staff but by following the longer route it also met requests for a service linking Iver Heath and Iver and to serve the local schools and hospital. It also relieved some inadequacy on route 457 at Iver Heath

Two very different one-man-operated Cub routes started in August. The first, on 9th August, was route 448A, a local town service running between Onslow Street and Pewley Way in Guildford. As so often happens with small projects, it absorbed a disproportionate amount of administrative effort because the route was to use a small section of private road. The Executive thought, mistakenly as it turned out, that it would need an indemnity from the trustees, the Poyle Estate, to protect it from liability for damage. The rather spartan service needed no extra buses as it was provided out of those allocated to route 448. In contrast route 381 which started on 30th August ran through the scantily populated Essex countryside to the east of Epping out to Toothill via Stewards Green and Collier's Hatch and was allocated its own Cub at Epping garage. Its introduction had been delayed while passing bays were installed in the narrow country lanes between Theydon Mount and Toothill and it still could not reach its intended terminus at Ongar because the roads were not yet suitable, even for a Cub.

The first route to venture onto Oxhey estate, which was being built to the west of the London to Birmingham main line, was the 332 which was extended from Bushey to Little Oxhey Lane on 7th June 1950 with the help of one 4Q4. This was an interesting operation because the estate was in its very early stages of development and host as yet only to what was described as 'temporary housing'. There were no made-up public roads from the outside world as yet and access to the

Literally one-man operated, the 336A had its own resident driver who kept the bus in the village, taking it to the garage for servicing on Fridays when he collected his wages, and paying his takings in each day at Rickmansworth station. Operating officially from Watford (Leavesden Road) garage, C 60 is in the car park at Rickmansworth station, surrounded by private cars of similar vintage. A.B. Cross

new houses entailed using a section of private road, Woodwaye, which needed special dispensation from the owners, but this routeing was abandoned later when Brookdene Avenue gave access to the estate.

Other areas newly served during 1950 included Larchwood Drive, Englefield Green (441 and 466A) from 18th January, Cottonmill Estate St Albans (355 diverted 10th May), Barrow Green Oxted (464/465 10th May), Wellpond Green (386 diverted 5th July), Becketts Avenue, Townsend (391 extended 27th September).

One favoured way of increasing the capacity of services economically was to substitute double-deckers for single-deckers wherever it was practicable to do so. Central Buses had converted Cricklewood's route 226 from 5Q5 to STL on 14th December 1949 and this was followed on 22nd February 1950 by the 234. In this case the terminus at Wallington had to be removed to the south side of the railway bridge in Beddington Gardens instead of Belmont Road. The 234A remained single-deck but also abandoned Belmont Road because it was extended to Hackbridge at the same time. The 234 conversion was of particular interest because the double-deckers were new RTs, according the route the esoteric honour of being the only case of single-deck LTs being replaced by RTs.

Country Buses followed the same policy, completing route 454 on 6th February (STL in place of 4Q4), but then waiting until 27th September to make its biggest conversion in style. It was made possible by the arrival of the first 20 RLHs which, by creating a surplus of lowbridge buses, provided the means to restore the through routes across Woking which had been broken when the northern halves had been converted to lowbridge STL in 1943. The southern portions had remained single-deck and, in 1950, were being operated with 6Q6 coaches but these were inadequate to cope with the heavy traffic particularly between Woking and Old Woking where more capacity was badly needed. The pre-1943 routes were not recreated because the frequency improvements introduced in 1946 altered the balance between the routes. The rump of the pre-1943 436, by now numbered 436B, was not therefore reunited with its old partner but with route 463, to give a through route running half-hourly from Walton to Guildford via Merrow. The 436 was instead attached to the 438, which had never been part of a through route, to give another half-hourly through service from Staines to Guildford via Burpham. The other rump, the 436A from Ripley,

was also linked with the 436 to restore the through route to Staines. The end result was a stronger cross-Woking service than had existed before 1943.

The 463 was a product of the 1946 restructuring and, as it did not go under any low bridges, was operated with standard highbridge STLs on a joint schedule with route 461A. Both now had to be converted to lowbridge. The redundant Godstone STLs provided the wherewithal for all this and shared their new unfamiliar haunts with the existing RLHs and STL19s. As the STs were used occasionally as spares, all four country types of lowbridge bus could be seen on this group until the older types were ousted by the second batch of RLHs in 1952.

Central Buses felt confident enough about the state of the fleet in May 1950 to stretch its wings

and try out a new venture, the operation of bus excursions on Sundays. Six routes were in the published programme for 21st May, three to Windsor and three to Whipsnade Zoo, from Clapham Common, Leyton, Barking, Hammersmith, Cricklewood and two or three intermediate points on route. These were so successful that more were added in June and July, with Ruislip Lido and Chessington Zoo added to the destinations. These were expanded considerably in subsequent years and broadened to include race specials and football excursions. Country Buses had introduced a small programme of excursions and tours in 1949, two Sunday excursions to Whipsnade from Ware and Windsor and a

Wednesday and Sunday circular tour of north Kent from Gravesend. The success of these led them to try a more ambitious programme of 38 in 1950, introduced in two stages on 17th May and 14th June. They covered a wide variety of destinations, including West Ham speedway and Brands Hatch motor racing. They too were a great success and continued to grow over the years.

The delivery of new buses slowed down drastically in 1951 and 1952 with the completion of all but the two main contracts and most of the extra vehicles were used for tram replacement rather than for service expansion. Central Buses expanded by only 99 scheduled runnings in 1951 and 24 in 1952, although by the start of 1951 most of the work of restoring a reasonable standard of adequacy had been done. The tasks now were to put services into those areas which had been waiting for a bus service since at least 1939 and to give services to the new areas built since the end of the war or then being built. Country Bus expansion was proportionately greater at 46 buses in 1951, and 24 in 1952 but nearly half of these must be attributed to the routes taken over from Eastern National in the Grays and Tilbury area. Green Line had mixed fortunes, going up by 20 in 1951 and down again by 14 in 1952. In fact 1952 was the first post-war year in which car miles run by the central departments was

Right In February 1951, route 166 was extended northward from Thornton Heath Pond to serve the housing lying between Norbury and Mitcham Common, but terminated short of anything useful at The Greyhound, Streatham

Common. Weymann-bodied RT 453, one of Croydon's first main batch, is stopping at a new Bus Stop in Purley with an as yet empty E sign gate, which suggests that preparations are in hand for the removal of the trams. *D.A. Jones/LTPS*

reduced, albeit only marginally but this was the beginning of an inexorable trend which was shared by Country Buses after 1953. Nevertheless, between 1945 and 1952, car mileage had increased by 36 per cent in the central departments and 89.5 per cent on Country Buses and Coaches, the comparable passenger mile increases being 17.2 and 75.5 per cent. Compared with pre-war, on the other hand, Central were running just over 4 per cent more while Country Buses and Coaches were up by 28.6 per cent.

Central Buses introduced 15 new or extended routes during 1951 and ten in 1952. Some of these were, or became, substantial operations. The first, though, was a long overdue service for Tulse Hill introduced on Sunday 7th January to coincide with the tram conversion route changes, from which it drew its resources. Numbered 195, it ran from Stockwell to West Norwood garage serving a mixture of pre-war LCC flats at the bottom of the hill and Victorian villas and houses further up. It had added interest in the vehicles used, the SRTs which had been released from routes 5 and 5A in the tram conversion that day. The next two routes made small-scale starts but both were set to grow considerably. On 10th January the 229 started on a route barely three-quarters of a mile long between Sidcup Station and Wren Road, using two SRTs. It was extended via St Mary Cray Estate to Orpington station on 17th October, tripling its length overnight and now using STLs, and then thrust northwards on 18th October 1952 through 1930s semis in Murchison Avenue, Arbuthnot Road and Townley Road to Bexleyheath. The 203 started between Hounslow Central and Hanworth (Duke of York) serving mainly pre-war housing between the railway and Mogden Sewage Works, in Bridge Road and Hall Road, but was extended at both ends on 25th July. This took it to Hatton Cross, where Heathrow Airport was beginning to develop in importance, giving Great South West Road its first bus route, again serving pre-war housing, and at the other end to Twickenham. It reached Bedfont on 3rd December 1952 and eventually got to Staines. Other areas served from 21st February were King Harold's Way and Parsonage Manor Way (122A), Swingate Lane (126), Galpins Road and Wide Way Streatham Vale (166).

The Goulds Green area of Hillingdon was put on the map on 25th July 1951 with the introduction of new route 204, running from Uxbridge to Hayes via Judge Heath Lane and Botwell Lane. The 240A was extended on the same day through Engel Park to Mill Hill East station.

Another LCC 'out-county' estate came into the fold on 17th October 1951, route 167 then being extended from Loughton garage through Pyrles Lane and Chester Road to terminate at the northern end in Willingale Road. This was also the day that the 207 brought buses to Plantagenet Road, Meadway and Manor Road on its way from New Barnet to Chesterfield Road. This route entered its own minor hall of fame by starting with two STLs and then being so successful that a third bus had to be added from 31st October. It also changed over to RTs, using vehicles which had been fitted experimentally with semaphore trafficators, because there were some awkward sight lines on the route. In the same programme, former tram route 168 was extended from Wandsworth up West Hill to Putney Heath (Green Man). The rather unsatisfactory western

Some trams were still running when route 168 was extended from Wandsworth up West Hill to Putney Heath. A queue waits at the unusual Tram E-sign at Waterloo Bridge for a car from the subway and Rehab HR/2 Car 1890 is on its way to reverse on the Savoy Street crossover, while RTL 1135 still looks like a sheepish newcomer squeezed between them. *C. Carter*

Looking for all the world a standard version, STL 2660 was one of the 34 unfrozen 17STLs, the only clue to this being its long radiator shell with slatted grille and its body was an STL14/2 which had started life on STL 2322 in 1937. It is in Watford High Street on the newly extended 332 to Oxhey estate. A.B. Cross

In a group of changes which tidied up and improved the network for Oxhey Estate, new route 346A replaced the southern end of the 332 which disappeared. Cravens-bodied RT 1415 is in Watford High Street, still looking much as it did when new, during the first summer of the new route's operation. A.B. Cross

terminus, short of the station and shops at Putney (this was long before the new estates at Roehampton were built), was an indication that resources and money were both still tight. West Hill had been served before the war by the 131, running from Hammersmith to Wandsworth via Barnes and Doverhouse Road.

The main thrust of Country Bus developments was to serve new estates and the burgeoning New Towns and it was an out-county LCC estate which came first. Route 370A was a new route from South Ockendon to Purfleet or Grays via Aveley, which served the southern flank of what was then known as Belhus Park estate, later Aveley estate, a development which Country Buses liked to describe as a 'quasi-Satellite Town', a curious distinction it shared with Slough and Oxhey. This was joined by new Green Line route 723A on 4th

July. The first real New Town to feature was Hemel Hempstead, but in a small way, on 13th June when single-deck route 320 was diverted intermediately to serve Longlands. The diversion of route 355 to serve part of Cottonmill Estate in 1950 had not met the needs of those living further into the estate near the railway and this deficiency was remedied from the same day by new route 325, a short simple route running from Trumpington Drive to St Albans garage.

Route 332 had been serving the eastern side of Oxhey estate as far as Little Oxhey Lane since June 1950 but the estate had soon spread westwards. From 26th September 1951 this area was served by the extension of some Kingswood to Oxhey Hall Farm short-workings on routes 345 and 346, which were diverted into the estate as far as Hallowes Crescent via Hayling Road. This left a messy mixture of three southern terminals and two intermediate routeings for the 345 and 346 but this was soon tidied up when the local routes were completely restructured on 5th March 1952. The 332 was withdrawn altogether, its northern end to Cassiobury Park being replaced by the 312 (from Little Bushey) diverted away from Chilcott Road, and its southern end by a new 346A from Kingswood to Little Oxhey Lane. Route 345 lost its Hallows Crescent bifurcation, was withdrawn between Oxhey (Hillcroft Crescent) and Harefield and rerouted at its northern end to cover the 312 to Chilcott Road, becoming simply Chilcott Road to Hillcroft Crescent via Wiggenhall Road. In turn, the 346 was withdrawn between Eastbury Road/Brookdene Avenue and Harefield to become Kingswood to Hallowes Crescent. The Harefield service was taken over by a new 347, which had its northern terminus at Chilcott Road and ran via Bushey Arches but it did not last long in that form. After only three months, on 11th June, it was withdrawn between St Albans Road and Chilcott Road and diverted over route 320 via Garston, Leverstock Green and Hemel Hempstead to Boxmoor. This brought double-deckers to these roads, at twice the former frequency, to carry the growing New Town traffic. All these changes took place against a background of persistent staff shortages in the area and the improvements were tempered by reductions in some services.

One more estate served for the first time in 1951 was Christianfields in Gravesend, just outside the London Transport statutory boundary; route 495 was extended from Kings Farm Estate on 26th September.

Country Buses' biggest expansion of 1951 had nothing to do with housing developments. On 30th September, the Executive took over the local services operated in Grays and Tilbury by the Eastern National Omnibus Company, the only one of a number of similar schemes which were under consideration at this time which came to fruition. All were designed to put right the more damaging effects of the way the LPTB boundary had been drawn through large urban areas in

1933. Such infringements of the statutory London Transport boundary, smaller examples of which have already been noted, were now possible by dispensation from the BTC which had powers under the 1947 Transport Act to run bus services anywhere in the country. Thirteen routes were transferred, together with the Eastern National garage in Argent Street and all continued to operate unchanged for three months. Twenty-eight buses were also borrowed, although not all of them were used by London Transport who started to move STLs into Argent Street right from the start. The borrowed ENOC buses were given London Transport fleet names on pasted labels and were fitted with garage and running number plate holders, and the staff working them were fitted out in the green uniforms of Country Buses. In all other respects things remained the same for three months. A full scheme of integration for the routes was installed on 2nd January 1952, including some new or restored links and giving them all route numbers in the London Transport 300 series. By this time the borrowed buses had all been replaced either by STLs or new RTs.

Central Buses had also expanded temporarily during the summer while the Festival of Britain was taking place. The Festival was opened by King George VI on 4th May which was the day the South Bank exhibition opened but the Festival Pleasure Gardens in Battersea Park did not open until 11th May. Eight special services were put on for the Festival, lettered A to H and all operated by STLs which had been stock-piled during the preceding year. Many of the STLs were also used to run supplementary schedules on ordinary routes serving the site and these were unusual in having double-ended blinds occupying the full depth of the 'via' aperture, the same arrangement being applied to the special services. There was also an architectural exhibition at the showpiece Lansbury estate in Poplar which opened a day earlier on 3rd May. This was served by a short special service D from West India Pier, where there was a service of water buses from the South Bank.

The other services linked the Festival Gardens with South Kensington station (A), Sloane Square

running from various suburban areas. The South Bank exhibition closed on 30th September and all the Waterloo routes were withdrawn. The Festival Gardens stayed open until November, when the A and B were withdrawn. These came back the following year and in subsequent years, eventually numbered as 45A and 137A.

The pace of change slowed down markedly in 1952 as the backlog of commitments was cleared away and before the development of the New Towns got up to speed. Central Buses responded to the enlargement of New Addington estate by extending the 130 from its original 1939 terminus at Salcot Crescent, to Homestead Way, a stone's throw from Croydon's southern boundary beyond which there was, and is, almost unspoilt open countryside. The new route 171 which replaced the 33 tram on 7th April served a quite different landscape. This was extended beyond the Manor House terminus, which owed its existence more to the fact that it was at the northern LCC boundary than to any traffic reason, through areas of Victorian housing in St Ann's Road, Black Boy Lane and Philip Lane, to Tottenham, Bruce Grove. This was not a pre-war route restored but an entirely new, some might say long overdue, venture.

On 14th May 1952 the 209 was introduced, serving a mixture of pre-war and post-war housing between Harrow Weald and South Harrow, through Long Elmes, Hatch End, Pinner, Cannon Lane, Rayners Lane Station, Clitheroe Avenue and Rayners Lane. It was one of the longest new routes to be started in this period and opened up

Below STLs 462, 1542 and one other working on Festival of Britain special services are at the newly opened Cornwall Road stand, Waterloo, with SRT 90 on the new 196 which has replaced the Kings Cross bifurcation on route 68, and RTW 283, newly installed on route 46 specially for the Festival. The STLs had special 'To & From' displays occupying the whole of the intermediate point box, as did all the STLs used as extras on ordinary routes. London Transport went through a brief period of using the word 'service' rather than 'route' at this time, and it was applied to the blinds on the FoB routes for some unexplained reason. D.W.K. Jones

station (B), the South Bank (C), Clapham Common car parks (F) and Patmore Street car park, Battersea (H). Two other routes serving the South Bank were from Victoria (Elizabeth Bridge) (E) and various car parks in the Waterloo area (circular – G). The 'park-and-ride' services, as they would now be called, were a complete flop and did not last long but the C in particular was a very popular route. There was also a route J which served none of these things but was put on specifically for the Festival and was the forerunner of what eventually became the Original London Sightseeing Tour. It ran on a 2½ hour circular route for 2s 6d (12½p) under the slogan 'Round the town for half-a-crown' and was operated by Old Kent Road with the four buses that had toured Europe in 1950. For a few subsequent years the J was supplemented by similar tours

Right Newly-built Coldharbour estate was served for the first time in June 1952 when route 498 was initiated. STL 1632, which had started life as an STL11 at Forest Gate in

Right Newly-built Coldharbour estate was served for the first time in June 1952 when route 498 was initiated. STL 1632, which had started life as an STL11 at Forest Gate in October 1936, had received this STL14 body by the time it was photographed in Gravesend a fortnight after the inception of route 498.
A.B. Cross

long stretches of road for the first time. This just left Honeypot Lane and Perivale Estate, served by routes 79/A from 6th August and the Farringdon Avenue and Petersfield Avenue route through Harold Hill (route 66A from 18th October).

The first lilliputian steps were taken in two of the New Towns early in 1952. The first was Harlow, on 20th February, when an undistinguished little operation using one Epping RT and numbered 396, was started between the 'Green Man' and 'Harlow New Town', a mere seven-minute journey terminating at a muddy heap known only as 'Road E'. The start at Stevenage on 26th March was only a little more substantial, new route 392 running from 'The White Lion' to Monks Wood via Haycroft Road, Greydells Road, Sish Lane, Bedwell and Rockingham Lane. The nine minute journey time allowed a 30-minute service to be operated with only one Hatfield RT. This was joined on 24th September by a 392A between Stevenage Station and Bedwell, taking over the route of the 392 which was simultaneously diverted to run direct via Sish Lane and also extended to the station.

Aveley estate had also been growing apace to stretch nearly a mile north of Stifford Road where its bus services were to be found, and changes were made on 30th April to bring buses into Foyle Drive. Route 328, which had come into existence only four months earlier when the co-ordination of Grays area routes had taken place, was completely altered. Instead of running from South Ockendon via Stifford Road, Aveley, West Thurrock and Grays to Woodside Estate, it became Aveley Estate (Elan Road) via North Stifford, Hogg Lane and Grays to Woodside Estate. A new 328A ran from Elan Road to Hall Avenue, with peak hour journeys to Purfleet. What had been the 328A (Purfleet–Woodside Estate) was renumbered 315 and to complete the confusion the 328s which had run from Ockendon Station to Purfleet were renumbered 328B.

On 14th May 1952, Sheerwater LCC Estate was served for the first time by a new route 420 from Woking Station and a little to the northwest, Holloway Hill enjoyed an extension of route 461A, both put on with only one additional STL at Addlestone. One extra STL was also enough to stock route 498 which was introduced on 11th June to serve Coldharbour, another Gravesend estate which was developing at this time. Northfleet actually got three STLs because the 4Q4s on route 497 were replaced at the same time. Along the Thames riverside to the west, Temple Hill estate had been encroaching further north across the marshlands above Dartford and had reached a stage which called for a bus service. On 3rd

December the 477 was extended from Westgate Road via Temple Hill, St Vincents Lane and Manor Way to terminate at Henderson Drive, penetrating an area previously visited only by hospital and works journeys. On the same day, New Greens Estate, St Albans was treated to an extension of route 391A from Townsend.

The story comes to an end with the introduction on 17th December of route 314A which ran from Hemel Hempstead The Parade (no bus station yet) to Bennetts End (Peascroft Road). It seems a fitting finale to this account of recovery and development that the last new route to be introduced in 1952 should be in a New Town, so symbolic must they be of post-war hopes and aspirations.

The last new route to start before the end of 1952 was the 314A, which served the Bennetts End area of the New Town. Now smartly turned out in the 1950 livery style with one cream band on an otherwise all-green bus, RT 622 was among those allocated to Two Waters in its first pioneering batch in August 1948.
A.B. Cross

BUSES FOR TRAMS

AT THE END of the war there was nothing to indicate that there was likely to be any change in the policy to replace trams with trolleybuses. In fact, the decision to buy 77 new trolleybuses seemed to point in the direction of continuity but this all changed during 1946 after a review had shown that the financial and operational benefits were marginally in favour of using oil-engined buses. On the basis of this review, the Board decided to change its policy and sought approval from the Minister of Transport, which he gave on 3rd October 1946 and on 15th November a public announcement was made that motor buses would replace the remaining trams. In some ways this should not have come as a complete surprise because right from the start of the programme there had been a strong implication in official pronouncements that the trolleybus was likely to be a transitional arrangement to make use of the remaining life of the fixed electrical infrastructure.

The tram conversion was planned to start in 1950 and some preparatory work was put in hand during 1949 but the planning for the route network had been going on since 1946, at about the time the policy decision was announced. There were two important obstacles to the complete integration of services with the rest of the bus system, the different rates of pay and agreements governing working conditions and the markedly different structure of fares on the trams compared with buses. Neither had mattered when the conversion was to trolleybuses, especially as Frank Pick had taken care to ensure that scheduled mileage was shared in due proportion when integration led to trolleybuses taking over bus mileage or buses taking over from trams. Now that there would be no form of electrically powered transport to switch mileage with, the distinctions became important. The solution of these problems was left until later and, for the time being, planning went forward on the basis that the buses which replaced trams would be regarded as a separate operation, even to the extent that the vehicles might be distinguished by painting them blue. Routes were therefore identified by their tram number with a 'T' prefix.

This minimised the scope for the kind of integration which had been practised before the war and most of the proposals kept very closely to the existing route patterns, with just a few extensions and a small amount of linking with existing bus routes. Most of the basic ideas laid out in 1946 saw their way through to the final schemes but there were a few interesting variations which are worth noting. In the first stage, route T12 (the eventual 44) would have replaced only the 12 tram, leaving trolleybus 612 unsullied, and the

New RTLs stored alongside E/1 trams in Clapham depot ready for new route 45. The use of CLAPHAM L.T. GARAGE as a destination display was dropped soon afterwards in favour of CLAPHAM COMMON STN.

T31 (170) would have been extended from 'Princes Head' to Clapham Junction, anticipating by nearly 30 years what eventually happened. As already recorded, the 31 tram was extended to Wandsworth in 1947 and this rather good idea fell through. In Stage 2, the T8 and T20 (57/57A) were to retain their Streatham/Tooting loop operation but broken in some way in Southcroft Road. In Stage 3 part of T42 (190) was to be linked with bus route 64 at West Croydon to run Thornton Heath – Addington and the existing route to Coombe Road would have become T42A. In Stage 7, The T68 (188) was to link with the 68 bus's King's Cross spur working and the 239 to run Greenwich to Tufnell Park. There were two additional links proposed in Stage 8: the extension of route 61 from Eltham to Greenwich, via Woolwich, to replace the special tram workings; and the extension of route 124 from Eltham to Woolwich. On the other hand, the T72 was intended as a direct replacement for the 72 tram, rather than the link with bus route 94 which eventually took place as the 186. In all cases the Embankment loop services were to have direct replacements but with provision for a break somewhere on Victoria Embankment. In the 1946 plan no provision was made for a separate service to cover the 36/38 journeys to Catford and this did not make an appearance until August 1948 when a Woolwich to Downham service was proposed. The revised plan also suggested a variation for the T72, which it was now proposed should run Eltham – West Kilburn, with a new Woolwich – Catford route covering Westhorne Avenue. The T66 (36A) then became Brockley Rise – Victoria.

One of the big problems encountered was finding places for buses to turn and stand. All the careful preparatory work done in readiness for the introduction of trolleybuses was to no avail as authority to approve routes and stands for buses vested in the Licensing Authority (formerly and later known as the Traffic Commissioner) and the existence of statutory authority for terminating trolleybuses was irrelevant. New arrangements had to be made at Grove Park, where an extension to Marvels Lane was not approved, and Victoria where the use of the Gillingham Street, Wilton Road, Vauxhall Bridge Road loop was not accepted. The planning team went to considerable lengths to solve what seemed to be an intractable problem at Southwark Bridge. The idea of a bus station somewhere north of the bridge had been sketched into early plans, but no site had been identified even though the trolleybuses were to have had a stand on London Transport property in Cloak Lane. There was also a site reserved for a bus stand in Upper Thames Street in the City of London Reconstruction Plan, but this seems to have fallen through simply because the cost of land was prohibitive.

Drastic alternative measures were worked out, the least destructive being a proposal for several of the routes to operate in a loop, either from Elephant via Borough, Southwark Bridge, Queen Victoria Street, Blackfriars Bridge to Elephant & Castle, or the reverse with routes being arranged to give a service both ways round at all times. Route T34 (45) was brought into this arrangement, extended around the reverse of the loop from Blackfriars to provide the necessary balance of operation. The plan also included linking T10 (95) and T26 (168) to run in a horseshoe from Tooting to Wandsworth via Streatham, Kennington, Elephant, Southwark Bridge, Victoria Embankment and Vauxhall. Two links with parts of existing bus services were also posited. The T52 (149) would have been extended via Blackfriars Bridge and Stamford Street to link with bus route 46 shorts at Waterloo to cross a third Thames bridge (Lambeth) and run Grove Park to Victoria. Route T60 (176A) would have been split with half extended to Liverpool Street via Bank and the rest via Queen Victoria Street and route 76 to Victoria. Between them these would have replaced the 76 Victoria – Liverpool Street spur working. As a simpler but more damaging alternative, a terminus on the south side of the river was sought, either in Sumner Street or in Great Suffolk Street. In the end, the City Corporation agreed to a stand on Dowgate Hill, well sited for passenger needs, but on a steep hill.

The future of Kingsway Subway was also given serious consideration. It would have needed rebuilding to allow the use of 8ft wide buses and the exit at the northern end would have been moved further south in Kingsway to improve the traffic arrangements at the Theobalds Road junction. Plans were prepared but the expense was found to be too great for the comparatively few benefits to be gained and an alternative surface route using Norfolk Street and Arundel Street was agreed with the authorities instead.

Contracts were let early in 1949 for the immense amount of work needed to make the tram depots ready for buses. All but Norwood,

The trams had to be kept going for at least five more years after the war but this was no problem once Charlton Works got into its stride and started turning out products that suggested the cars could be kept running for much longer. E/1 class 1582 was one of the two hundred Brush cars built in 1910/1911 and was therefore nearly 40 years old by the time it was photographed at Kennington Gate, leading an HR/2 on route 58, twenty years its junior. F.W. Ivey

No replacement was originally planned for the 36/38EX special journeys between Woolwich and Catford, represented here by Car 2 in Lewisham Road near Albion Hill. This tram was famous for being the only 'new' car built for London Transport, an entirely new body having been mounted on the underframe and trucks from Car 1370 which had been severely damaged in an accident in 1933. D.A. Thompson

which was to be abandoned, and Wandsworth, which already had an internal layout suitable for bus operation, were to be completely rebuilt and two entirely new garages were to be built at Rye Lane, for the Grove Park services, and Stockwell, to replace Norwood.

In January 1950 the Transport & General Workers' Union was given details of the proposed phasing of the scheme which, as originally planned, would have been in nine stages, working progressively across south London from Wandsworth to finish with the Woolwich Road

routes, the same sequence as had been planned for the intended changeover to trolleybuses. They were also told that staff would receive Central Bus rates of pay when they started working on the buses. This removed one of the two big stumbling blocks to integration. The other, the matter of workmen's fares, was solved by a reform of the system of fares and charges which was introduced on the day of the first stage of the conversion. Workmen's fares were abolished but a new Early Morning Single Fare was introduced which applied to all journeys by Central or Country bus, tram or trolleybus completed before 8am. Although former users of workmen's fares suffered a considerable increase for some journeys, early morning passengers over the rest of the system found themselves the beneficiaries of some substantial bargains. The scale of EMS fares started at 2d, for journeys normally costing between 3d and 1s 1d (journeys of up to ten miles). Return and transfer fares were all withdrawn but Cheap Midday Fares were increased in

Finding a terminal point for the replacement bus services on the Southwark Bridge routes was a major headache during the planning of the south London tram conversion scheme. Brush Car 96, new in 1928 to The County Borough of East Ham, is seen on the bridge shortly after leaving the terminal crossover on the north side, which was some way short of the pre-war site in Queen Street because of unrepaired bomb damage to the track. F.W. Ivey

price rather than being withdrawn immediately. The new scales not only overcame the problem of integration, they also laid the ground for the introduction of mechanised ticket issue.

The organisation of the central departments was changed on 12th July 1950, in readiness for the changeover. The Central Bus and Tram & Trolleybus departments were merged as Central Road Services under one Operating Manager, John Burnell and the former five Divisions, three bus and two tram and trolleybus, were re-arranged as four. The old bus divisional office at Kingsland Road was closed and the new Divisional headquarters were set up at Cricklewood, Manor House, Camberwell and Vauxhall. Eight depots and two bus garages whose names clashed with another establishment were renamed at the same time:

Old name	New name
Hammersmith (Bus)	Riverside
Hanwell (Bus)	Southall
Camberwell	Walworth
Hackney	Clapton
Hendon	Colindale
Holloway	Highgate
Hounslow	Isleworth
Leyton	Lea Bridge
Streatham (Telford Avenue)	Brixton
Sutton	Carshalton

All the tram and trolleybus depots were also given codes and trolleybuses were fitted with the same type of code and running number holders as buses. Trams did not show the codes during their remaining years.

Storage space for the buses which had to be stockpiled for each stage of the conversion was set aside in the yard alongside Edgware garage. The first of the new buses arrived there during August 1950, a total of 133 being accumulated for the first stage, a mixture of RTs and RTLs. At first these were delivered with masking on the indicator glasses but this was later removed and subsequent deliveries appeared with provision for full blind displays. These were to make their belated re-appearance on Central Road Services' vehicles with this conversion, Country Buses having made a start earlier in the year.

Tram routes 12, 26, 28, 31 and 34 and trolleybus route 612 were replaced by motor buses on 1st October 1950. Two through services which had been broken during the conversion to trolleybuses in 1937 were restored in this stage but two others were not and were destined never to be. Bus route 44 ran from a new stand in London Bridge Street, London Bridge Station, a short extension from the Hop Exchange tram terminus, to Mitcham (Three King's Pond) incorporating both tram route 12 and trolleybus route 612. Route 612 had come into the reckoning at a fairly late stage, as it was no part of the original plan to replace any trolleybuses, but the scope for economy by eliminating the overlap between Battersea and Wandsworth, while restoring

through journey opportunities, was a siren voice that could not be ignored. But for this, Wandsworth would have continued as a joint bus/trolleybus garage. The other restoration was bus route 170 which ran from Wandsworth to Hackney (Well Street), thereby covering all but a short section of tram route 31 as it had existed before December 1939 but not to the full extent of Leyton which it had served before June 1939.

The 26 tram was replaced in two parts, by route 168 extended in the west to Wandsworth (High Street) but cut back in the east to Farringdon Street, where it occupied a new stand in Stonecutter Street. The section east of Blackfriars was covered by an extension of tram route 72 from Savoy Street to Hop Exchange. This last tram route extension in London was a temporary arrangement until the plan to extend part of the 70 from Tooley Street could be effected. Another new stand used by route 168 was in Horse Guards Avenue, the rather unsatisfactory replacement for the Savoy Street tram terminus, which was used by shortworkings and on Sundays. An application had been made to use Temple Place, as had been the intention under the pre-war trolleybus plans, but this was unacceptable to the authorities. The operation of buses through Whitehall Court in particular was a constant irritant to the rather influential residents and London Transport was under a continuous bombardment of complaints which led eventually to the working being altered at night to avoid Whitehall Court.

Tram 28 was directly replaced by the identical 169, although the stand at Clapham Junction was moved further up St John's Hill to the Southern Region Goods Yard forecourt; and at Victoria buses made a U-turn in Vauxhall Bridge Road some way short of the old terminus. Route 45, replacing the 34 tram, shared the Farringdon Street stand with route 168, a short but useful extension from Blackfriars, and should have been

The short workings on route 46 between Victoria and Waterloo might have been absorbed into a tram replacement route T52 from Victoria to Grove Park via Lambeth Bridge, Waterloo, Blackfriars Bridge, Southwark Bridge and Old Kent Road if London Transport had not found a suitable stand for the Southwark Bridge services. RTW 202 is seen on route 46 after their transfer onto the route in time for the Festival of Britain in 1951. A.B. Cross

Clapham Junction to Wandsworth, replacing that part of the 628 nighter. The remaining bits of the 612 and 628 were joined together to form a Tooting to Hammersmith service numbered 630. There is no record of why the simpler option of extending the 288 to Tooting was not chosen.

The two connections that were not restored were of the 26 and 28 trams to the 626 and 628 trolleybuses, which had been split in 1937. At one stage during the planning process the idea was discussed of converting the two trolleybus routes to oil bus operation so that through operation could be re-established. One of the perceived merits of this would have been that it would not then have been necessary to buy more new trolleybuses to replace the earlier life-expired vehicles, the ones that were eventually replaced by the second batch of Q1s. Nothing came of the proposal because there were still plenty of older motor buses in need of replacement.

To replace the trams 133 new buses were needed, 77 RTs at Wandsworth, 37 RTLs at Clapham and 19 temporarily at Camberwell. Wandsworth was in a Leyland engineering group but was allocated AECs for the time being because not enough RTLs were being delivered at the appropriate time to meet all the needs of both stage one and the rest of the fleet. This was remedied in stage three. The new Stockwell garage should have featured in Stage 1 as the operator of route 170 but work had been delayed while new homes were found for the tenants of some of the houses on the site. It was not to be ready until April 1952 and in its absence route 170 went into Wandsworth. To make room, the buses for part of route 168 and the whole of 169 were accommodated temporarily in a newly laid out yard at

Weymann-bodied RT 3265 at the new stand specially established for route 44 at Three Kings Pond, Mitcham. The timetable panel on the Holden-designed TCP Bus Stop post contains a poster announcing the changeover from tram to bus on 1st October 1950. The conductor was presumably unaware that a separate intermediate point display had been provided for the shorts from Mitcham to Battersea. F.G. Reynolds

extended to South Kensington station but was temporarily curtailed at Battersea (Parkgate Road). This arrangement was necessary because Battersea Bridge had been closed since 16th March when it had been damaged by a collier colliding with one of its piers, and traffic, including buses, had been diverted via Chelsea Bridge. Tram route 34 had spent its last five months terminating on the south side of the bridge.

Night services in the area were restructured. Tram route 3 was replaced by new route 288 which was extended from Battersea ('Princes Head') to Wandsworth to cover the 612, and the night 168, replacing 26, was extended from

Camberwell garage intended to provide extra capacity for the expansion of bus services. They were transferred into Clapham in stage two.

Tram routes 2, 4, 6, 8, 10, 20, 22 and 24 were replaced by buses on 7th January 1951, the 2/4 being the first of the Embankment loop routes to be converted. The system of numbering devised to distinguish the alternative routeings around the loop was deceptively simple, the idea being not to have two different numbers but to use the suffixes 'B' for via Blackfriars and 'W' for Westminster added to the basic route number, in this case 155. This replaced the 2 and 4 trams on an identical route except for a short extension in Wimbledon to reach a stand in St George's Road. In the event the effort needed to ensure that the correct number and intermediate point displays were showing defeated the conductors and the system became a shambles. It seems strange that tram staff, accustomed far more than were bus staff to changing from route to route and who had always seemed to cope well with the various boards and blinds on trams, were defeated by this, maybe because they were not properly briefed. The 155 proved be the only case where this system was attempted.

The linking of the northern end of tram route 6 to the rump of bus routes 5 and 5A went ahead in line with the 1946 plan, the resulting routes unaccountably being given the new numbers 189 and 189A (North Cheam/Raynes Park – Cannon Street). Daytime services around the Southcroft Road loop were split, but not in the way envisaged in 1946. New routes 57, from Victoria to Tooting via Streatham, and 57A, Victoria to Streatham (St Leonards Church) via Tooting, replaced the 8 and 20. At Streatham, the 57A was given a

new stand in Babington Road, irritatingly short of the main shopping area. The replacements for the 22 and 24 lost their Southcroft Road section completely, their replacements being 50, Embankment (Horse Guards Avenue) – Streatham (Telford Avenue) via Brixton and 104 Horse Guards Avenue to Tooting (Mitre) via Clapham. The 10 was covered by an almost identical 95 with short extensions at each end to reach the stands in Dowgate Hill, for Cannon Street, and Coverton Road, Tooting. The 287 was a direct replacement of night tram 1, which managed without the special suffix letters, perhaps because the intricacies of the double loop working defied simple

Metro-Cammell-bodied RTL857, temporarily allocated to Camberwell until the garage at Clapham could be made ready, is on the stand at Armoury Way, Wandsworth. It is incorrectly displaying the intermediate point blind for route 169 which includes the name 'South Lambeth', a place which most people had not heard of before these new blinds appeared on the streets.
The Omnibus Society

Below RTs and RTLs stored in the yard at Edgware garage for Stage I.

description. It did have individual intermediate point blinds for each variation and in this case they seem to have worked. Because it was such a busy route, the 287 was the only night service to be given an enhanced frequency, the half-hourly tram being covered by a bus every 24 minutes.

The new garage replacing Telford Avenue depot, misleadingly named Brixton, was far from ready to receive its new buses and a temporary site was set up in a car park behind Streatham Hill Theatre. It was a fully operational self-contained base complete with makeshift offices and staff facilities and with a fuel tank mounted on the chassis of G 99. This and other delays to garage building, other than the special case of Stockwell, which were experienced throughout the conversion programme were due in no small part to the continuing shortages of essential materials, particularly steel. In fact, the revolutionary design of Stockwell and the similar use of reinforced concrete at Peckham owed their exis-

tence to the need to find alternative materials to replace steel.

Brixton's new buses were forty-two RTs for routes 50 (shared with Clapham), 57, 95 and 287 (also shared with Clapham), while Clapham, to which routes 50 (part), 57A, 104, 155B, 155W, 189, 189A and the rest of 287 were allocated, became one of the largest bus garages overnight. Eighty-five new RTLs joined those already there for route 45 and the nineteen transferred from Camberwell with routes 168 and 169, to give the impressive total of 140, although at that stage the building was still unfinished and many of these buses had to be parked in the open.

Only two new bus routes started on 8th April, replacing the Croydon tram routes 16, 18 and 42, but between them they needed 112 buses, 55 RTs at Brixton and 57 at Thornton Heath. Only a handful of these were new, the majority coming second-hand from Wandsworth where the opportunity was taken to change its stock to Leylands. During the days leading up to the conversion, Wandsworth received 61 new RTLs, 57 of which were in one continuous sequence (RTL 1119–1175), along with some nearly new transferred from Nunhead. Its RTs were shared between Brixton and Thornton Heath whose needs were topped up by 18 and 19 new ones respectively. All but one of Wandsworth's new RTLs had Park Royal bodywork, but the exception was of unusual interest in being the last of the 450 supplied by Metro-Cammell, RTL 1000. By this time MCCW had started to build the fleet of 700 RFs, the first of which had been received by London Transport four days earlier.

The RTLs contributed by Nunhead had an interesting background. As recorded in Chapter 7, the unfrozen STDs at Victoria had been withdrawn at short notice in February 1951 when the drivers refused to operate them any longer. London Transport decided to replace them with post-war STDs, drafted in from Leyton, which in turn received second-hand RTs from Nunhead. To release the RTs, Nunhead had received new RTLs, a surprising assignment as it was an AEC garage in an AEC engineering group.

An interesting coincidence at this time was that, just as the trams were being replaced by RT family buses along the Brighton Road, so the main trunk bus routes along the same corridor, all until then operated by STLs, were also being restocked. Route 133 had received new RTs at Croydon and Streatham garages in the autumn of 1950, after which Streatham had continued to take in RTs, fitfully it must be said because the needs of the tram conversion kept getting in the way. These were for route 159 which was completed when Old Kent Road received its allocation in April 1951. Another closely related route, the 3, was also similarly treated when RTs began to arrive at Norwood garage in October 1950, followed by RTLs at Chalk Farm. The reason for this sudden flush of new buses was that the headroom at both Norwood and Streatham had now been

Below Brixton's RT 2026 heads from Tooting to Cannon Street station, where it will use the new stand in Dowgate Hill which replaced the Southwark Bridge tram terminus. W.J. Haynes

Bottom RTL 879 on the stand in Dowgate Hill at Cannon Street station about a year after route 189 replaced tram route 6, alongside one of the many bombed sites still to be seen in the City of London in the 1950s. Route 48 behind had been brought forward from Stage 7. J.H. Aston

increased so that RT family buses could enter the two garages, opening the belated opportunity for these important routes to be modernised. Not apparently directly connected with these events, the other main Brighton Road route, the 59A, had its STLs from Camberwell replaced by RTLs in the spring of 1951. Camberwell was assigned more new buses than was needed for this purpose, the surplus being used to replace older RTLs for use as trainers in the tram conversion programme. These RTLs replaced the RT3s which had been the tram driver training fleet since the start of the conversion.

Route 109 replaced the 16 and 18 trams on exactly the same route, with a new terminal in High Street, Purley, and needed a total of 88 buses. The attempt at distinguishing the direction taken around the Embankment loop with a suffix letter was abandoned and instead a single route number was applied. To distinguish the two routes around the loop special blind displays reading WESTMINSTER & EMBANKMENT, or BLACKFRIARS & EMBANKMENT were used, with such success that the formula was never changed during the whole time such operations existed. Route 155 followed suit officially with the summer schedules on 2nd May, but there is evidence that the change actually took place earlier, probably to coincide with the start of the 109. This was a last minute decision, as could be seen from the offside route number plates which had the number offset to make room for the suffix. The contemporary map also showed the routes as 109B and 109W and a special amendments leaflet was issued. The 42 was replaced by route 190, not a clever choice of number alongside 109, which had short extensions at each end to Zion Road, Thornton Heath

and the 'Swan & Sugar Loaf', South Croydon, where it used a new stand in Nottingham Road. The 109 became instantaneously one of London's most frequent bus routes, its fifty-six an hour on the section between Brixton and Kennington even coming close to rivalling the legendary 101.

Thornton Heath garage was still being built but was in a more advanced state of completion than other new garages because the trams had been moved out to Purley depot the previous year to give the builders a fully cleared site. The buses were able, therefore, to move in immediately, which was still not the case at Brixton. Apart from the arrangements already mentioned in connection with stage two, some of Brixton's buses were housed temporarily at the former Brixton Hill tram depot, near Christchurch Road, for which there was no planned future use. No facilities were provided and it was used merely as a bus park but this arrangement was to continue until 7th November 1953.

Below left Newly shipped in from Wandsworth RT 1854 and RT 1878 stand amidst the clutter of the unfinished, but habitable, Thornton Heath garage. The new destination display and the all-purpose intermediate point blind show what has replaced the use of suffix letters for the Embankment loop working.

Below Electric trams had run on a route virtually identical to the new 190 bus for 49 years and horse trams for at least another 20 before that but the simple pattern of operation was to be disrupted within 18 months and in later years became very complicated. RT 1857, seen at the London Road end of Brigstock Road, was one of the buses brought in second-hand from Wandsworth, where they were replaced by new RTLs.
The Omnibus Society

Few buses in the 1946 livery style went into service with full blind displays but some had the masking removed when they were reallocated to garages where full displays were standard or more common, which is what has happened to RT 3073, seen on tram replacement route 70. It had been allocated to Willesden for route 8 in March 1950, and was one of a number which went to Bromley in exchange for RTWs in February 1951. It left there on 2nd May for Peckham in the big round of reallocations associated with the opening of the new garage, in which Bromley lost double-deck work. The use of ONLY on a journey which extended beyond the end of the route was only one example of the many eccentricities which plagued this practice and led to its ultimate downfall.
A.B. Cross

The next stage should have seen the conversion of the Norwood routes and of route 35, to bring north London operation to an end, but Stockwell garage still did not exist and there was nowhere else within striking distance available to park the buses. On the other hand, in Deptford, trams had been using a temporary bridge over Deptford Creek for some time, and completion of its permanent replacement was imminent. The decision was made therefore to exchange Stage 4 with 7, bringing forward to 10th/11th July 1951 the conversion of routes 68 and 70. Wednesday was chosen, rather than a Sunday as was usual for these conversions, because there was a substantial amount of change to existing bus routes. Their schedules traditionally changed on a Wednesday and the Trade Union had asked for an exception to be made to avoid too much disruption to rotas.

The bus route changes were complicated for such a simple network but were in broad accordance with the spirit, if not the detail, of the 1946 plan except in one important respect. There had been a belated change of policy about the numbering of the routes and from this stage onwards, wherever possible, numbers which matched or included the tram route number were used, instead of the random selection originally made. In consequence, bus route 70, not the planned 48, covered the tram route of that number, with an extension to Waterloo, rather than Horse Guards Avenue. The latter was covered instead by a 70A which ran only in peak hours. The replacement for the 68 tram (Greenwich – Waterloo) was numbered 188, instead of 69, and took over the northern end of the 68A from Waterloo to Chalk Farm, rather than the '239' (latterly 196) to Tufnell Park. The 196 was extended instead over

the southern part of the 68A to Norwood Junction. At the same time it took over most of the regular short workings from route 68, including the last vestige of the venerable spur working to King's Cross, making it the dominant route in this corridor. An incidental benefit of the new schedules was that a more frequent peak service was installed on route 68 between Upper Norwood and South Croydon and on the 196 to Norwood Junction and north of King's Cross. One other small change was the extension of route 4 from Bermondsey to Surrey Docks Station.

One of the curious byways of this stage was the decision to include VIA ELEPHANT or VIA HOP EXCHANGE on destination blinds to distinguish the routes of the 70/A and 188 which somebody apparently thought impenetrably confusing to the lay mind. This might have remained a mere harmless curiosity but for the fact that it had recently been decided to add the word ONLY to short working destinations. When these two accretions were combined, especially on the narrow blind of a roof-box RT or on rear blinds, the result was almost unreadable. One of the worst examples was SURREY DKS STN ONLY / VIA HOP EXCH. The use of ONLY quickly fell into such disrepute, because there were so many absurdities and anomalies, that the idea was dropped within a couple of years.

This conversion was well ahead of any work being done to house buses at New Cross and it was necessary to make alternative arrangements for routes 70, 70A and 188. As it happened, a new garage had opened on 2nd May 1951, on the site of the former Bull Yard premises of Thomas Tilling Ltd at Peckham (PM). This was nothing to do with the tram conversion but part of a programme to build new garages or enlarge existing ones to make room for the many buses then being parked in streets or open parking areas and for further expansion of the bus fleet. It had a parking area capable of accommodating 150 buses but when it opened it had responsibility only for route 36 (transferred from Camberwell and Catford) and the former Nunhead allocation of route 78, a total of seventy-one buses. It also provided a home for some of the buses used on Festival of Britain special services but still had plenty of room for the thirty-eight new RTs needed on the former tram routes. In total, forty-eight new RTs were licensed, four at Holloway, six at Turnham Green and thirty-eight at Peckham. A start had just been made on replacing the partial allocation of Leylands at Turnham Green by RTs and six of the displaced RTLs were sent to Chalk Farm to replace SRTs on the 196, the four RTs allocated to Holloway being for the same purpose. The rest of the buses for the peak vehicle requirement of forty-five on the 196 were transferred from route 68 at Chalk Farm and both the 68 and 68A at Camberwell.

The SRTs taken off the 196 started an important sequence of events. They were transferred to

Forest Gate garage, its second flirtation with the class following the collapse of the 1949 programme. This time they were for use on route 66 where they took the place of STLs, which, directly or indirectly, started the replacement of Guys at Hornchurch. This launched the continuous programme of withdrawal which, with considerable help from the STLs released from Festival of Britain duties in the late summer of 1951, eventually led to the disappearance of the Guys in December 1952.

On 7th October 1951 buses replaced the trams on routes 56/84, 58, 60, 62 and 66 and, brought forward from Stage 6, on the special workings on routes 36/38 between Woolwich and Catford. The replacement bus routes varied from published plans in a number of ways. Tram 66 was replaced not by a 177 from Forest Hill to Victoria but, in a reversion to one of the earliest plans, by a new 36A which linked the section replacing the trams to short workings on route 36 to form a Brockley Rise to West Kilburn service. The 56 and 84 took the more sensible number 184, rather than the planned 136B/136W and was also extended from Peckham Rye to a more useful but far less picturesque terminus at Brockley station, to serve the pre-war Honor Oak LCC estate. Unfortunately it was not possible for the number 136 to be earmarked instead for the replacement of the 36/38 in Stage 8 because it had been surrendered to British Transport Films for use in their products. Route 60 became 176A, instead of 163, the 176 being the replacement for route 62. At Forest Hill, the 176 used another new terminal at 'The Railway Telegraph', which it approached via Rockbourne Road. The 185 bus was a straight replacement for the 58 and night route 7 became 286. A new route 180 replaced the special service of 'Extras' on routes 36 and 38 between Woolwich (Parsons Hill) and Catford Garage.

An additional 109 buses were scheduled for these routes, shared between Camberwell, Catford and Walworth garages. The fifty RTLs for Walworth were not new but a mixed bag of vehicles reclaimed from tram driver training duties which looked decidedly dowdy and lacklustre and, the majority, buses which had been replaced by RTs at Alperton, Palmers Green and Southall and held in store at Edgware. Camberwell was allocated an additional sixteen RTLs for the 36A, sharing the operation with a similar number of RTs from Peckham transferred from the 36. The 180, with twelve new RTs, went into Catford.

Although much of the site at Walworth had been cleared and pits filled in, no serious work on the building of the new garage was possible until the trams had been removed so the parking space available was not enough for all its commitments. The 185 was therefore garaged across the road at Camberwell although nominally allocated to Walworth. The staff were assigned to Walworth and were able to report to its new office block in Camberwell New Road to sign on and off and pay in their takings. Schedules used the code WL(Q) to denote the special arrangement which continued until the next stage of conversion on 6th January 1952.

'The Admiral Hardy' in College Approach Greenwich affirms an appropriate historic connection behind RT 2552, one of the 38 new buses allocated to Peckham for routes 70, 70A and 188 in July 1951. The inclusion of VIA ELEPHANT on the destination blinds enforced some strange abbreviations, like CHALK FM, as seen here, and SURREY DKS. F.W. Ivey

The release of SRTs from route 196 had the unrelated consequence of triggering the replacement of the wartime Guys either directly, or indirectly by using displaced STLs. SRT154, in South Street Romford, has replaced a Hornchurch Guy on route 66. A.B. Cross

The abandonment of the Grove Park routes took place on 5/6th January 1952. The original plans for the conversion had assumed that the replacing buses would provide at least the same seating capacity as the trams but no detailed assessment of usage had been made in advance and, as the scheme developed, it became clear that this had been unnecessarily ambitious. By the time of stage six the frequencies of replacement services were much less lavish and the number of buses needed was substantially below what had been forecast. This enabled two of the Norwood routes which had been waiting for the still unready Stockwell garage, 48 and 78, to be brought forward into this stage, together with Grove Park routes 5 (night), 52, 54 and 74,

With one exception the new bus services had different route numbers from the published plan. Tram 48 became bus 48, not the planned 188, the 52 became 149, not 178, the 54 became 69 not 70 and the 78 became 178, rather than 149. The exception was route 74 which was replaced by the intended 179. Night route 5 became 285. Again with one exception, the routes were identical to the tram routes they replaced, the only route to be varied, apart from the different terminal arrangements, was route 178. It was extended along Robson Road to 'The Rosendale' in West Norwood to restore the service provided before the war as a bifurcation of route 2. This stretch was interesting as it was served by garage journeys on route 3 and had bus stops specially labelled to that effect, the only example of bus stops being provided purely for garage runs.

There was to have been another variation. The 1946 proposals had assumed that the pre-war plan to extend the trolleybuses replacing route 54 to the junction of Marvels Lane and Chinbrook Road would be carried forward into the post-war plans. In the event, this was not to be and London Transport instead negotiated the purchase of a parcel of railway land in Baring Road, so that a bus stand could be built on a raft. This was the

only purpose-built bus stand in the whole south London conversion programme, quite a contrast with the many supplied for trolleybuses in the 1930s.

A new garage had been built specially for the Grove Park routes, mostly on land previously occupied by the tramway permanent way depot but including a number of other properties. To enable the site to be cleared the PW department was transferred to premises in Bowles Road, next to Old Kent Road garage, for the remaining years of tramway operation, and the electrical engineers were housed at Camberwell. The new garage, which took the inaccurate name Rye Lane (RL), was in Bellenden Road, only a stone's throw from the recently opened and still under-used Peckham garage. If London Transport had had its way, there would have been an entrance to the garage directly onto Peckham High Street between Rye Lane and Bellenden Road. Not surprisingly, Camberwell Borough Council would not countenance so many vehicle outlets onto the main road in such a short space and withheld planning consent, so the shops at numbers 42–54 (even) which would have been demolished were given a reprieve which had still not run out fifty years later.

In addition to the four Grove Park routes, the garage also took responsibility temporarily for route 178 which thereby acquired itself a garage run, which it made in service, almost as long as the scheduled route. Route 48 went into Camberwell, a more sensible allocation than Stockwell, where it became a fixture for the few years that it survived. Altogether 111 buses were needed, eighty-seven RTs at Rye Lane, fifteen RTs at Peckham, for route 36 which had been increased in frequency as part of the replacement of the 54 tram, and nine at Camberwell. Only seventy-seven of Rye Lane's RTs were new, the balance of ten being made up with ten second-hand from Holloway and Nunhead each of which had received five experimental RTs. Camberwell did

A solitary HR/2 nears the summit of the impressively four-tracked Dog Kennel Hill, while a tram driver learns new hill-descending skills on RTL 2 at its foot. The Omnibus Society

not receive any new buses because the 36A and 185 were now able to move into their natural home at Walworth and they left nine of their RTLs behind for the 48, Walworth receiving nine new ones instead.

This left only the subway routes 33 (West Norwood – Manor House) and 35 (Forest Hill – Archway) to be dealt with in Stage 7 on 5/6th April 1952. They were replaced respectively by bus routes 171 and 172, following the same surface route above the subway as the 170, and the night service on the 35 by route 292. The 171 was to have been extended from Manor House, a terminus dictated by the municipal boundary rather than by any great traffic objective nearby, to Turnpike Lane Station. This would have been a better objective, but during the gestation period of the scheme the Executive decided to extend it instead into uncharted territory through St Anns Road, Black Boy Lane and Philip Lane, areas long overdue for a service, to Bruce Grove Station. The 292 was also extended beyond the Bloomsbury terminus of the night tram to Charing Cross Underground. station, which was by now a centre for night services to south London.

The sixty-two buses needed for the two routes were allocated to three garages, none of which had been tram depots, in a complicated series of moves. Stockwell garage had opened at long last on the previous Wednesday, since when its vast chamber had been home to route 178, which had been transferred from Rye Lane. Its twelve RTLs had come second-hand from Hendon, yet another garage whose Leylands were being replaced by new RTs. Hendon sent another 22 which joined four taken out of store at Finchley to provide the rolling stock for the southern allocation of route 171. Route 172's southern base was not Stockwell as planned but Rye Lane, where the twelve RTs left behind by the 178 were joined by sixteen new ones. Both routes had a small allocation at Holloway, which took them over from Highgate, for which it was allocated eight RTs.

The network of routes between London and Woolwich were to have been replaced in two further stages, the 40, 44, 46 and 72 in July and the 36/38 in October. In the event the two stages were merged into one on 5th/6th July. The decision was prompted by the improved rate of delivery of new buses but it was also heavily influenced by the better service reliability being achieved, the measurable increase in the numbers of passengers using the services that had already been converted and by their good financial results.

The 162 scheduled tram runnings were replaced by a substantially diminished motor bus schedule of 113. Some of the former tram routes had been considerably underused, in many cases because they had lost so much traffic through bombing and the general decline in population in inner London. Also, the historic decline in the use of public transport had been in progress now for four years and the trams had not been spared their share.

Left Route 178 enjoyed an allocation of RTs for only three months between its introduction in January and its transfer to Stockwell in April 1952, after which it remained an RT route for the rest of its Victoria – West Norwood life. RT 3390 is in Vauxhall Bridge Road on its way to The Rosendale in West Norwood, an extension which restored the service along Robson Road withdrawn early in the war. Aviation & Transport Photographs

Centre left RTL 1262 runs alongside the tram terminal stub at West Norwood in the early days of operation of route 171 in a scene where the number of buses is the same as the number of other motor vehicles in sight. The RTL was one of thirty-four sent south from Hendon, where they had been replaced by new RTs, to provide the starting stock for the new Stockwell garage. C. Carter

Broadly speaking, the bus route pattern that emerged on 6th July was in line with the plans of 1946, other than the, by now, usual alterations to the route numbers. Only three routes were given direct replacements on an identical route. Routes 36 and 38, which were to have been 184B/184W, were replaced by the 177, and the 46 was covered by the 182 which like other Southwark Bridge routes was extended to Cannon Street. However, instead of a daily through operation, the 182 had a complicated route pattern which, in summary, meant that it did not run between Eltham and Woolwich in Monday–Friday off-peak hours, and ran only as far west as New Cross on Saturday evenings and Sundays. The service on the London side of New Cross was made up by route 21, which had its Saturday frequency doubled and was extended from Eltham to London Bridge on Sundays. Tram route 40 was replaced by the 163 (planned as 181) which, instead of running to Wickham Lane Plumstead, continued beyond Woolwich to Plumstead Common replacing and absorbing the foreshortened 53 motor bus. It was supported in this task by route 180 which was similarly extended. Tram 44 was merged as intended with bus route 161 but instead of the route number changing unnecessarily to 154, it sensibly kept 161. The 161 also had a Monday-Friday peak hour extension to Greenwich Church, which continued the 'round-the-corner' service introduced on the trams during the war but at an enhanced level to help with the replacement of route 53. The section of route 44 from Eltham Church to The Yorkshire Grey was not replaced directly and the peak hour non-stop operation on route 161 between Eltham and Woolwich, introduced as a wartime measure, was discontinued.

RT 2844 was one of the new buses assigned to Rye Lane for route 172, the replacement for subway tram route 35, which ran between identical terminals. W.J. Haynes

The 72 tram was not replaced between Lewisham and Savoy Street. Instead, the service from Woolwich was extended from Lewisham over bus route 94 via Brockley and Forest Hill to Crystal Palace under the number 186. The 94 was cut back to Lewisham except on Saturday afternoons when it continued to run to Brockley Rise. The Eltham – Woolwich service was also topped up by changes to route 21A which, like the 161, had run between Woolwich and Eltham non-stop in peak hours. Normal stopping arrangements were introduced on this section which now ran additionally on Saturday afternoons and the route was withdrawn between Sidcup and Farningham. To cover this, an all day daily service to Farningham was scheduled on route 21 including a through service from Moorgate to Farningham for the first time for many years.

The allocation of the replacing buses was complicated to say the least, starting with the fact that the vehicles used were not all new. This had not been the plan but the Trade Union had approached London Transport earlier in the year asking for priority to be given to the allocation of new buses to routes 86 and 106 rather than the tram conversion and this had been agreed. This drained away sixty-eight vehicles but the situation was then complicated by a Government decision to restrict vehicle production for the home market in order to increase exports. This cut the number of new buses delivered up to June by thirty-two. The shortfall was made up by using fifty-three surplus pre-war STLs which had been reconditioned in preparation for the Coronation the following year. Although not much younger than the trams they were replacing, they were at least smart and in good condition. The twenty-nine RTLs which had been in use as trainers and

were now sent to Abbey Wood were distinctly unkempt. They were joined by nine RTLs transferred from Enfield, which was receiving new RTs at the time. The remaining buses for New Cross were RTs, fifteen new ones and nineteen 2RT2s which, although recovered from the training fleet, looked a good deal smarter than the RTLs. New Cross was the fourth and last Central Area garage to have an official allocation of 2RT2s

Neither garage was ready to receive its full complement of buses. Although Abbey Wood was the further advanced, it started with only twenty RTLs for route 177, the fifteen RTLs for the 186 being allocated temporarily to Plumstead. They were kept in a yard nearby called Saunders Yard until they could be taken into Abbey Wood on 3rd September. New Cross had a nominal peak vehicle requirement of seventy-nine but no buses could be kept on the site because it was not in a fit state to be used while still in the midst of rebuilding. Instead the STLs for route 163 were allocated to Rye Lane and Camberwell, while the RTs for the 177 and STLs for the 182 were allocated to Peckham. The official allocation was New Cross and schedules showed the codes NX (RL), NX (Q) or NX (PM). The buses should have carried NX plates but in practice the host garage often used its own plates, particularly at weekends when they covered the STL workings with their own RTs. The 2RT2s at Peckham were also known to stray onto route 70. New Cross began to take its routes under its own roof on 22nd October and completed the job on 12th November. The replacement by RTs of the temporary allocation of STLs began in December and was completed in March 1953, but the 2RT2s were to stay until the type was withdrawn completely.

With the completion of the tram conversion,

Nominally 18 years old, STL 443, seen at New Cross, is smartly turned out after overhaul and has a chassis fully up to the latest standards of STL technology, having been upgraded to 2/16STL when it was fitted with an oil engine in 1939. The STL18 body was of the same type as the one originally fitted in 1934.
C. Carter

London Transport had finished the task of replacing its 'obsolete fleet' of buses, trolleybuses and trams. The 1947 estimate that 1,052 buses would be needed to replace the trams, and even the later reduced estimate of 982 made when detailed plans were prepared in 1950, were shown in the event to be a considerable overestimate. In total, 824 buses had been used and this reduction was also reflected in the scheduled mileage, down $16\frac{1}{2}$ per cent on the estimate, and in the number of additional drivers and conductors needed, which was down by 387. All of this was a portent of the cold economic winds which would soon be blowing around the public transport industry.

B Y THE END OF 1952 the RT family and the RLHs were covering 85 per cent of all double-deck bus scheduled requirements and even the single-deck schedules were already 54 per cent RF operated. Compared with May 1945, the peak vehicle requirement for all buses had gone up by over 2,000, of which 1,653 were double-deckers, 338 large single-deckers and 14 20-seaters. About 800 of the double-deckers had replaced trams and were not therefore a true increase, while thirty-one more and 232 of the single-deckers operated Green Line which did not exist in 1945. This represents a 23 per cent increase if Green Line is included or 18 per cent without.

The growth in the size of the fleet owned was even more phenomenal, having gone up from a total of 6,448 to 8,928, a 40 per cent increase. These figures are slightly distorted by the fact that 160 STLs were in store for use during the Coronation celebrations in 1953 and a large number of withdrawn buses were still in stock awaiting disposal. Allowing for this the fleet available long-term was more like 8,550 strong, an increase which, with spares, matches the up-lift in scheduled operations. The trolleybus fleet had also grown from the 1945 total of 1,747 to a record 1,811, although again this was inflated because the second batch of Q1s was being delivered and there was some lagging in withdrawals.

No fewer than seven of the 15 routes on which RTWs operated passed through the Bank intersection, which was therefore dominated by the class, as is apparent from this June 1952 scene. The absence of full blind displays on the RTWs indicates that they have yet to have their first overhaul. The absence of any significant amount of traffic other than buses, is remarkable to the modern eye. L.T. Museum

A brisk return visit to the walk around town in 1946, recorded in Chapter 5, will serve to illustrate just how much had changed in the intervening six years. The date chosen is 7th July 1952, the first working day after the last trams had been withdrawn. At Oxford Circus, as elsewhere in the centre of London, not much had happened to the bus route patterns. The main changes were the switch of northern terminals between the 53A and the 59A/159, the withdrawal of the 25C and the renumbering of 25B to 25, but two of the Green Line routes had gone, the 724 and 725 having been swallowed up by the 709, 710 and 711 in 1947. The vehicle scene, on the other hand, was unrecognisable. Only two routes had anything other than RT family vehicles on them. Merton garage had yet to receive a single RT family bus, this honour being withheld until later in the year, because the Daimlers were considered good enough to outlast all the other utility types. Route 88 therefore still had a complete allocation of Daimlers from Merton garage, although it was possible to see the occasional STL too, alongside Riverside's RTLs. The other exception was route 113, which was still carrying on with the pre-war STDs, a class which, despite being non-standard was to maintain a presence until the very last day of operation by pre-war buses. As recently as January 1952, the 13 too had still been graced by these excellent machines but the undoubted affection in which they were held by the Hendon drivers had begun to wear thin as they realised that theirs was one of the few garages which had not shared in the post-war bonanza. In response to their discontent, the STDs had been replaced by RTLs (soon themselves replaced by RTs) but given a new lease of life at Enfield operating on routes 107 and 107A.

Otherwise at Oxford Circus, RTWs could now be found on routes 6, 8 and 15, RTs on the 3, 7, 7A, 12, 13, 17, 25, 53A, 60, 73, 137, and 159, and RTLs on 3, 12, 17, 23, 53A, 59A, 60, 73 and 137. These allocations are quoted in full as the mixture was fairly typical of the central London scene. The Green Line routes were populated exclusively by RFs which, in these early days when they were still new, were fitted with the pilot injection system which was claimed to reduce diesel knock and make the engine quieter. They were certainly very quiet and the sound developed by the injection system was quite different from that of the same 9.6 litre unit in the RTs. A little variety was provided at Orchard Street where it was still possible to see 2RT2s running on route 30, alongside Hackney RTLs, but the 74 had long since lost its RTs in favour of RTWs. Although the 2RT2s still had their same distinctive looks, their sound effects were now quite different as they had all had their pot cavity engines replaced by toroidal and were identical in sound to the 3RT.

All the Green Line routes at Marble Arch as elsewhere were run by the ubiquitous RF but the garages were not yet in possession of their full complements of spares and, on a lucky day, it was possible to see the odd 10T10 or TF standing in for an RF in for docking. It was also possible to see coaches carrying Luton garage plates, a new feature in central London which had come into being in 1951 when route 714 had been extended to Luton to cover the 727. Another bit of variety to be found at Marble Arch, which it would have been easy enough to miss, were the SRTs, barely distinguishable as they were from the RT. They ran in large numbers on route 16 passing at the rate of up to thirty-eight an hour in peak hours, and brought a different, more vintage, STL-like sound to the aural scene contrasting with the purr of the RTs and the harsher roar of the RTLs and RTWs. More 2RT2s could be encountered at

Hyde Park Corner where route 96 could be found in addition to the 14 and 30 but what stood out here were the post-war STDs still running on route 38A. Loughton still had a full complement of these, which they were destined to keep for another three years so earning the questionable distinction of being the last garage to get post-war RTs.

At Piccadilly Circus, the Ds on route 88 met the STDs on the 38A and 2RT2s on the 14 and 96 to add a little spice to the swirl of post-war standard types. Down the road at Trafalgar Square, however, there was even greater variety, albeit on a small scale, amongst all the RTs, RTLs and RTWs. The first official allocation of STLs encountered on the walk could be found here, on routes 77 and 77A from Victoria, who also supplied some post-war STDs, and between them the 77, 77A and 88 provided the biggest concentration of Daimlers to be found in central London. Route 96 was a showcase for the 2RT2s and route 24 made a small dent in standardisation with its SRTs from Chalk Farm garage.

At the next port of call, Victoria Embankment, the transformation was greater than anywhere. Gone were the 138 trams an hour of all kinds on seventeen routes which had been observed in 1946. In their place, on a road that did not have a single bus in 1946, was a procession of RTs and RTLs at the rate of 148 buses an hour in each direction on the thirteen bus routes that had replaced them. Honours were about even between RTs and RTLs but here, perhaps unexpectedly, it was possible to see more STLs, this time on brand new route 163 running under NX plates but actually operating from Camberwell and Rye Lane garages. Also a surprise were the 2RT2s, mixed in with post-war RTs and RTLs on route 177, running from Peckham but carrying New Cross garage plates.

Some more unfamiliar bus routes would be encountered at Aldwych, where route 68A had given way to new routes 188 (RTs) and 196 (RTLs) while the 170 and 171, which were mainly RTL with a handful of RTs, and the 172 (RT) could be seen sneaking up from the Embankment through Norfolk Street and back again down Arundel Street. At Ludgate Circus there were more newcomers, buses on routes 45, 168 (both RTLs) and 179 (RTs), former tram routes, making their way to and from the new terminus at Stonecutter Street. The next new encounter would have been in Cannon Street where the buses replacing the Southwark Bridge trams could be seen slipping along the short section from Dowgate Hill to Queen Street. Here again there were more STLs, drafted in on tram replacement duties, this time on route 182, based at Peckham standing in for New Cross. At Aldgate, even the double-deck Green Line routes had succumbed to RTs, while the single-deckers, now including new route 723A, were all RF. In this changed world, however, the trolleybuses seemed eternal, nothing of substance having changed. But even they bore

signs of the times in the form of their aluminium depot code and running number plates which looked so alien on their cream relief bands.

So, this almost unvarying bus scene was repeated all over London and there were few reminders of the earlier times. Return to Bloomsbury, though, and there the observer would find a massive reminder of the past which was destined to survive for at least another forty-eight years, the northern exit slope from Kingsway Subway. There too, in theory at least, it would have been possible, fleetingly, to see a background of Daimlers and STLs on the 77 and 77A and perhaps a post-war STD crossing into Theobalds Road on the 38A as though nothing had changed. Within three years all that too was to be swept away to leave the RT family to reign alone, completing the post-war transformation and leaving the days of struggle a distant memory.

Post-war STD 154 at Victoria on the 38A, one of three routes operated exclusively by the type, which had a greater life expectancy than the other stop-gaps. Loughton was the only garage not to receive RTs during the main delivery programme.

The most numerous non-standard bus to be seen in the West End was the wartime Daimler, found on routes 77, 88 and, as here at St Pancras station, the 77A. D 24 was a Duple-bodied specimen, new in September 1944 and had been turned out in the 1950 mostly red livery. Replacement of the class did not start until the last quarter of 1952. Robert F. Mack

THE SCHEDULED FLEET

This table shows the number of buses of each type, trams and trolleybuses scheduled for service during the Monday to Friday peak at the end of each year. In practice, particularly in the earlier years, the buses actually operated varied considerably from the schedule as described in the main text.

Vehicle type			year ending: 1945	1946	1947	1948	1949	1950	1951	1952
CENTRAL BUSES										
LT (DD) ...	...	...	1066	1065	944	632	49	—	—	—
ST (highbridge)	...	...	467	580	574	416	64	—	—	—
STL (highbridge)	...	...	1908	1915	1874	1775	1444	406	364	327
STD	...	...	104	149	159	160	162	153	149	150
B	...	...	10	28	28	28	**34	28	23	10
D (highbridge)	...	...	114	211	222	216	221	235	258	216
G	...	...	336	410	409	413	411	370	134	1
RT	...	...	136	137	315	820	1426	2138	2658	3049
SRT	...	...	—	—	—	—	140	155	155	159
RTL	...	...	—	—	—	*57	509	927	1142	1266
RTW	...	...	—	—	—	—	177	491	484	489
Double-deck (h/b) ...	Total		4141	4495	4525	4517	4637	4903	5367	5667
ST (lowbridge)	...	...	—	—	—	—	—	—	1	—
STL (lowbridge)	...	...	14	11	11	11	11	11	12	—
D (lowbridge)	...	...	6	9	9	9	9	9	9	—
RLH	...	...	—	—	—	—	—	—	—	22
Double-deck (l/b) ...	Total		20	20	20	20	20	20	22	22
Double-deck	**Total**		**4161**	**4515**	**4545**	**4537**	**4657**	**4923**	**5389**	**5689**
LT (SD)	...	...	172	171	165	141	94	82	84	23
T	...	...	55	114	101	80	77	81	82	82
TD	...	...	—	—	29	53	131	131	131	126
Q	...	...	60	59	53	76	73	87	87	70
RF	...	...	—	—	—	—	—	—	—	85
Single-deck (TMO) ...	Total		287	344	348	350	375	381	384	386
C (OMO)...	...	...	7	9	11	11	5	—	—	—
Single-deck...	**Total**		**294**	**353**	**359**	**361**	**380**	**381**	**384**	**386**
Central Bus ...	**Total**		**4455**	**4868**	**4904**	**4898**	**5037**	**5304**	**5773**	**6075**
COUNTRY BUSES										
LT (DD) ...	...	...	—	—	7	3	1	—	—	—
ST (highbridge)	...	...	147	164	170	42	2	—	—	—
STL (highbridge)	...	...	462	446	434	417	386	233	152	64
RT	...	...	—	—	—	152	226	395	500	616
Double-deck (h/b) ...	Total		609	610	611	614	615	628	652	680
ST (lowbridge)	...	...	6	6	6	6	6	—	—	—
STL (lowbridge)	...	...	16	19	19	19	19	17	17	—
RLH	...	...	—	—	—	—	—	19	19	45
Double-deck (l/b) ...	Total		22	25	25	25	25	36	36	45
Double-deck	**Total**		**631**	**635**	**636**	**639**	**640**	**664**	**688**	**725**
T	...	...	83	97	104	132	121	132	139	141
4Q4	...	...	93	87	70	60	66	63	65	15
5Q5	...	...	10	12	12	—	—	—	—	—
6Q6	...	...	—	—	16	15	15	10	9	—
TF	...	...	—	—	—	4	4	6	6	51
LTC	...	...	—	—	3	—	—	—	—	—
Single-deck (TMO) ...	Total		186	196	205	211	206	211	219	207
C	...	...	34	36	34	40	44	48	56	55
Single-deck	**Total**		**220**	**232**	**239**	**251**	**250**	**259**	**275**	**262**
Country Bus ...	**Total**		**851**	**867**	**875**	**890**	**890**	**923**	**963**	**987**
GREEN LINE										
STL	...	...	—	5	—	—	—	—	—	—
RT	...	...	—	1	—	—	—	30	31	31
D	...	...	—	32	38	38	38	—	—	—
Double-deck	**Total**		**—**	**38**	**38**	**38**	**38**	**30**	**31**	**31**
10T10	...	...	—	144	152	153	143	155	113	—
6Q6	...	...	—	43	28	23	24	26	27	—
TF	...	...	—	49	46	44	52	54	61	—
RF	...	...	—	—	—	—	—	—	44	232
Single-deck	**Total**		**—**	**236**	**226**	**220**	**219**	**235**	**245**	**232**
Green Line ...	**Total**		**—**	**274**	**264**	**258**	**257**	**265**	**276**	**263**
Country Bus & Coach	**Total**		**851**	**1141**	**1139**	**1148**	**1147**	**1188**	**1239**	**1250**
MOTOR BUSES	**Total**		**5306**	**6009**	**6043**	**6046**	**6184**	**6492**	**7012**	**7325**
Trams	**Total**		**733**	**733**	**747**	**748**	**737**	**650**	**323**	**—**
Trolleybuses ...	**Total**		**1599**	**1606**	**1606**	**1615**	**1616**	**1602**	**1610**	**1603**
GRAND TOTAL ...	...		**7638**	**8348**	**8396**	**8409**	**8537**	**8744**	**8945**	**8928**

* The figure shown for RTL was the official allocation for 31.12.48 but this exceeds the number licensed on that day.
** Includes 15 Tilling Bristols at West Green.

APPENDIX 2

SUMMARY OF PASSENGER FLEET OWNED

The table alongside shows the number of motor buses of each type owned by London Transport at the end of each year from 1945 to 1952. The figures for 1945 include those vehicles still on loan to other operators (ST class), or which had been requisitioned by the government for ambulance duties (9T9, 10TIO, 6Q6, LTC and TF classes), or which were still held by the American armed forces (10T10 class). For more information about these, see Chapter 2.

Vehicle type			year ending:	1945	1946	1947	1948	1949	1950	1951	1952
Double-deck											
LT	...	...	...	1203	1202	1161	815	74	—	—	—
ST	...	...	...	1042	1033	989	764	146	9	8	8
Q (DD)	...	...	...	4	—	—	—	—	—	—	—
STL (pre-war)	...	...	...	2564	2563	2552	2491	2137	1097	905	889
STL (unfrozen)	...	...	...	34	34	34	34	34	28	28	25
18STL20	...	...	...	10	20	20	20	20	20	20	20
1STD1 and 1/1	...	...	...	100	100	100	100	100	100	100	100
3STD2	...	...	...	11	11	11	11	11	11	11	11
4STD3	...	...	...	—	65	65	65	65	65	65	65
B	...	...	...	29	29	29	29	29	29	29	27
G	...	...	...	416	435	435	435	436	436	283	115
D	...	...	...	141	281	281	281	281	281	281	236
1RT1 & 2RT2	...	...	...	151	150	150	150	148	148	147	147
3RT	...	...	...	—	—	182	911	1664	2757	3422	3845
RTC	...	...	...	—	—	—	—	1	1	1	—
SRT	...	...	...	—	—	—	—	149	160	160	160
RTL	...	...	...	—	—	—	43	550	1080	1278	1386
RTW	...	...	...	—	—	—	—	213	500	500	500
RLH	...	...	...	—	—	—	—	—	20	20	76
Double-deck	...	**Total**		**5705**	**5923**	**6009**	**6149**	**6058**	**6742**	**7258**	**7610**
Single-deck											
LTL	...	...	...	190	190	190	190	120	98	96	86
1T1	...	...	...	45	45	43	43	26	26	26	24
3T3	...	...	...	12	12	12	12	1	1	1	1
7T7	...	...	...	25	23	23	22	11	—	—	—
8T8	...	...	...	1	1	1	1	1	—	—	—
9T9	...	...	...	49	49	49	49	49	49	49	9
10T1O	...	...	...	254	254	254	254	254	254	253	253
11T11	...	...	...	29	29	29	29	29	29	29	24
14T12	...	...	...	—	50	50	50	50	50	50	50
15T13	...	...	...	—	—	—	30	30	30	30	30
1Q1	...	...	...	1	—	—	—	—	—	—	—
4Q4	...	...	...	102	102	102	102	102	102	102	85
5Q5	...	...	...	80	80	80	80	80	80	79	79
6Q6	...	...	...	50	49	49	49	49	49	49	49
LTC	...	...	...	24	24	24	24	24	24	24	23
TF	...	...	...	77	76	76	76	76	76	76	71
TD	...	...	...	—	10	31	55	131	131	131	131
RF	...	...	...	—	—	—	—	—	—	110	425
RFW	...	...	...	—	—	—	—	—	—	15	15
Large Saloon single-deck		**Total**		**939**	**994**	**1013**	**1066**	**1033**	**999**	**1120**	**1355**
C	...	...	...	75	74	74	74	74	74	72	71
CR	...	...	...	48	48	48	48	47	47	29	20
20-seater	...	**Total**		**123**	**122**	**122**	**122**	**121**	**121**	**101**	**91**
Single-deck	...	**Total**		**1062**	**1116**	**1135**	**1188**	**1154**	**1120**	**1221**	**1446**
GRAND TOTAL	...	...		**6767**	**7039**	**7174**	**7337**	**7212**	**7862**	**8479**	**9056**

APPENDIX 3A

HIRED TILLING BUSES

Summary of Tilling Group buses borrowed by London Transport, including garages where they operated.

Loaning company	Fleet numbers	Registration numbers	Type	Operating garages
Brighton Hove & District Omnibus Co. Ltd	6400–6406	EAP8–11/EPM1–3	K5G	Tottenham
Caledonian Omnibus Co	325/326	HSM644/645	K5G	Hammersmith (R), Upton Park
Crosville Motor Services Ltd	MB319–340 MB369–378	JFM72–93 KFM245–254	K6A	Chalk Farm, Dalston*, Camberwell†, Godstone, Harrow Weald*, Merton, Mortlake*, Plumstead, Reigate, West Green
Eastern Counties Omnibus Co. Ltd	LKH94–98 LKH107–138	HPW94–98 HPW107–138	K5G	Clayhall, Croydon, Palmers Green, Potters Bar, Putney Bridge, Tottenham, Victoria
Eastern National Omnibus Co. Ltd	4000–4007 4030–4034	NNO100–107 ONO51–55	K5G	Camberwell, Catford, Norwood, Nunhead,
Hants & Dorset Motor Services Ltd	TD876–895 TD896–914	HLJ25–44 HRU844–862	K6A	Amersham, Barking, Camberwell*, Godstone, Harrow Weald*, Hounslow, Merton, Mortlake, Reigate, Upton Park,
Southern National Omnibus Co Ltd	906–913	HOD90–97	K5G	Camberwell, Dalston, Hammersmith (R), Holloway, Nunhead
Southern Vectis Omnibus Co Ltd	729, 730	FDL297, 298	K5G	Harrow Weald, Nunhead
United Automobile Services Ltd	BDO92–100 BDO101–109	KHN392/493–500 LHN101–104/305–309	K5G	Amersham*, Catford, Cricklewood, Godstone*, Hanwell (HW), Norwood
United Counties	651–658	EBD220–227	K5G	Amersham*, Camberwell, Cricklewood, Hammersmith (R), Leyton, Norwood*, Nunhead*, Willesden
Western National Omnibus Co Ltd	882–894	HOD9–21	K5G	Hammersmith (R), Harrow Weald, Leyton, Willesden
	878–881 895–899	HOD5–8 HOD22–26	K6A	Dalston, Mortlake, Plumstead, West Green
Westcliff-on-Sea Motor Services Ltd	(None)	CJN324–326	K5G	Hammersmith (R)*, Holloway, Leyton

* Not an initial allocation – received re-allocated buses later.
† Second delivery of Crosville buses.

Operating garage	Routes known to have been operated by Tilling Bristols	Additional routes authorised for Tilling Bristol operation
Amersham	336,353	
Barking	62,87	
Camberwell	137 – later 42	4A, 35 (later deleted and replaced by 36)
Catford	36,75	54,94
Chalk Farm	68	31,39
Clayhall	8, 8A, 60	
Cricklewood	2,16	
Croydon	68,166	166A (Special instructions issued not to use on route 12 due to low bridge at Bingham Road.)
Dalston	11	(Instructions issued for route 106 to be included on blinds for use when on loan to Hackney'. Not believed to have happened.)
Godstone	410	
Hammersmith	11,72	91
Hanwell	97	55,120
Harrow Weald	140,230	
Holloway	19	27,27A
Hounslow	110	111
Leyton	38	35, 106 (167 added 13.12.49)
Merton	118,127	49
Mortlake	33	111
Norwood	2, 68A	68
Nunhead	63	
Palmers Green	102	
Plumstead	53,99,122	54, 75, 153 (53A was included on blinds but was on the police embargo list.)
Potters Bar	84	134 shown on blinds but not on authority list.
Putney Bridge	93	
Reigate	405	430 (Also operated on 411 but not on blinds.)
Tottenham	73, 76/34B¶	67¶
Upton Park	40	101
Victoria	10, 77, 77A	
West Green	144, 144A, 144B, 29 (not added to list until 30.11.49)	
Willesden	52	

¶ Not at first authorised